CONCISE
CROSSWORD
DICTIONARY

CONCISE
CROSSWORD
DICTIONARY

First published 1986

Reprinted 1989, 1990

This edition 1992

© 1986 HarperCollins Publishers

HarperCollins Publishers,
77-85 Fulham Palace Road,
Hammersmith, London W6 8JB.

ISBN 1 85501 247 2
Printed in Great Britain by
HarperCollins Manufacturing, Glasgow

CONTENTS

v

CONTENTS, *cont.*

FOREWORD

This new version of the popular GEM DICTIONARY FOR CROSSWORD PUZZLES has been completely revised and reorganized. The content has been expanded by increasing the word length to include words of up to 15 letters, thus making the coverage more relevant to the standard cryptic crossword grid. The word count now totals over 55,000 items.

This increased content has been arranged in a larger number of separate fields — 81 in all — alphabetically arranged, from Abbreviations to Writers. This greater degree of subdivision should significantly reduce the search time required. Additional help in this respect is provided by a short Index which relates some possible alternative categories to their relevant fields.

The fact that the author is a practising crossword compiler has meant that he has been able to draw on his experience in this area to tailor the content to items that crossword solvers actually meet. Irrelevant items have been excluded and the coverage has been generally updated to include the kind of material today's compilers make use of.

These improvements make this new

FOREWORD

Crossword Dictionary the ideal aid for all crossword fans.

NOTE: In order to facilitate scrutiny for letter placement within words a special typeface has been used that keeps the letters of each word vertically in line with those of the words above and below it.

To preserve this helpful columnar arrangement the following symbols have been used:

| = word space, as in speed|the|plough

, = hyphen, as in dairy,farm

' = apostrophe, as in lady's|finger

Abbreviations

3D	CB	DJ	GI	JP	mk
AA	CC	DM	Gk	Jr	ml
AB	cc	do	GM	KB	mm
AC	CD	DP	gm	KC	MM
a c	CF	Dr	GP	KG	MN
AD	c f	DS	GR	km	MO
a d	CH	DV	gr	KO	MP
AG	Ch	EC	GS	kr	MR
AI	ch	Ed	g s	KT	Mr
am	CI	ed	GT	Kt	MS
AV	c l	eg	gu	LA	Ms
a v	cm	EP	HC	l b	Mt
BA	c / o	ER	HE	l c	mv
BB	CO	Ex	hf	Ld	MW
BC	Co	Ez	HM	l h	NB
BD	CP	FA	ho	LM	nd
bf	cp	FD	HP	LP	NE
bk	CR	f f	HQ	LT	NI
BL	cr	f l	hr	Lt	n l
BM	CS	FM	HT	LV	no
bn	c t	FO	i b	MA	nr
BP	Cu	FP	i / c	mb	NS
Bp	cu	f p	i d	MB	NT
BR	c v	Fr	i e	MC	NW
Br	DA	f r	in	MD	NY
br	DC	FT	IQ	mf	NZ
Bt	DD	f t	Ir	MG	OB
CA	DF	GB	Is	mg	o b
c a	DG	GC	I t	MI	OC

1

OE	qr	SU	yr	Aug	CBI
OK	qt	SW	AAA	AVM	CCF
OM	qv	TA	ABC	bar	Cdr
OP	RA	TB	Abp	BBC	CET
op	RB	TD	acc	BCC	cfi
OR	RC	Th	act	BEd	CGS
OS	RD	tp	ADC	BEF	ChB
OT	Rd	tr	adj	BEM	Chr
OU	rd	TT	adv	bhp	CIA
oz	RE	Tu	AEC	BHS	Cia
pa	RF	TV	aet	BIM	CID
PA	rh	UK	AEU	BMA	Cie
PC	RI	UN	AFC	BMJ	CIe
pc	RN	UP	AFM	BMW	cif
pd	ro	US	agm	BOC	CMG
PE	RS	UU	agr	bor	CMS
PG	RT	ux	AID	BOT	CND
pH	RU	vb	aka	Bro	COD
pl	RV	VC	Ald	BRS	cod
pm	ry	VD	alt	BSA	COI
PM	s/c	VE	amp	BSc	Col
PO	sc	VJ	amt	BSM	col
po	sd	vo	ans	BST	con
pp	SE	VP	aob	BTA	Cor
PR	SF	vs	aor	BTU	cos
Pr	SI	vt	APR	Btu	cot
pr	SJ	VW	Apr	BVM	Cpl
PS	SM	wc	APT	BWV	CPR
Ps	SO	WD	ARP	CAB	CRE
PT	SP	WI	arr	cal	CSE
pt	sp	wk	ASA	Cal	CST
PU	sq	WO	ASH	CAP	CSV
pw	Sr	wp	ATC	cap	CTC
QC	SS	WS	ATS	car	CUP
ql	St	wt	ATV	CAT	CVO
QM	st	yd	AUC	CBE	CWS

cwt	DTs	Feb	GPI	int	lit
Dan	EBU	fec	GTC	IOM	LLB
dau	ECG	fem	GUS	IOU	log
DBE	ECO	fig	Hab	IOW	loq
dbl	EDC	FIS	HAC	IPC	LPO
DCL	EEC	fob	Hag	IRA	LSA
DCM	EEG	foc	HCF	ITN	LSD
DDR	EFL	for	Heb	ITV	LSE
DDT	EIS	FPA	her	Jan	LSO
DEA	EMI	Fri	HGV	Jas	LTA
Dec	ENE	FRS	HLI	JCR	Ltd
dec	Eng	fur	HMC	jct	LWT
def	eng	fut	HMG	Jer	mag
deg	ENT	fwd	HMI	Jno	Maj
del	Eph	Gal	HMS	Jnr	Mal
DEP	ESE	GBA	HMV	Jud	Mar
Dep	ESN	gbh	HNC	Jul	max
dep	ESP	GBS	HND	KBE	MBE
DES	esp	GCB	Hon	KCB	MCC
DFC	Esq	GCE	hor	KGB	Mc/s
DFM	est	GDP	Hos	KKK	MEP
Dip	ESU	GDR	HRH	KLM	met
Dir	ETA	GEC	HSE	km/h	mfd
div	etc	Gen	HTV	ktl	MFH
DIY	ETD	gen	IBA	Lab	Mgr
DNA	ETU	Geo	IBM	lab	Mic
DNB	Exc	ger	ICI	Lat	mil
dob	fam	GHQ	ICS	lat	Min
DOE	FAO	Gib	ill	lbw	min
dom	fas	GLC	ILO	LCC	mis
doz	FBA	GMC	ILP	LCJ	MIT
DPP	FBI	GMT	IMF	lcm	MLR
DSC	FCA	GNP	imp	LDS	Mme
DSO	FCO	GOC	inc	LDV	MOD
dsp	fcp	GOM	ind	LEA	mod
DTI	FDR	Gov	inf	Lev	MOH

ABBREVIATIONS

Mon	NSW	PLA	rep	SDP	TSB
MOT	NUJ	PLC	rev	Sec	TUC
mph	NUM	PLO	RFA	SEN	Tue
MPS	Num	PLP	RFC	Sen	TVA
MRA	NUR	PLR	RFU	seq	UAE
MRC	NUS	PMG	RGS	ser	UAR
Mrs	NUT	PMO	RHA	SET	UDC
MSC	NYO	pop	RHS	SFA	UDI
msl	OAP	pos	RIC	sfz	UDR
mss	OAS	POW	RIP	sin	UFO
MTB	OBE	ppc	Rly	SMO	UHF
mus	obj	PPE	RMA	SMP	UHT
MVO	Oct	PPS	RMO	SNP	ult
Nat	oct	PRO	RMP	sob	UNO
nat	OED	psc	RMS	Soc	USA
nav	ONC	PTA	ROC	sol	USN
NBC	OND	Pte	Rom	sop	USS
nbg	ono	PTO	RPI	SOS	usu
NCB	opp	PVC	RPM	sqn	usw
NCO	Ops	QED	rpm	SRN	VAD
NEB	opt	QEF	RPO	SSE	val
NEC	ord	QEH	RRE	SSW	var
neg	OSB	QMG	RSA	STD	VAT
Neh	OTC	QPR	RSM	std	VDU
NFS	OUP	qty	RTE	str	veg
NFT	Oxf	RAC	RTZ	TV	vel
NFU	pap	rad	RUC	sub	Ven
NGA	par	RAF	RYS	Sun	VHF
NHI	pat	RAM	sae	tan	vid
NHS	PBI	RBA	SAM	TCD	VIP
NNE	PCC	RCM	Sam	tel	viz
NNW	PEN	RCO	SAS	ten	voc
nom	PEP	RCT	Sat	Thu	vol
NOP	PGA	RDC	SCE	Tim	VSO
Nov	PhD	rec	SCM	Tit	WEA
NPL	phr	ref	SCR	TNT	Wed

wef	biog	cosh	FIFA	kilo	orig
WHO	biol	coth	floz	lang	ORTF
WNW	bldg	CPRE	FRCP	L|of|C	OUDS
wpb	BMus	CRMP	FRCS	Lond	Oxon
wpm	BNOC	CSYS	GATT	long	pass
WSW	BOAC	DAAG	GCMG	LRAM	PAYE
WVS	Brig	D|day	GCVO	LRCP	PDSA
YOP	Brit	decl	Gdns	LRCS	perf
abbr	Bros	dept	gent	mach	perh
ABTA	BThU	derv	geog	marg	pers
ACAS	BUPA	Deut	geol	masc	Phil
ACGB	caps	DHSS	geom	math	phon
AERE	Capt	dial	Glam	Matt	phot
AIDS	CARD	diam	Glos	mech	phys
AMDG	Card	dict	guin	memo	pinx
ammo	Cath	diff	HIDB	MIRV	plup
anat	cath	dist	hist	Mlle	plur
anon	CCPR	DMus	hi|fi	Mods	Preb
arch	CEGB	DUKW	HMSO	MORI	prep
asap	cent	Ebor	Hons	morn	Pres
Asst	cert	Eccl	IATA	MRCP	Prin
at|no	chap	Edin	ibid	NADA	prob
at|wt	Chas	EFTA	ICBM	NATO	Prof
AUEW	Chem	El|Al	ILEA	naut	prop
AWOL	choc	ELDO	incl	Nazi	Prot
AWRE	CIGS	elec	INRI	NCCL	Prov
BAOR	C|in|C	ENSA	Inst	NEDC	prox
Bart	circ	EOKA	IOUS	neut	PSBR
B|Ca l	co|ed	EPNS	Irel	NFER	RADA
B|Com	C|of|E	Esth	ital	non|U	RADC
Beds	C|of|I	et|al	Josh	Obad	RAEC
Belg	C|of|S	exec	Judg	obdt	RAMC
B|ès|L	comp	Exon	junc	OCTU	RAOC
B|ès|S	conj	Ezek	KCMG	OEEC	RAPC
BFPO	co|op	FIAT	KCVO	OHMS	RAVC
Bibl	Corp	FIDO	KGCB	OPEC	RCMP

ABBREVIATIONS

recd	Thur	Assoc	in|loc	SOGAT
regt	TocH	ASTMS	intro	SSAFA
REME	trig	BALPA	Lancs	STOPP
rhet	Trin	B|and|B	LASER	subst
RIBA	Tues	b|and|s	Leics	SWALK
RNAS	UCCA	Bart's	Lieut	SWAPO
RNIB	UEFA	BASIC	Lincs	theol
RNLI	Univ	Berks	Lt,Col	Thess
RNVR	USAF	BLitt	Lt,Gen	trans
ro,ro	USSR	Bucks	maths	treas
RSPB	VSOP	Cambs	meths	UMIST
RSVP	VTOL	CAMRA	Middx	UNRRA
SALT	vulg	CENTO	NAAFI	UWIST
SATB	WAAC	Chron	Notts	V|and|A
Scot	WAAF	circs	NSPCC	vocab
SDLP	WACS	COBOL	op|cit	WAACS
sect	WAVE	COHSE	OXFAM	WAAFS
Sept	W/Cdr	Comdr	P|and|O	Wilts
Serg	WFTU	contd	PLUTO	Worcs
sing	WRAC	cosec	pro,am	WRACS
sinh	WRAF	cresc	pseud	Xtian
SNCF	WRNS	cusec	R|and|A	Yorks
Solr	WRVS	D|and|C	R|and|D	ab|init
SPCK	Xmas	Dip|Ed	ROSLA	approx
SPQR	YMCA	DLitt	RoSPA	attrib
STOL	AAQMG	DPhil	RSPCA	Cantab
subj	ad|lib	ERNIE	Rt|Hon	cet|par
Supt	admin	et|seq	Rt|Rev	cosech
syst	ad|val	ex|lib	Salop	Dunelm
tanh	ALGOL	G|and|S	Sarum	E|and|OE
TASS	Anzac	h|and|c	sci|fi	Fid|Def
TCCB	ANZUS	Hants	SCUBA	Hon|Sec
tech	appro	Herts	SEATO	incorp
temp	arith	Hunts	SHAEF	indecl
TGWU	Asdic	indef	SHAPE	Lit|Hum
Thos	ASLEF	indiv	SLADE	loc|cit

Londin	SABENA	Nat|West
Lonrho	sculpt	non|obst
Man|Dir	Staffs	per|cent
Messrs	transf	Pol|Econ
mod|con	UNESCO	prox|acc
Mus|Bac	UNICEF	Reg|Prof
Mus|Doc	Winton	var|lect
Nat|Sci	Benelux	verb|sap
nem|con	Cantuar	infra|dig
NIBMAR	COMECON	Interpol
non,com	Consols	Northumb
Noncon	Dip|Tech	Oxbridge
non|seq	Euratom	Cominform
Norvic	FORTRAN	Comintern
pro|tem	intrans	Northants
QARANC	nat|hist	
quango	NATSOPA	

Agriculture

ear	corn	mare	silo	ditch	mower
hay	crop	milk	skep	drill	mulch
lea	dung	neat	soil	fruit	ovine
mow	farm	neep	till	grain	plant
rye	herd	oats	vega	grass	ranch
bale	husk	peat	weed	graze	rumen
barn	jess	pest	baler	guano	sheep
bull	kine	rake	bothy	haulm	shoat
byre	lamb	rape	calve	hedge	stock
calf	lime	root	churn	horse	straw
cart	loam	seed	crops	humus	tilth
clay	lush	shaw	dairy	maize	tuber

AGRICULTURE

veldt	potato	prairie
wagon	reaper	rancher
wheat	roller	reaping
yield	sheave	rearing
animal	silage	rustler
arable	sowing	savanna
barley	stable	stubble
binder	trough	subsoil
butter	turnip	tillage
cattle	warble	tilling
cereal	weevil	tractor
clover	anthrax	wagoner
colter	bullock	agronomy
cowman	cabbage	breeding
cutter	calving	clippers
digger	combine	cropping
fallow	compost	drainage
farmer	cowherd	elevator
fodder	cowshed	ensilage
forage	digging	farmyard
furrow	drought	forestry
gimmer	erosion	gleaning
grains	farming	hayfield
grange	fertile	haymaker
harrow	harvest	haystack
heifer	haycart	landgirl
hopper	hayrick	loosebox
manger	lambing	pedigree
manure	lucerne	pigswill
meadow	milkcan	rootcrop
merino	milking	rotation
millet	newmown	rotavate
piglet	paddock	rotovate
pigsty	pasture	shearing
plough	piggery	sheepdip
porker	poultry	vineyard

allotment
cornfield
dairy,farm
dairymaid
fertility
grassland
harvester
haymaking
husbandry
implement
incubator
livestock
pasturage
phosphate
pig,trough
ploughing
root,house
rotavator
rotovator
shorthorn
sugar|beet
swineherd
threshing
wasteland
winnowing
agronomist
battery|hen
cattle|cake
cultivator
fertilizer
harvesting
husbandman
irrigation
weed|killer

agriculture
chicken|farm
cultivation
farm|produce
germination
insecticide
pasture|land
poultry|farm
agricultural
horticulture
insemination
market|garden
smallholding
agriculturist
agrobiologist
cattle|breeder
cattle|farming
chicken|farmer
electric|fence
horticultural
kitchen,garden
sheep,shearing
stock,breeding
tea,plantation
viticulturist
collective|farm
market,gardener
milking,machine
milking|parlour
speed|the|plough
agriculturalist
market,gardening
rotation|of|crops

Animals

ai	moo	byre	hoof	paca	toad
ox	nag	cage	horn	pack	tusk
ape	pad	calf	howl	pard	tyke
ass	paw	cavy	hump	peba	unau
bat	pet	chow	ibex	pelt	ursa
bay	pig	claw	jill	pest	urus
cat	pod	colt	kine	pika	urva
cob	pom	cony	kudu	poll	vole
cow	pug	coon	lair	pony	wolf
cry	pup	deer	lamb	prad	yelp
cub	ram	dray	ling	prey	yoke
cur	rat	drey	lion	puma	yowl
dam	run	fang	lynx	puss	zebu
den	set	fawn	mane	rein	addax
doe	sow	Fido	mare	roan	apery
dog	sty	foal	meow	roar	beast
elk	teg	form	mews	rout	billy
ewe	tod	frog	mink	runt	biped
fox	tom	gaur	moke	saki	bison
fur	tup	goat	mole	seal	bitch
gam	yak	hack	mona	sett	bleat
gnu	zoo	hare	mule	stag	bongo
hob	Arab	hart	musk	stot	borer
hog	beak	herd	mutt	stud	boxer
kid	bear	hern	myna	tail	brock
kit	boar	hide	neat	teal	brood
kob	bray	hind	oont	team	Bruin
low	buck	hock	oryx	tike	brush
mew	bull	hole	oxen	titi	brute

5/6 LETTERS

bunny	horse	panda	stray	basset
burro	hound	pidog	swine	bayard
camel	husky	piggy	tabby	beagle
caple	hutch	pinto	takin	beaver
capul	hutia	pongo	talon	bellow
catch	hyena	pooch	tapir	beluga
civet	hyrax	potto	tatou	bharal
coati	izard	pouch	tiger	bident
coney	jenny	pound	tigon	bobcat
coypu	Jumbo	pride	troop	borzoi
crawl	kaama	puppy	trunk	bovine
cuddy	kiang	pussy	udder	bow,wow
daman	kitty	rache	urial	Briard
dhole	koala	rasse	vixen	bridle
dingo	kulan	ratel	waler	bronco
dogie	lapin	reins	whale	burrow
drill	leash	rhino	whelp	cackle
drove	lemur	sable	zebra	canine
earth	liger	saiga	zibet	castor
eland	llama	sasin	zoril	cat,nap
fauna	loris	satyr	zorro	cattle
feral	manis	sheep	agouta	cayman
field	manul	shire	agouti	chacma
filly	miaow	shoat	albino	circus
fitch	moose	shrew	alpaca	coaita
flock	morse	skunk	angora	cocker
fossa	mount	slink	antler	collie
gayal	mouse	sloth	aoudad	colugo
genet	nanny	snarl	argali	corral
genus	Neddy	snort	aye,aye	cougar
girth	neigh	snout	baboon	coyote
grice	okapi	spitz	badger	coypou
growl	orang	stall	baleen	cruive
grunt	otary	steed	bandog	curtal
hinny	otter	steer	barren	cus,cus
hippo	ounce	stoat	barton	dassie

11

ANIMALS

desman	hog.rat	margay	saddle
dewlap	hooves	marmot	saluki
dikdik	houdah	marten	sambar
dobbin	howdah	merino	school
donkey	humble	merlin	sea.ape
dragon	hummel	monkey	sea.cow
dugong	hunter	mouser	sea.dog
embryo	hyaena	mousse	serval
entire	hybrid	mulish	setter
equine	impala	musk|ox	shelty
ermine	instar	muster	simian
farrow	jackal	muzzle	sleuth
feline	jaeger	nilgai	sorrel
fennec	jaguar	nilgau	sphinx
ferine	jennet	ocelot	stable
ferret	jerboa	onager	string
fossil	jumart	pallah	summer
fox.bat	jungle	pariah	tarpan
garron	kennel	pastor	taurus
gee.gee	killer	phylum	teetee
genera	kindle	piglet	teledu
gennet	kit|fox	pig.rat	tenrec
gerbil	kitten	pig|sty	tomcat
gibbon	koodoo	poodle	toy|dog
gnawer	langur	porker	tracer
gobble	lap|dog	possum	tusker
gopher	lionet	pug|dog	ursine
grison	litter	pye.dog	vermin
grivet	lowing	quagga	vervet
guenon	lowrie	rabbit	vicuna
gun|dog	lupine	racoon	walrus
hackee	mad|dog	ranger	wapiti
hackle	mammal	red|fox	warren
he.goat	manati	reebok	weasel
heifer	manege	rhesus	wether
hogget	manger	rodent	whinny

wild|ox	chimera	griffin	manatee
wombat	colobus	griffon	Manx|cat
wyvern	coon|cat	gryphon	markhor
ant,bear	courser	grysbok	marmose
asinine	cowshed	guanaco	mastiff
aurochs	croaker	guereza	meerkat
barking	dasyure	habitat	metazoa
basenji	deerdog	hackney	milk|cow
bear,cat	deer,hog	half,ape	mole|rat
beavery	deerlet	hamster	mongrel
bestial	denizen	hanuman	monster
big|game	dew|claw	harness	mouflon
bighorn	dolphin	harrier	muridae
bird,dog	echinus	hexapod	musimon
blesbok	epizoon	hindleg	musk,hog
blue|fox	ewe|lamb	hindpaw	musk,rat
brocket	extinct	hircine	mustang
buffalo	fetlock	hog,deer	nandine
bull,bat	finback	hogwash	narwhal
bulldog	fitchet	ice|bear	nosebag
bullock	fitchew	jacchus	opossum
bush|cat	foreleg	jackass	pack|rat
caracal	forepaw	karakul	paddock
carcase	foumart	keitloa	painter
carcass	fur,seal	lambkin	palfrey
caribou	gambrel	land,rat	palmcat
catling	gazelle	lemming	panther
cattalo	gelding	leonine	pastern
centaur	gemsbok	leopard	peccary
cervine	giraffe	leveret	Pegasus
cetacea	gizzard	linsang	piebald
chamois	glutton	lioness	pig,deer
charger	gnu|goat	lurcher	pit|pony
cheetah	gorilla	macaque	pointer
Cheviot	grampus	madoqua	pole|cat
chikara	grey|fox	mammoth	polypod

ANIMALS

porcine	twinter	brancard	dog|pound
pricket	unicorn	brown|rat	dog's|life
primate	urodele	bull,calf	dormouse
raccoon	vaccine	bull,frog	duckbill
rathole	vampire	bush,baby	earth|hog
rattler	vulpine	bush,buck	edentate
red|deer	wallaby	cachalot	elephant
redpoll	warthog	cachelot	elkhound
Reynard	water|ox	cannibal	entellus
roebuck	web,toed	capuchin	entrails
roe,deer	whippet	capybara	fin,whale
rorqual	whisker	carapace	foxhound
rotifer	wild|ass	carcajou	frogling
saimiri	wild|cat	cariacou	fruit,bat
Samoyed	wistiti	castrate	Galloway
sapajou	withers	cave,bear	grey|mare
sea,lion	wolf,dog	cavicorn	grey|wolf
she,goat	wood,rat	ceratops	hair,seal
shippon	aardvark	Cerberus	hair,tail
siamang	aardwolf	cetacean	hedgehog
sirenia	abattoir	chestnut	hedgepig
sondeli	Airedale	chimaera	hoggerel
sounder	animalia	chipmuck	horse,box
sounder	anteater	chipmunk	hound,dog
spaniel	antelope	chowchow	house|dog
spouter	Antilope	civet|cat	humpback
sumpter	argonaut	coach|dog	hydrozoa
sun,bear	bactrian	cowhouse	Irish|elk
tadpole	black|cat	creature	jenny|ass
tamarin	black|fox	dairy|cow	kangaroo
tanager	black|rat	deer|park	keeshond
tarsier	blauwbok	demi,wolf	kinkajou
terrier	blinkers	Derby|dog	kitty,cat
tigress	blow,hole	dinosaur	kolinsky
tree,fox	blue,buck	Doberman	labrador
trotter	blue,hare	dog|house	lancelet

leporine	predator	turnspit
lion's den	protozoa	turn tail
longhorn	pussy cat	ungulate
loosebox	rabbitry	viscacha
mandrill	reindeer	vivarium
man eater	rhizopod	wanderoo
mangabey	river hog	war horse
marmoset	ruminant	warragal
mastodon	sand mole	watchdog
maverick	sapi utan	water cow
Minotaur	sauropod	water dog
mongoose	sea horse	water rat
monk seal	sealyham	wharf rat
mule deer	sea otter	whistler
musquash	sea swine	white fox
nautilus	serotine	wild boar
neat herd	sheep dog	wild goat
night ape	shepherd	wild life
nose band	Shetland	wolf pack
oliphant	skewbald	woof woof
omnivore	spitz dog	yeanling
ouistiti	squirrel	yearling
pack mule	stallion	amphibian
palomino	stegodon	Angora cat
pangolin	steinbok	Arctic fox
Pekinese	stray cat	armadillo
penny dog	stray dog	arthropod
pinniped	suborder	babirussa
pinscher	suricate	babyrussa
platanna	tabby cat	badger dog
platypus	terrapin	bandicoot
polar fox	theropod	bangsring
polliwog	tiger cat	beaver rat
polo pony	tortoise	billy goat
porkling	tree frog	binturong
porpoise	troutlet	black bear

ANIMALS

Black|Bess   dog|collar   lamp|shell
blackbuck   dog|kennel   latration
blue|sheep   dray|horse   lion|heart
blue|whale   dromedary   livestock
boarhound   dziggetai   Lowrie|Tod
brood|mare   earth|wolf   mammalian
brown|bear   Eskimo|dog   manticora
brush|deer   feralized   manticore
brush|wolf   fill|horse   March|hare
buck|hound   flying|fox   mare's|nest
burro|deer   frog|spawn   marsupial
caballine   gazehound   marsupium
Caffre|cat   gift|horse   megathere
camass|rat   ginger|tom   menagerie
caparison   Great|Dane   monoceros
carnivore   greyhound   monotreme
cart|horse   grimalkin   mouldwarp
catamount   ground|hog   mouse|deer
cat|and|dog   guinea|pig   mousehole
caterwaul   herbivore   mule|train
ceratodus   herpestes   musk|shrew
chickaree   high|horse   Nandi|bear
chihuahua   honey|bear   nanny|goat
coleopter   hoofprint   native|cat
cotton|rat   horse|shoe   neat|house
crocodile   horse|whip   neat|stall
curry|comb   Houyhnhnm   on|the|hoof
dachshund   ichneumon   orangutan
dairy|herd   iguanodon   oviparous
Dalmatian   Incitatus   pachyderm
dark|horse   infusoria   pademelon
deerhound   Jersey|cow   palm|civet
deer|mouse   Judas|goat   pariah|dog
deer|tiger   jungle|law   Pekingese
desert|rat   Kerry|blue   percheron
dinothere   koala|bear   phalanger

pinnipede	tiffen|bat	black|sheep
pipistrel	tiger,wolf	blood,horse
pocket|rat	Tod|Lowrie	bloodhound
polar|bear	toy|poodle	bottle,nose
police|dog	tree|shrew	Bucephalus
poodle|dog	trilobite	bull,roarer
porcupine	ululation	Burmese|cat
prayer|dog	waterbuck	camelopard
predatory	water,bull	camel|train
proboscis	water,deer	cannon,bone
pronghorn	water,mole	cattle,grid
protozoan	water,vole	cephalopod
quadruped	Welsh|pony	chevrotain
racehorse	whalebone	chimpanzee
razor,back	white|bear	chinchilla
red|setter	wild|sheep	Clydesdale
rescue|dog	wolfhound	coach|horse
retriever	wolverine	cottontail
ridgeback	woodchuck	crio,sphinx
Rosinante	wood,mouse	dachshound
sarcodina	woodshock	dapple,grey
scavenger	yellow,dog	dermoptera
schnauzer	youngling	dog's|chance
sea,canary	zeuglodon	dumb|animal
sea,squirt	Angora|goat	dumb|friend
shorthorn	angwantibo	equestrian
shrew,mole	animalcule	Evangeline
silver|fox	animal|life	fallow,deer
skunk,bear	arthropoda	fatted|calf
sloth,bear	babiroussa	field,mouse
springbok	Barbary|ape	flagellata
staghound	bear|garden	fox|terrier
St|Bernard	Bedlington	freemartin
stegosaur	bell|the|cat	giant|panda
studhorse	bellwether	golden,mole
tarantula	bezoar,goat	ground,game

17

ANIMALS

hammerhead	pig|in|a|poke	sucking|pig
hartebeest	pine|marten	Syrian|bear
heterocera	Pomeranian	tailwagger
hippogriff	pouched|rat	tantony|pig
hippogryph	prairie|dog	tardigrade
honey|mouse	prairie|fox	thill|horse
horned|toad	raccoon|dog	Tiergarten
horn|footed	radiolaria	timber|wolf
horseflesh	rat|terrier	toy|spaniel
horse|sense	rhinoceros	toy|terrier
hunting|dog	right|whale	trace|horse
Iceland|dog	river|horse	tracker|dog
Indian|pony	rock|badger	Turkish|cat
jack|rabbit	Russian|cat	vampire|bat
jaguarundi	sabre|tooth	vertebrate
Kodiak|bear	saddleback	water|mouse
kookaburra	sand|hopper	Weimaraner
leopardess	sausage|dog	white|whale
lion's|share	schipperke	wild|animal
loggerhead	sea|blubber	wildebeest
Maltese|cat	sea|leopard	woolly|bear
Maltese|dog	sea|monster	xiphopagus
martingale	sea|unicorn	Afghan|hound
megalosaur	sheep's|eyes	basset|hound
molluscoid	Shire|horse	beast|of|prey
neat|cattle	short|sheep	Belgian|hare
omnivorous	shrew|mouse	black|cattle
ornithopod	Siamese|cat	bloodsucker
otterhound	snaffle|bit	buffalo|wolf
otter|shrew	sperm|whale	bull|mastiff
pack|animal	springbuck	bull|terrier
pack|of|dogs	spring|hare	bunny|rabbit
pantheress	springtail	Buridan's|ass
paradoxure	stock|horse	Cape|buffalo
Persian|cat	stone|horse	cardophagus
phyllopoda	sub|species	carriage|dog

cat's pyjamas	plantigrade	catamountain
cat squirrel	pocket mouse	cat's whiskers
Cheshire cat	prairie wolf	cattle market
church mouse	rabbit hutch	cinnamon bear
crown antler	red squirrel	dog in a manger
dairy cattle	reservation	draught horse
daisy cutter	rhynchodont	dumb creature
Diana monkey	saddle girth	field spaniel
eager beaver	saddle horse	French poodle
Egyptian cat	sand skipper	gazelle hound
elephantine	sea elephant	goat antelope
entire horse	shepherd dog	grey squirrel
fishing frog	sleuth hound	Guinea baboon
flickertail	snaffle rein	hare and hound
flying lemur	snow leopard	harvest mouse
globigerina	social whale	hippopotamus
green turtle	sorrel horse	hoofed animal
grizzly bear	sporting dog	horse blanket
ground sloth	stone marten	Irish terrier
hibernation	sumpter mule	jumping mouse
Highland cow	swamp rabbit	jumping shrew
hircocervus	titanothere	king of beasts
honey badger	wheel animal	marmalade cat
horned horse	white ermine	mating season
insectivore	wishtonwish	mountain goat
Irish setter	wolf whistle	mountain hare
kangaroo rat	American lion	mountain lion
Kilkenny cat	Archangel cat	national park
killer whale	baby elephant	Newfoundland
land spaniel	bay at the moon	pantophagous
lion hearted	beard the lion	platanna frog
Malayan bear	bonnet monkey	pocket gopher
orang outang	bottom animal	quarter horse
ornithosaur	brontosaurus	rhesus monkey
paper sailor	Cairn terrier	rock squirrel
Pavlov's dogs	Cashmere goat	Saint Bernard

ANIMALS

Shetland pony
Spanish horse
Spanish sheep
spider monkey
Suffolk punch
sumpter horse
thoroughbred
tree squirrel
ursine monkey
Virginia deer
water buffalo
water spaniel
Welsh terrier
Aberdeen Angus
affenpinscher
ailourophilia
ailourophobia
animalisation
animal kingdom
animal worship
baggage animal
beast of burden
Boston terrier
cocker spaniel
Dandie Dinmont

draught animal
echinodermata
gadarene swine
mountain sheep
nature reserve
rogue elephant
Scotch terrier
sheep and goats
tortoise shell
Clumber spaniel
domestic animal
Highland cattle
horse of the year
Indian elephant
man's best friend
pedigree cattle
Aberdeen terrier
animal magnetism
golden retriever
miniature poodle
Newfoundland dog
Scottish terrier
Sealyham terrier
springer spaniel

Architecture

3D	bay	inn	rib	arch	barn
RA	cot	kip	tie	area	base
wc	den	nef	adit	aula	bead
bar	hut	pub	apse	balk	beam

bell	list	site	cabin	helix	plaza
bema	loft	slab	cella	hinge	porch
berm	mews	slum	cheek	hoist	pylon
boss	mill	span	close	hotel	quoin
byre	moat	step	coign	hotel	ranch
cell	mole	stoa	court	house	range
coin	naos	tent	croft	hovel	revet
cote	nave	tige	crown	hutch	ridge
cove	nook	tile	crypt	igloo	riser
cusp	ogee	toft	decor	ingle	rooms
cyma	pale	tope	ditch	inlay	salle
dado	pane	vane	domus	Ionic	salon
dais	park	wall	Doric	jetty	scale
digs	path	weir	dowel	joint	sewer
dome	pier	well	drain	joist	shack
door	pile	wing	drive	jutty	shaft
drip	plan	yard	eaves	kiosk	shore
drum	post	zeta	entry	ledge	slate
eave	quad	abbey	facia	level	slums
exit	rail	abode	fanal	lobby	socie
face	ramp	adobe	fence	lodge	sough
farm	raze	adyta	flats	lotus	speos
flag	reed	agora	floor	mains	spire
flat	rima	aisle	flush	manor	splay
flue	rind	alley	flute	manse	stage
fort	rise	ancon	folly	mitre	stair
foss	road	arena	forum	motel	stall
fret	roof	arris	fosse	newel	stele
gate	roof	attic	foyer	niche	stile
haha	room	berth	gable	ogive	stoep
hall	sash	booth	glass	order	stone
head	seat	bothy	glebe	oriel	stria
home	shed	bower	glyph	ovolo	strut
jamb	shop	brick	grate	panel	study
keep	sill	broch	groin	patio	stupa
lift	silo	brogh	hatch	pitch	suite

ARCHITECTURE

talon	castle	fillet	listel	rafter
tepee	cellar	finial	loggia	recess
torus	cement	fleche	lounge	refuge
tower	centre	fluted	louvre	reglet
trave	chalet	founds	lyceum	regula
tread	chapel	fresco	maison	relief
trunk	church	frieze	mantel	rococo
tupek	circus	garage	marble	rubble
tupik	closet	garden	metope	saloon
usine	coffer	garret	milieu	school
vault	column	gazebo	module	sconce
villa	concha	ghetto	mortar	scotia
adytum	convex	girder	mosaic	screen
alcove	coping	godown	mosque	scroll
annexe	corbel	gopura	mud|hut	shanty
arbour	corner	Gothic	muntin	sluice
arcade	corona	gradin	museum	soffit
aspect	course	grange	mutule	spence
atrium	cranny	granny	oculus	spiral
avenue	crenel	gravel	office	spring
awning	cupola	griffe	pagoda	square
bagnio	damper	grille	palace	stable
barrow	dentil	ground	palais	storey
barton	donjon	gutter	paling	street
batten	dormer	hangar	parget	stucco
bedsit	dorsal	hawhaw	parvis	studio
belfry	dosser	header	pharos	suburb
billet	dry|rot	hearth	piazza	summer
bistro	duplex	hostel	picket	tablet
bridge	durbar	hostel	pillar	taenia
brough	estate	impost	plinth	tavern
by|room	exedra	insula	podium	temple
camber	fabric	kennel	portal	thatch
camera	facade	lancet	posada	tholos
canopy	facing	lean|to	prefab	tholus
canopy	fascia	lintel	purlin	timber

toilet	capital	estrade	low|rise
torsel	caracol	eustyle	lunette
trench	carving	factory	mansard
tunnel	cavetto	fencing	mansion
turret	ceiling	festoon	marquee
vallum	chamber	fitment	masonry
volute	chambre	fixture	megaron
wicket	chancel	fluting	minaret
wigwam	chapter	Fossway	mirador
window	charnel	free|end	moellon
zoning	chateau	fusarol	mudsill
academy	chez|moi	galilee	mullion
address	chimney	gallery	munting
air|duct	choltry	garland	mutular
archlet	cipolin	gateway	narthex
archway	cistern	godroon	necking
areaway	citadel	gradine	new|town
armoury	cloison	granary	nursery
arsenal	cob|wall	granite	obelisk
asphalt	concave	grating	offices
astylar	conduit	grounds	ossuary
balcony	console	hallway	outlook
barmkin	contour	hip|roof	outwork
baroque	cornice	hospice	palazzo
barrack	cottage	housing	pannier
beading	crocket	hydrant	pantile
bearing	cubicle	keyhole	parapet
bedroom	culvert	kitchen	parlour
boudoir	cushion	klinker	parquet
box|room	derrick	lagging	passage
bracing	dinette	landing	pendant
bracket	doorway	lantern	pension
bulwark	dungeon	larmier	pergola
cabaret	echinus	lattice	plafond
canteen	edifice	library	plaster
cantina	entasis	lodging	ponceau

ARCHITECTURE

portico	terrace	banister	curb|roof
postern	theatre	bannerol	cymatium
purlieu	tie,beam	barbican	dark,room
pyramid	tracery	bartisan	dead|wall
railing	transom	base|line	detached
rampart	trefoil	basement	diggings
Rathaus	trellis	basilica	domicile
reredos	tribune	bathroom	doorhead
roofage	tumulus	bell|tent	doorjamb
roofing	upright	best|room	doorpost
rooftop	veranda	blinding	doorsill
roomlet	viaduct	brattice	downpipe
rosette	vitrail	building	driveway
rostrum	abamurus	bulkhead	dwelling
rotunda	abatjour	bull's,eye	ebenezer
sanctum	abatvoix	bungalow	entrance
Schloss	abbatoir	buttress	entresol
sea|wall	abutment	canephor	epistyle
shebeen	acanthus	cantoned	erection
shelter	acrolith	capstone	espalier
shelter	air,drain	caracole	estancia
shingle	anteroom	caryatid	exterior
shore|up	aperture	casement	extrados
shoring	apophyge	catacomb	fanlight
shutter	aqueduct	chapiter	farmyard
sinkage	arcature	chaptrel	fastness
skew,put	archives	chez|nous	faubourg
skid|row	artefact	cincture	fire|plug
slating	astragal	clithral	fireside
station	Atlantes	cloister	fire|stop
steeple	aularian	colossus	flat|arch
storied	back|door	concrete	flat|roof
subbase	baguette	corridor	flooring
sundial	baluster	cross,tie	fortress
surbase	bandelet	cul,de,sac	fossette
Telamon	banderol	cupboard	fountain

funk‚hole	outhouse	subtopia
fusarole	palisade	suburbia
gable‚end	palmette	sun|porch
game|room	Pantheon	tectonic
gargoyle	parabema	tenement
gatepost	parclose	teocalli
hacienda	parterre	terraced
handrail	pavilion	thalamus
headpost	peak|arch	tile|roof
headsill	pedestal	tolbooth
high‚rise	pediment	top|floor
hospital	pilaster	town|hall
hothouse	pinnacle	transept
housetop	platform	trap|door
interior	playroom	traverse
intrados	pointing	triglyph
isodomon	property	triptych
keystone	prospect	tympanum
kingpost	quarters	underpin
lavatory	rocaille	upstairs
lich‚gate	sacristy	verandah
lodgings	scaffold	voussoir
lodgment	scullery	wainscot
log|cabin	semi‚dome	wall|tent
lotus‚bud	shoulder	windmill
love‚nest	shutters	woodworm
magazine	side|door	ziggurat
martello	skewback	acoustics
mess|hall	skylight	acropolis
messuage	slum|area	alignment
monolith	snack|bar	almshouse
mon|repos	solarium	angle‚iron
monument	spandril	anthemion
ogee|arch	stairway	apartment
open|plan	stockade	architect
ornament	storeyed	archivolt

ARCHITECTURE

Attic|base
banderole
banquette
bas|relief
bay|window
bead|house
bell|tower
belvedere
blueprint
bolection
bottoming
bow|window
box|girder
breezeway
brickwork
bunkhouse
butt|joint
cafeteria
campanile
cartouche
cartulary
cathedral
cauliculi
chophouse
clapboard
classical
cleithral
cloakroom
clubhouse
coal|house
coffer|dam
coffering
colonnade
Colosseum
columella
composite

converted
courtyard
cross|beam
crossette
crown|post
cubby|hole
cubiculum
curtilage
curvature
cyma|recta
decastyle
door|frame
door|panel
doorstone
dormitory
doss|house
drainpipe
dripstone
dry|fresco
earthwork
edificial
elevation
esplanade
estaminet
extension
fan|window
farmhouse
fastigium
fireplace
fixed|arch
flagstone
flathouse
floor|plan
flophouse
footstone
forecourt

framework
front|door
front|room
fundament
gable|roof
garderobe
glory|hole
green|belt
guildhall
guttering
gymnasium
headboard
headmould
headpiece
hexastyle
homecroft
homestall
homestead
hoodmould
houseboat
house|plan
impromptu
inglenook
ingleside
inner|city
landscape
low|relief
marquetry
masonwork
mausoleum
mezzanine
mock|Tudor
modillion
mouldings
neo|Gothic
Nissen|hut

octastyle	stateroom	battlement
open|floor	still,room	bedchamber
outskirts	stone|wall	bidonville
paintwork	storm|door	blind|alley
panelling	structure	breakwater
Parthenon	stylobate	bressummer
partition	sunk|fence	canephorus
pedentive	sun|lounge	cantilever
penthouse	swing|door	cauliculus
peridrome	synagogue	cellar|door
peristyle	telamones	chimney,pot
pontlevis	threshold	cinquefoil
proseuche	tierceron	clearstory
prothesis	tollbooth	clerestory
reception	tollhouse	clock|tower
refectory	town|house	coffee|shop
reservoir	tree,house	common|room
residence	triforium	compluvium
revetment	truss|beam	conversion
ridgepole	Tudor|arch	Corinthian
rigid|arch	vallation	covered|way
ring|fence	vestibule	crosswalls
roadhouse	wallboard	damp|course
rough|arch	warehouse	denticular
roughcast	whitewash	diaconicon
round|arch	window|bay	dining|hall
rus|in|urbe	window|box	dining|room
sally|port	acroterion	doll's|house
scagliola	arched|door	Doric|order
scantling	arched|roof	downstairs
shopfront	architrave	drawbridge
skew,table	art|gallery	earthworks
slate|roof	auditorium	excavation
staircase	balustrade	family|seat
stairhead	barge,board	fan,tracery
stanchion	base|course	fire|escape

27

first|floor
first|story
foot|bridge
French|roof
garden|wall
glass|house
glebe|house
Greek|Ionic
greenhouse
ground|plan
groundsill
groundwork
habitation
hammer|beam
hipped|roof
Ionic|order
ivory|tower
jerry|built
lancet|arch
Lebensraum
lighthouse
living|room
luxury|flat
maisonette
manor|house
mantel tree
masonry|pin
mitre|joint
monolithic
opera|house
orthograph
orthostyle
passageway
paving|flag
pebble|dash
pentastyle

pied|à|terre
pigeonhole
pile|bridge
portcullis
priest|hole
projection
proportion
propylaeum
proscenium
quadrangle
quatrefoil
Quonset|hut
ranch|house
real|estate
repository
restaurant
retrochoir
ribbed|arch
ridge|strut
rising|arch
rising|damp
road|bridge
Roman|Doric
Romanesque
rose|window
rumpus|room
Saxon|tower
screenings
scrollhead
sewing|room
skew|bridge
skew|corbel
skyscraper
split|level
storehouse
stronghold

structural
sun|parlour
terra|cotta
trust|house
tumbledown
turret|room
undercroft
university
ventilator
watch|tower
wicket|door
wicket|gate
antechamber
atmospheric
barge|couple
barge|stones
barrel|vault
buttressing
campaniform
caravansary
chimney|tops
coffee|house
common|stair
compartment
concert|hall
coping|stone
cornerstone
country|seat
crazy|paving
crenellated
cyma|reversa
drawing|room
duplex|house
eating|house
entablature
fan|vaulting

foundations
gambrel|roof
ground|floor
ground|table
hanging|post
hearthstone
ichnography
inhabitancy
kitchenette
lancet|style
latticework
laundry|room
leaded|glass
lecture|hall
linen|closet
little|boxes
mansard|roof
mantelpiece
mantelshelf
masonry|arch
mews|cottage
morning|room
Norman|tower
oeil,de,boeuf
oriel|window
outbuilding
pantile|roof
paving|stone
pendant|post
picket|fence
pitched|roof
plasterwork
pointed|arch
public|house
rampant|arch
restoration

roofing|tile
room|divider
scaffolding
service|lane
service|lift
shingle|roof
sitting|room
smoking|room
stately|home
step|terrace
street|floor
summerhouse
sunken|fence
trefoil|arch
Tuscan|order
urban|sprawl
utility|room
ventilation
wainscoting
waiting|room
water|closet
weathercock
willow|cabin
window|frame
window|glass
wrought|iron
amphitheatre
architecture
assembly|hall
audience|hall
Bailey|bridge
balustrading
bead|moulding
billiard|room
breastsummer
building|line

buttress|pier
caravanserai
chapter|house
charnel|house
chimney|shaft
chimney|stack
city|planning
common|bricks
conservatory
construction
country|house
dividing|wall
Dormer|window
double|glazed
double|scroll
entrance|hall
espagnolette
false|ceiling
fluted|column
French|Gothic
french|window
frontispiece
galilee|porch
garden|suburb
head|moulding
hitching|post
hotel|de|ville
hunting|lodge
inner|sanctum
lake|dwelling
lancet|window
lodging|place
machicolated
Maiden|Castle
main|entrance
mansion|house

meeting house	dormitory town
Nelson column	double glazing
phrontistery	dwelling house
pier buttress	dwelling place
plaster board	emergency exit
porte cochere	ferroconcrete
prefabricate	fire resisting
privy chamber	floodlighting
rooming house	furnished flat
salle à manger	Gothic revival
semi detached	housing estate
shutting post	jerry building
smallholding	lattice girder
snubbing post	master builder
stained glass	open plan house
string course	owner occupied
substructure	palais de danse
swinging post	partition wall
thatched roof	picture window
town planning	prefabricated
underpinning	public gallery
urban renewal	public library
weatherboard	retaining wall
accommodation	revolving door
architectonic	shooting lodge
architectural	sound proofing
assembly rooms	triumphal arch
boarding house	wattle and daub
building block	apartment house
building board	apartment to let
butler's pantry	banqueting hall
chimney corner	bed sitting room
community home	consulting room
council estate	country cottage
county council	funeral parlour
cross vaulting	housing problem

housing project	banqueting house
interior design	clustered column
listed building	community centre
office building	discharging arch
picture gallery	dormitory suburb
pleasure ground	foundation stone
prefabrication	married quarters
slaughterhouse	owner occupation
superstructure	reception centre
system building	spiral staircase
air conditioning	state apartments
architectonical	unfurnished flat

Artists

Arp	Wren	Monet	Duccio
Low	Bacon	Orpen	Giotto
Adam	Berry	Piper	Ingres
Cuyp	Blake	Pugin	Knight
Dali	Bosch	Rodin	Laszlo
Etty	Clark	Scott	Lavery
Eyck	Corot	Smith	Ledoux
Gill	Crome	Soane	Mabuse
Gogh	David	Steer	Millet
Goya	Degas	Watts	Morris
Hals	Dürer	Wyatt	Panini
Hunt	Frith	Bewick	Pisano
John	Giles	Braque	Renoir
Klee	Kelly	Casson	Romney
Lely	Lippi	Claude	Rubens
Nash	Lowry	Corbet	Ruskin
Opie	Manet	Cotman	Seurat

ARTISTS

Sisley

Spence

Stubbs

Tadema

Titian

Turner

Van|Ryn

Warhol

Bassano

Bellini

Bernini

Boucher

Cellini

Cézanne

Chagall

Chardin

Cimabue

Courbet

Daumier

Da|Vinci

De|Hooch

El|Greco

Epstein

Gauguin

Gibbons

Gillray

Gropius

Hobbema

Hockney

Hogarth

Holbein

Matisse

Memlinc

Millais

Murillo

Pasmore

Phidias

Picasso

Poussin

Raeburn

Raphael

Sargent

Sickert

Spencer

Tenniel

Tiepolo

Uccello

Utrillo

Van|Dyck

Van|Eyck

Van|Gogh

Vermeer

Watteau

Zoffany

Angelico

Brancusi

Brangwyn

Brueghel

Hepworth

Landseer

Leonardo

Mantegna

Montegna

Munnings

Perugino

Pissarro

Rossetti

Rousseau

Vanbrugh

Veronese

Vlaminck

Whistler

Beardsley	Mackintosh
Canaletto	Praxiteles
Constable	Rowlandson
Correggio	Sutherland
Delacroix	Tintoretto
Donatello	Fra|Angelico
Fragonard	Ghirlandaio
Giorgione	Le|Corbusier
Hawksmoor	Gainsborough
Rembrandt	Michelangelo
Velásquez	Winterhalter
Botticelli	Leonardo|da|Vinci
Caravaggio	Toulouse|Lautrec

Astronomy

sky	apsis	Orion	Auriga	Hyades
sun	Ariel	phase	bolide	Hydrus
Argo	Cetus	Pluto	Boötes	meteor
Bora	comet	Rigel	Caelum	Nereid
Hebe	Dione	saros	Castor	Oberon
Juno	Draco	solar	Caurus	Octans
Lynx	Hydra	Spica	corona	Pictor
lyra	Indus	stars	Corvus	planet
Mars	Lepus	Titan	cosmic	Pollux
moon	lunar	umbra	cosmos	quasar
nova	Lupus	Venus	Cygnus	Saturn
Pavo	Mensa	albedo	dipper	Selene
Rhea	Musca	Antlia	Dorado	Sirius
star	nadir	apogee	galaxy	starry
Vega	Norma	Aquila	gnomon	syzygy
Algol	orbit	astral	heaven	Tethys

ASTRONOMY

Triton	transit	red|dwarf
Tucana	Achernar	red|giant
Uranus	aerolite	Sculptor
Vulcan	Almagest	sidereal
zodiac	aphelion	solarium
Antares	Arcturus	sunspots
appulse	asteroid	universe
apsides	Canicula	upper|air
azimuth	Cepheids	Aldebaran
Canopus	Circinus	Andromeda
Cepheus	Cynosure	anthelion
Columba	ecliptic	astrolabe
day|star	empyrean	astrology
dog|star	Erodanus	astronomy
eclipse	evection	celestial
equinox	fenestra	Centaurus
faculae	flocculi	coelostat
gibbous	full|moon	corposant
heavens	galactic	cosmogony
Jupiter	ganymede	cosmology
Lacerta	half|moon	Delphinus
Neptune	heavenly	ephemeris
new|moon	Hercules	fenestral
Pegasus	hyperion	firmament
perigee	isochasm	fixed|star
Perseus	luminary	flocculus
Phoenix	Milky|Way	giant|star
Polaris	mock|moon	Great|Bear
Procyon	moonbeam	heliostat
Regulus	night|sky	light|year
Sagitta	nutation	lunar|halo
Serpens	parallax	lunar|rays
sextile	penumbra	meteorite
stellar	Pleiades	meteoroid
sunspot	Pointers	Monoceros
Titania	pole|star	moonlight

moonshine	perihelion
Ophiuchus	phenomenon
parhelion	precession
planetary	quadrature
planetoid	selenology
polar|star	solar|cycle
quasi,star	solar|flare
radio|star	star|stream
refractor	terminator
satellite	tropopause
scintilla	waning|moon
solar|wind	waxing|moon
starlight	Andromedids
supernova	Baily's|beads
telescope	coronagraph
uranology	cosmography
Ursa|Major	cosmosphere
Ursa|Minor	evening|star
Vulpecula	falling|star
almacantar	Gegenschein
Canis|major	Kelper's|laws
Canis|minor	league|table
Cassiopeia	lunar|crater
Chamaeleon	major|planet
collimator	midnight|sun
double|star	minor|planet
geocentric	morning|star
green|flash	observatory
Horologium	occultation
ionosphere	Orion's|sword
Lesser|Bear	photosphere
light,curve	planetarium
luminosity	planisphere
Orion's|belt	polar|aurora
outer|space	polar|lights
paraselene	radio,source

solar|corona
solar|energy
solar|system
star|cluster
stella|maris
stratopause
tail|of|comet
Telescopium
translunary
astronomical
astrophysics
Canis|majoris
Charles's|wain
chromosphere
crescent|moon
Halley's|comet
heavenly|body
man|in|the|moon
meteor|crater
meteorograph
selenography
shooting|star
space|station
spectrograph

spectroscope
spectroscopy
star,spangled
stratosphere
variable|star
vertical|rays
constellation
extragalactic
printed|matter
Southern|Cross
annular|eclipse
astrogeologist
heavenly|bodies
northern|lights
partial|eclipse
radioastronomy
radio,telescope
southern|lights
St|Anthony's|fire
Astronomer|Royal
Hubble's|constant
Nautical|Almanac
sun,|moon|and|stars

Biblical Names

Ur	Ham	Abel	Amon	Cana	Gath
Dan	Job	Adam	Amos	Eden	Gaza
Eli	Lot	Agag	Baal	Edom	Jael
Eve	Nod	Ahab	Boaz	Esau	Jehu
Gad	Abba	Ahaz	Cain	Ezra	Joel

John	Hosea	Dorcas	Pilate
Jude	Isaac	Elijah	Rachel
Leah	Jonah	Elisha	Reuben
Levi	Jacob	Emmaus	Romans
Luke	James	Esther	Salome
Magi	Jesse	Eunice	Samson
Mark	Joppa	Exodus	Samuel
Mary	Jubal	Festus	Simeon
Moab	Judah	Gehazi	Sisera
Noah	Judas	Gibeon	Thomas
Omri	Laban	Gideon	Abaddon
Paul	Micah	Gilboa	Abigail
Ruth	Moses	Gilead	Abilene
Saul	Nahum	Gilgal	Abraham
Seth	Naomi	Goshen	Absalom
Shem	Peter	Haggai	Adullam
Aaron	Sarah	Hannah	Ananias
Abihu	Sheba	Hebron	Antioch
Abner	Silas	Isaiah	Antipas
Abram	Simon	Israel	Azariah
Annas	Sinai	Jairus	Babylon
Asher	Sodom	Jethro	Calvary
Babel	Titus	Jordan	Cherith
Barak	Uriah	Joseph	Cleopas
Caleb	Zadok	Joshua	Corinth
Cyrus	Zimri	Josiah	Deborah
Dagon	Amalek	Judaea	Delilah
David	Andrew	Kishon	Didymus
Dinah	Ararat	Martha	Eleazar
Elias	Balaam	Miriam	Elkanah
Elihu	Belial	Mizpah	Ephesus
Endor	Bethel	Naaman	Ephraim
Enoch	Canaan	Naboth	Ezekiel
Haman	Carmel	Nathan	Gabriel
Herod	Daniel	Nimrod	Galilee
Hiram	Darius	Patmos	Genesis

BIBLICAL NAMES

Gentile	Caiaphas
Goliath	Chorazin
Hebrews	Damascus
Ichabod	Ebenezer
Ishmael	Gadarene
Japheth	Gamaliel
Jericho	Gehennah
Jezebel	Golgotha
Jezreel	Gomorrah
Lazarus	Habakkuk
Malachi	Herodias
Matthew	Hezekiah
Meshach	Immanuel
Messiah	Iscariot
Michael	Issachar
Nineveh	Jephthah
Obadiah	Jeremiah
Pharaoh	Jeroboam
Rebekah	Jonathan
Solomon	Manasseh
Stephen	Matthias
Timothy	Naphtali
Zebedee	Nazareth
Abednego	Nehemiah
Abinadab	Potiphar
Adonijah	Abimelech
Akeldama	Ahasuerus
Amorites	Arimathea
Appelles	Bathsheba
Ashkelon	Beelzebub
Barabbas	Beer₁sheba
Barnabas	Bethlehem
Behemoth	Bethphage
Benjamin	Bethsaida
Bethesda	Boanerges
Caesarea	Capernaum

Elimelech	Armageddon
Elisabeth	Bartimaeus
Esdraelon	Belshazzar
Galatians	Colossians
Jerusalem	Gethsemane
Magdalene	Methuselah
Nicodemus	Shibboleth
Pharisees	Bartholomew
Sadducees	Jehoshaphat
Samaritan	Philippians
Zacchaeus	Philistines
Zachariah	Sennacherib
Zechariah	Thessalonians
Zephaniah	Nebuchadnezzar

Biological Sciences

lab	bursa	order	bionic
ova	class	ovate	biotin
sac	clone	ovoid	botany
alar	cyton	ovule	coccus
axil	fauna	petri	cohort
cell	fibre	slide	colony
cone	flora	spore	cytode
cyte	gemma	still	embryo
gene	genes	taxis	enzyme
germ	genus	virus	fibrin
ovum	group	zooid	foetus
talc	hypha	aerobe	foment
tank	linin	agamic	gamete
algae	lymph	amoeba	gas|jar
bifid	lysin	biogen	hybrid

39

lacuna	ecology	section	entozoon
lamina	egg｜cell	shellac	epiblast
lanate	enation	stimuli	eugenics
lipase	fertile	synapse	feedback
nekton	fistula	synergy	fistular
ovisac	flaccid	syringe	follicle
phylum	forceps	trypsin	genetics
plasma	gametes	vaccine	geotaxis
staple	genesis	vascula	homogamy
system	gliadin	vitamin	inositol
theory	habitat	yolk｜sac	involute
tissue	haploid	zoology	isotropy
zymase	histoid	zootomy	lenticel
acyclic	lactase	adhesion	meniscus
aerobic	lamella	adhesive	mutation
albumen	lateral	amitosis	mycology
albumin	microbe	aquarium	nucleole
amylase	mitosis	autology	organism
anatomy	monitor	basidium	plankton
anomaly	myology	bioblast	prophase
aquaria	nascent	biometer	rudiment
atavism	network	biophore	sex｜ratio
benthos	obovate	blastema	sitology
biology	obovoid	body｜cell	specimen
blubber	oxidase	carotene	sphenoid
booster	paracme	cell｜wall	stimulus
breeder	pedicel	co｜enzyme	sub｜order
calorie	pigment	cohesion	synapsis
cell｜sap	plastid	conchate	syndesis
congeal	primary	cyclosis	taxonomy
cordate	primate	cytology	thiamine
culture	protein	demersal	transect
deltoid	radicle	diastase	trencher
dentine	saltant	diatomic	unciform
diploid	scanner	ectogeny	vascular
dissect	science	effluent	virology

8/10 LETTERS

vitamin|A	gestation	telophase
vitamin|B	halophily	threshold
vitamin|C	herbarium	toast¡rack
vitamin|D	heterosis	vitelline
vitamin|E	histology	yolk|stalk
vitellus	incubator	zoobiotic
xenogamy	initiator	zoogamete
zoospore	injection	achromatin
ambergris	isotropic	albuminoid
anabolism	klinostat	anisotropy
anaerobic	lactation	antecedent
archetype	life¡cycle	antibodies
atavistic	limnology	antitoxins
attenuate	luciferin	biochemics
bifarious	metaplasm	biochemist
bigeneric	microsome	biogenesis
bilateral	microtome	biometrics
bionomics	morphosis	biophysics
bisulcate	myography	biorhythms
body|clock	nutrition	blastoderm
chromatin	occlusion	blastomere
coenobium	ovulation	cacogenics
conjugate	paralyser	carcinogen
convolute	petri|dish	catabolism
cytoplasm	phenology	cell|tissue
dichotomy	phenotype	centrosome
dimorphic	phycology	chromosome
duplicate	phytotron	consequent
ectoplasm	potometer	culture|jar
effluvium	processed	deep|freeze
endoplasm	protogyny	depilatory
endosperm	prototype	dissection
endospore	pyrogenic	egg¡albumen
evolution	scientist	embryology
folic|acid	subdivide	entomology
geobiotic	symbiosis	enzymology

ephemerist	agglutinate	Y|chromosome
etiolation	attenuation	zoochemical
exobiology	auxanometer	zooplankton
formic|acid	benthoscope	acceleration
generation	bioengineer	anthropogeny
growth|ring	bipartition	anthropology
homochromy	cellulation	anthropotomy
incubation	chlorophyll	antithrombin
involution	chloroplast	astrobiology
katabolism	chromoplast	bacteriology
laboratory	coagulation	biochemistry
maturation	cod|liver|oil	biosatellite
metabolism	culture|tube	biosynthesis
microscope	eccrinology	carbohydrate
microscopy	elimination	cell|division
morphology	environment	cross|section
mother|cell	generic|name	cryoplankton
odontogeny	heterotopes	culture|flask
organology	homogenizer	dietotherapy
osteoblast	hygroscopic	disinfectant
pasteurise	insecticide	essential|oil
petri|plate	lactalbumin	eurythermous
physiology	lactoflavin	experimental
primordial	lipoprotein	fermentation
protogenic	microscopic	formaldehyde
protoplasm	monomorphic	immune|bodies
riboflavin	pure|culture	keratogenous
scientific	sensitivity	microspecies
sensitizer	somatic|cell	mitotic|index
somatology	stimulation	monomorphous
spirometer	synoecology	palaeobotany
sterilizer	systematics	pyridoxamine
vital|stain	thermolysis	radiobiology
viviparous	thermolytic	reflex|action
zoophysics	unicellular	regeneration
accelerator	X|chromosome	serum|albumin

simple|tissue
specific|name
trace|element
ultramicrobe
vitaminology
water|culture
zoochemistry
zoogeography
acotyledonous
biodegradable
biogeographer
blastogenesis
crossbreeding
fertilisation
hermaphrodite
heterogenesis
heterogenetic
micro|organism

sterilisation
aerobiological
anthropologist
bacteriologist
biodegradation
bioengineering
breeding|ground
electrobiology
microbiologist
natural|history
natural|science
photosynthesis
plant|formation
anthropological
bacteriological
biological|clock
dissecting|table

Birds

auk	owl	chat	eyry	kiwi	rail
caw	pen	claw	fowl	kora	rhea
coo	pet	coop	game	lark	rook
cry	pie	coot	guan	loon	ruff
daw	roc	crow	gull	lory	skua
emu	tit	dodo	hawk	mina	smew
fly	tui	dove	honk	mute	sord
hen	zoo	down	hoot	nest	swan
jay	bevy	duck	ibis	nide	tail
kea	bill	erne	kaka	pavo	tern
moa	bird	eyas	kite	pern	weka

BIRDS

wing	hobby	serin	darter
wisp	homer	skart	dipper
wren	jenny	skein	drongo
aerie	junco	snipe	dunlin
agami	larus	solan	eaglet
argus	macaw	squab	elanet
avian	madge	stilt	falcon
booby	mavis	stork	flight
brace	merle	torsk	fulmar
brant	moray	trill	gaggle
capon	moult	tweet	gambet
cavie	murre	veery	gander
charm	nandu	vireo	gannet
cheep	nidus	wader	garrot
chick	ornis	aquila	garuda
chirp	ousel	argala	godwit
cluck	ouzel	auklet	gooney
covey	owlet	aviary	grouse
crake	oxeye	avocet	henrun
crane	peggy	bantam	herald
crest	pekan	barbet	honker
diver	pewit	blenny	hooper
drake	picus	bonito	hoopoe
eagle	pipit	bulbul	howlet
egret	pitta	canary	jabiru
eider	poker	chough	jacana
eyrie	Polly	clutch	kakapo
finch	poult	condor	lanner
geese	quack	corbie	linnet
genus	quail	coucal	magpie
glede	raven	covert	martin
goose	reeve	cuckoo	mopoke
grebe	robin	culver	motmot
harpy	roost	curlew	nandoo
hatch	rotch	cushat	oriole
heron	saker	cygnet	oscine

44

osprey	willet	goldeye	peafowl
ox,bird	ynambu	gorcock	pelican
palama	antbird	gor,crow	penguin
parrot	barn|owl	goshawk	phoenix
passer	bittern	gosling	pinguin
pavone	blue,eye	grackle	pinnock
peahen	blue|jay	grey|hen	pintado
peewee	blue|tit	greylag	pintail
peewit	brooder	grey|owl	plumage
petrel	bunting	haggard	pochard
phoebe	bush,tit	halcyon	pollack
pigeon	bustard	hawk|owl	poulard
plover	buzzard	hen,coop	poultry
pouter	cariama	hennery	puttock
puffin	catbird	hoatzin	quetzal
pullet	chewink	hoot|owl	redbird
rallus	chicken	hornowl	redwing
redcap	chirrup	ice|bird	rookery
roller	coal|tit	jacamar	rooster
scoter	colibri	jackdaw	rosella
sea,cob	cotinga	kestrel	ruddock
seamew	cowbird	killdee	sage|hen
sea,owl	creeper	lapwing	sea,bird
shrike	dopping	lich,owl	seadove
simurg	dor,hawk	mallard	seaduck
siskin	dovecot	manakin	seagull
thrush	dunnock	marabou	sea,hawk
toucan	egg,bird	martlet	sea,lark
towhee	emu,wren	migrant	seriema
trogon	fantail	moor,hen	simurgh
turdus	feather	mud,lark	sirgang
turkey	fern,owl	oilbird	skimmer
volary	flapper	ortolan	skylark
warble	flicker	ostrich	sparrow
weaver	gadwall	Partlet	staniel
wigeon	gobbler	peacock	striges

BIRDS

sturnus	bell,bird	flamingo	philomel
sun,bird	berghaan	forewing	podargus
swallow	bird,bath	gamecock	poorwill
tattler	bird,cage	garefowl	popinjay
tiercel	birdcall	garganey	puff,bird
tinamou	bird's,egg	great,auk	rara,avis
titlark	blackcap	grosbeak	rare,bird
titling	bluebill	guacharo	redshank
tumbler	bluebird	hangbird	redstart
twitter	bluewing	hawfinch	reedbird
vulture	boatbill	henhouse	rice,bird
wagtail	boattail	hernshaw	ringdove
warbler	bobolink	hind,wing	ringtail
waxwing	bobwhite	hornbill	rock,bird
web,foot	brown,owl	killdeer	rock,dove
widgeon	bush,wren	kingbird	rock,lark
wood,owl	caracara	king,crow	sage,cock
wren,tit	cardinal	kiwi,kiwi	sand,lark
wryneck	cargoose	lame,duck	sand,peep
aasvogel	cockatoo	landrail	screamer
accentor	cockerel	lanneret	sea,snipe
adjutant	curassow	laverock	shelduck
aigrette	dabchick	lovebird	shoebill
albacore	dead,duck	megapode	skua,gull
alcatras	didapper	moor,cock	snowbird
amadavat	dobchick	moor,fowl	songbird
anserine	dotterel	musk,duck	starling
anserous	dovecote	mute,swan	sun,grebe
ant,pipit	duck,hawk	nightjar	surfbird
apterous	duckling	night,owl	swiftlet
aquiline	duck,mole	nuthatch	tapaculo
arapunga	duck,pond	ovenbird	tawny,owl
avifauna	eagle,owl	ox,pecker	teal,duck
baldpate	fauvette	parakeet	thrasher
barnacle	feathers	pavonian	throstle
bee,eater	fish,hawk	pheasant	titmouse

tragopan	bottle|tit	heath|cock
trembler	bower|bird	heronshaw
troupial	brambling	horned|owl
waterhen	bull|finch	jacksnipe
wheatear	campanero	Jenny|wren
whimbrel	cedarbird	king|eider
whinchat	chaffinch	kittiwake
white|cap	chickadee	little|auk
wild|duck	cockatiel	merganser
wildfowl	cock|robin	migration
wingspan	cocks|comb	migratory
woodchat	columbary	mound|bird
woodcock	columbine	nightbird
wood|duck	crossbill	night|crow
wood|ibis	currawong	night|fowl
woodlark	dicky|bird	nighthawk
wood|wren	eagle|eyed	nocturnal
yoke|toed	eider|duck	on|the|wing
yoldring	fieldfare	ossifrage
aepyornis	fieldlark	owl|parrot
albatross	firecrest	parrakeet
ant|thrush	flute|bird	partridge
bald|eagle	frogmouth	passerine
beaf|eater	gallinazo	peregrine
bean|goose	gallinule	phalarope
beccafico	gerfalcon	pine|finch
birdhouse	gier|eagle	ptarmigan
bird's|nest	goldcrest	quail|dove
bird|table	goldeneye	razorbill
blackbird	goldfinch	redbreast
blackcock	goldspink	redbreast
blackgame	goosander	red|grouse
blackhead	grey|goose	rifle|bird
black|swan	guillemot	ringouzel
black|tern	guinea|hen	rock|pipit
blue|heron	gyrfalcon	salangane

BIRDS

sanctuary	aberdevine	hen harrier
sandpiper	aviculture	herald duck
sapsucker	battery hen	honey eater
scamp duck	bird of prey	honey guide
scrubbird	bluebreast	hooded crow
sea dragon	blue pigeon	hoodie crow
sea parrot	bluethroat	house finch
sedge bird	brent goose	Indian kite
sedge wren	budgerigar	indigo bird
seed snipe	burrow duck	jungle fowl
sheldrake	bush shrike	kingfisher
shore bird	butter bird	meadow lark
snake bird	canvas back	missel bird
snow fleck	Cape pigeon	mutton bird
snow goose	cheep cheep	night churr
solitaire	chiff chaff	night heron
sooty tern	chittagong	night raven
spoonbill	cow bunting	nutcracker
stilt bird	crab plover	parrotbill
stock dove	crested jay	parson bird
stonechat	deep litter	pigeon hawk
stone hawk	demoiselle	pigeon loft
talegalla	dickeybird	poll parrot
tom turkey	didunculus	pratincole
trumpeter	ember goose	quack quack
turnstone	fallow chat	Quaker bird
water bird	flying fish	ring plover
water cock	get the bird	road runner
water fowl	goatsucker	rock hopper
water rail	greenfinch	rock pigeon
web footed	green goose	sage grouse
wheatbird	greenshank	sailorbird
whitehead	grey parrot	sanderling
whitewing	guinea cock	sand grouse
wild goose	guinea fowl	sand martin
windhover	harpy eagle	screech owl

sea swallow	butcher bird	singing bird
sea vampire	Canada goose	sitting duck
setting hen	carrion crow	snow bunting
shearwater	Chanticleer	song sparrow
sheathbill	Cochin china	Spanish fowl
sickle bill	cock a doodle	sparrowhawk
solan goose	cock sparrow	stilt plover
song thrush	columbarium	stone curlew
stone snipe	dead as a dodo	stone falcon
summer duck	fallow finch	stone plover
summer teal	fan tail dove	swallowtail
sun bittern	gnatcatcher	tree swallow
tailor bird	golden eagle	Vanga shrike
talk turkey	green linnet	wattled crow
tawny eagle	ground robin	weaver finch
thick knees	honey sucker	whitethroat
tropic bird	king penguin	wood swallow
turkey cock	king vulture	wood warbler
turtle dove	lammergeier	adjutant bird
wading bird	man o war bird	barndoor fowl
water ousel	meadow pipit	barnyard fowl
weaver bird	muscovy duck	bird's eye view
willow wren	nightingale	bramble finch
wood grouse	pied wagtail	brown pelican
woodpecker	pigeon house	burrowing owl
wood pigeon	pigeon's milk	bustard quail
wood shrike	Pretty Polly	capercaillie
wood thrush	pterodactyl	capercailzie
wren thrush	purple finch	cardinal bird
yellow bird	reed bunting	chicken house
zebra finch	reed sparrow	chimney swift
accipitrine	reed warbler	cliff swallow
bastard wing	rock sparrow	crested swift
black grouse	rooster fish	crowned eagle
black martin	scissorbill	cuckoo roller
brush turkey	sea dotterel	cuckoo shrike

BIRDS

diving petrel
domestic fowl
elephant bird
falcon gentil
fighting cock
flowerpecker
fully fledged
gallinaceous
golden oriole
golden plover
ground cuckoo
hedge sparrow
hedge warbler
hermit thrush
homing pigeon
honey buzzard
mandarin duck
marsh harrier
merrythought
missel thrush
mistle thrush
mourning dove
painted snipe
rifleman bird
ring dotterel
sedge warbler
serpent eater
stonechatter
stormy petrel

stubble goose
tropical bird
ugly duckling
umbrella bird
velvet scoter
water wagtail
whip poor will
wingless bird
wood pheasant
yellow hammer
barnacle goose
bird of passage
carrier pigeon
ornithologist
oyster catcher
spring chicken
trumpeter swan
turkey buzzard
willow warbler
yellow bunting
bird of paradise
bird of paradise
ornithological
Rhode Island Red
robin redbreast
wild goose chase
birds of a feather
peregrine falcon

Capacity

cran	dry|quart
gill	hogshead
peck	spoonful
pint	teaspoon
homer	decalitre
litre	decilitre
pinta	fluid|dram
quart	kilolitre
barrel	centilitre
bushel	millilitre
chopin	tablespoon
cupful	thimbleful
gallon	teaspoonful
magnum	imperial|pint
dry|pint	cubic|capacity

Cereals

awn	corn	durra	pulse
ear	crop	field	spear
lea	husk	flour	spike
oat	oats	glean	straw
rye	reap	grain	wheat
sow	rice	maize	barley
soy	soya	paddy	cereal

CEREALS

farina	soy|flour	ground|rice
groats	wild|oats	Indian|corn
hominy	broomcorn	kaffir|corn
lentil	buckwheat	paddy|field
mealie	corn|bread	rolled|oats
millet	corn|field	wheat|field
corncob	cornflour	whole|wheat
harvest	corn|salad	corn|in|Egypt
oatmeal	ear|of|corn	corn|in|Israel
tapioca	rice|paddy	corn|on|the|cob
wild|oat	sweetcorn	decorticated
ripe|corn	barley|corn	
semolina	brome|grass	

Character Types

ass	doll	rake	puppy	Amazon
cad	dolt	scab	rogue	apache
fop	drip	snob	saint	beauty
hag	dude	thug	scamp	bibber
ham	dupe	toff	scold	cadger
hex	fool	twit	shrew	canter
oaf	gull	wimp	siren	carper
pal	guru	joker	sneak	codger
rat	heel	Judas	spark	con|man
rip	hick	knave	sport	coward
sot	hype	macho	stoic	dodger
wit	liar	miser	toady	dotard
bore	lout	moron	toper	duffer
brat	minx	mouse	trier	egoist
chum	ogre	nomad	vixen	faggot
cove	prig	prude	wally	fantod

6/7 LETTERS

fawner	sinner	dilutee	king|pin
fellow	square	doubter	know|all
fibber	stooge	dreamer	liberal
gasbag	vandal	drifter	lie|abed
gay|dog	virago	drop|out	lounger
genius	voyeur	dullard	low|brow
gossip	Watson	egghead	Luddite
grouch	worthy	egotist	lunatic
hassle	wretch	epicure	man's|man
hep|cat	zealot	eremite	marxist
hippie	zombie	faddist	meddler
humbug	a|bad|egg	fall|guy	Mr|Right
jet|set	also|ran	fanatic	niggard
junkie	ancient	fathead	nut|case
layman	ascetic	flaneur	oddball
leader	avenger	gabbler	old|fogy
loafer	babbler	gallant	old|maid
madman	beatnik	glutton	outcast
martyr	bonkers	gourmet	paragon
nobody	bounder	groupie	parvenu
nutter	bucolic	haggler	patriot
ogress	buffoon	half|wit	Paul|Pry
old|boy	bumpkin	hangdog	peasant
pariah	charmer	hard|man	playboy
pedant	chauvin	has|been	prodigy
pundit	cheater	hellcat	puritan
puppet	copy|cat	hellier	radical
purist	coxcomb	heretic	recluse
rabbit	cry|baby	hoodlum	ruffian
rascal	cuckold	hothead	runaway
roamer	culprit	hotspur	sad|sack
Romany	dabbler	hustler	saviour
rotter	dallier	hyped|up	sceptic
rustic	darling	infidel	Scrooge
sadist	devotee	Jezebel	showman
sexist	diehard	Joe|Soap	show|off

shyster	blighter	imbecile
slacker	bluenose	impostor
sponger	Bohemian	innocent
suspect	braggart	intruder
swinger	busybody	jabberer
thinker	carouser	jailbird
tippler	cenobite	jawsmith
tosspot	crackpot	John Bull
traitor	criminal	laid back
trueman	deceiver	lame duck
twister	defector	layabout
upstart	derelict	live wire
villain	dirty dog	lone wolf
vulture	dogooder	low lifer
wastrel	drunkard	machismo
welcher	everyman	man hater
welsher	evildoer	martinet
whipcat	feminist	Napoleon
windbag	fine lady	nepotist
wiseguy	folk hero	nihilist
workshy	follower	nuisance
wrecker	frontman	numskull
absentee	funnyman	objector
aesthete	gadabout	offender
agitator	gamester	optimist
agnostic	gaolbird	outsider
alarmist	gourmand	pacifist
alterego	greatman	paleface
altruist	groupnik	paramour
antihero	hangeron	parasite
antipope	hectorer	partisan
apostate	hedonist	penitent
banterer	highbrow	perjurer
beginner	hooligan	plebeian
betrayer	humorist	poltroon
bignoise	idolater	poor soul

popinjay	battleaxe	goodmixer
prattler	Bluebeard	gradgrind
quackery	blusterer	greenhorn
quisling	boywonder	harebrain
rakehell	careerist	Hellenist
renegade	careerman	honestman
romancer	character	honourman
romantic	charlatan	hypocrite
saucebox	chatterer	ignoramus
scalawag	chiseller	inamorata
skinhead	churchman	inebriate
slattern	comforter	introvert
somebody	consenter	jetsetter
sorehead	coughdrop	ladiesman
spitfire	darkhorse	lateriser
stranger	defeatist	lazybones
swindler	defrauder	libertine
sybarite	demagogue	logroller
telltale	desperado	lostsheep
theorist	dignitary	loudmouth
tightwad	dissenter	manofmark
truckler	dogmatist	manofnote
turncoat	dollybird	masochist
twotimer	earlybird	nonentity
underdog	eccentric	nonsmoker
vagabond	Edwardian	oddmanout
whizzkid	exploiter	pacemaker
wiseacre	extravert	patrician
wisefool	extrovert	Pecksniff
accessory	familyman	peculator
adulterer	favourite	persuader
adversary	fireeater	pessimist
alcoholic	flagwaver	plutocrat
auntsally	fossicker	poetaster
bacchanal	freeagent	poisonpen
barbarian	gentleman	pothunter

CHARACTER TYPES

pretender	aficionado	lawbreaker
queer|fish	anglophile	left|winger
racketeer	anglophobe	lotus|eater
reprobate	antagonist	malefactor
roisterer	aristocrat	malingerer
roughneck	benefactor	man|of|straw
Samaritan	best|friend	mastermind
sassenach	Big|Brother	matchmaker
scapegoat	blackguard	merrymaker
scoundrel	black|sheep	Methuselah
screwball	bobbysoxer	middlebrow
simpleton	bootlicker	militarist
skylarker	career|girl	misogynist
slowcoach	chatterbox	mountebank
sob|sister	chauvinist	ne'er|do|well
socialist	church|goer	non|starter
socialite	Cinderella	old|soldier
star|pupil	confidante	past|master
strongman	daydreamer	peeping|Tom
sundowner	delinquent	philistine
suppliant	Don|Quixote	pragmatist
swaggerer	drug|addict	prima|donna
swellhead	Dutch|uncle	psychopath
sycophant	enthusiast	recidivist
tactician	fly|by|night	ringleader
termagant	fuddy|duddy	secularist
terrorist	gastronome	shoplifter
underling	gentlefolk	smart|aleck
visionary	girl|Friday	sneak|thief
warmonger	girl|friend	social|lion
womanizer	gold|digger	spoilsport
womenfolk	goody|goody	squanderer
wrongdoer	human|wreck	street|arab
xenophobe	jackanapes	sugar|daddy
young|fogy	Jesus|freak	taskmaster
adventurer	lady|killer	time|server

troglodyte	gate,crasher	soliloquist
tub,thumper	grave|robber	spendthrift
upper|crust	guttersnipe	stool|pigeon
utopianist	hard|drinker	suffragette
vacillator	helping|hand	sympathiser
vegetarian	homo|sapiens	teacher's|pet
wallflower	human|nature	teeny,bopper
well,wisher	imperialist	town,dweller
wine,bibber	lickspittle	Walter|Mitty
woman,hater	lifemanship	artful|dodger
young|blood	line,shooter	awkward|squad
Young|Fogey	living|image	babysnatcher
adventuress	man|of|genius	backwoodsman
animal|lover	materialist	bible,thumper
beachcomber	mental|giant	blue|stocking
Bible|reader	merry,andrew	bobby,dazzler
blackmailer	misanthrope	carpet,knight
blue,eyed|boy	name,dropper	collaborator
braggadocio	nationalist	Colonel|Blimp
cattle|thief	nosey,parker	conservative
centenarian	opportunist	cosmopolitan
chain|smoker	personality	doppelganger
cheese,parer	pettifogger	eavesdropper
Cinemascope	philanderer	featherbrain
close|friend	prodigal|son	flittermouse
common|scold	quacksalver	flower|people
connoisseur	rapscallion	grey|eminence
country|girl	rationalist	hair,splitter
deadly|enemy	reactionary	headshrinker
dipsomaniac	reparteeist	humanitarian
eager|beaver	right,winger	kleptomaniac
femme|fatale	Sabbatarian	lounge,lizard
francophile	scaremonger	mad|as|a|hatter
francophobe	self,made|man	man,about,town
freethinker	simple|Simon	modest|violet
gallows|bird	sleep,walker	moneygrubber

one upmanship	compassionate
poor relation	conceitedness
prevaricator	condescending
right hand man	condescension
rolling stone	conscientious
rough diamond	consternation
salvationist	controversial
scatterbrain	country cousin
single person	courteousness
somnambulist	deserving poor
street urchin	determination
stuffed shirt	dishonourable
swashbuckler	dispassionate
transgressor	distinguished
transvestite	double crosser
troublemaker	double dealing
truce breaker	dyed in the wool
ugly customer	egocentricity
ugly duckling	egotistically
woolgatherer	excitableness
absence of mind	exhibitionism
accident prone	exhibitionist
Anglo American	foolhardiness
angry young man	fool's paradise
anthropomorph	forgetfulness
anthropophagi	fortune hunter
antichristian	fresh air fiend
anythingarian	frivolousness
apple pie order	gentle hearted
barbarousness	gentlemanlike
bare faced liar	gentlewomanly
bargain hunter	go as you please
best of friends	good influence
clapperclawer	good Samaritan
clishmaclaver	go the whole hog
companionship	grandiloquent

hair₁splitting
half₁heartedly
heartlessness
hole₁and₁corner
hunger₁marcher
hypercritical
hypochondriac
idiosyncratic
impassiveness
imperturbable
impetuousness
impulsiveness
inconsiderate
inconsistency
incorruptible
indefatigable
individualist
infant₁prodigy
in₁honour₁bound
insignificant
insubordinate
intransigence
introspective
irrepressible
irresponsible
lackadaisical
Lady₁Bountiful
latchkey₁child
laughing₁stock
long₁suffering
lunatic₁fringe
misadventurer
misanthropist
mischief₁maker
over₁confident
overcredulous

overexcitable
overindulgent
pain₁in₁the₁neck
panic₁stricken
penny₁pinching
perspicacious
plain₁speaking
procrastinate
prophet₁of₁doom
pusillanimous
quiet₁as₁a₁mouse
ray₁of₁sunshine
remittance₁man
riotous₁living
rough₁and₁ready
rough₁customer
round₁the₁twist
sanctimonious
scandalmonger
self₁appointed
self₁approving
self₁assertive
self₁conceited
self₁conscious
self₁deceitful
self₁important
self₁indulgent
self₁satisfied
sense₁of₁humour
sense₁of₁values
sharp₁practice
short₁tempered
sign₁the₁pledge
sit₁on₁the₁fence
smooth₁tongued
soap₁box₁orator

sober as a judge
social climber
social outcast
sophisticated
soul searching
stick in the mud
stiff upper lip
supercritical
superstitious
sweet tempered
swelled headed
swollen headed
sycophantical
temperamental
tender hearted
tongue in cheek
unadventurous
uncomplaining
uncooperative
undisciplined
unenlightened
ungentlemanly
unimaginative
unintelligent
unsympathetic
untrustworthy
unworkmanlike
well respected
well thought of
wheeler dealer
willing helper
willing worker
auto suggestion
back scratching
back seat driver
beat generation

changeableness
characteristic
class conscious
claustrophobia
common or garden
credibility gap
crocodile tears
culture vulture
disciplinarian
dog in the manger
doubting Thomas
easy come, easy go
factitiousness
fastidiousness
fish out of water
flower children
formidableness
free spokenness
frolicsomeness
full of mischief
glutton for work
good for nothing
gracious living
hell for leather
high handedness
high mindedness
high principled
holier than thou
hot air merchant
hypersensitive
impressionable
inveterate liar
jealous husband
larger than life
Macchiavellian
male chauvinist

man|in|the|street
man|in|the|street
man|of|many|parts
man|of|substance
man|of|the|moment
mods|and|rockers
nasty|bit|of|work
nimble|fingered
obstructionist
overscrupulous
petit|bourgeois
philanthropist
pleased|as|Punch
pleasure|seeker
pluck|up|courage
practical|joker
presence|of|mind
public|nuisance
public|spirited
rich|as|a|Croesus
salt|of|the|earth
scatter|brained
self|advertiser
self|controlled
self|interested
self|sufficient
sensationalist
sentimentalist
someone|or|other
straight|as|a|die
supersensitive
tail|end|Charlie
terror|stricken
three|bottle|man
total|abstainer
traditionalist

troubleshooter
unconventional
unenterprising
universal|aunts
unostentatious
unprofessional
ambulance|chaser
ancestor|worship
antivivisection
awkward|customer
bats|in|the|belfry
birds|of|a|feather
connoisseurship
conservationist
conventionalist
conversationist
cool|as|a|cucumber
cryptocommunist
cuckoo|in|the|nest
dual|personality
eternal|triangle
flibbertigibbet
good|naturedness
half|heartedness
hope|against|hope
humanitarianism
little|Englander
middle|of|the|raod
model|of|industry
non|professional
paragon|of|virtue
philanthropical
pillar|of|society
platitudinarian
quite|a|character
ready|and|willing

second|childhood
self,considering
self,destructive
self,opinionated
sensation,monger
snake|in|the|grass
stable|companion
stage,door|Johnny
stand|on|ceremony
stark,|staring|mad
strong,|silent|man
thorn|in|the|flesh
too|clever|by|half
to|the|manner|born

tower|of|strength
unaccommodating
uncommunicative
undemonstrative
under,privileged
undistinguished
unprepossessing
unsportsmanlike
unstatesmanlike
well,intentioned
whited|sepulchre
with|bated|breath
yours|faithfully

Chemical Sciences

pH	muon	borax	oxide	action
dye	neon	boron	ozone	air|gas
gas	norm	dregs	poise	alkali
gel	otto	ester	radon	amylum
ion	rust	ether	resin	anneal
lab	soda	ethyl	rosin	atomic
sol	zein	flask	salts	barite
acid	agene	fluid	toxin	barium
alum	agent	hexad	uredo	baryta
amyl	alkyl	inert	U,tube	beaker
atom	amide	latex	vinyl	boffin
buna	amine	leach	xenon	borate
calx	argon	monad	xylem	bunsen
dyad	assay	nitre	yeast	calcar
etna	basic	nylon	acetic	calxes

carbon	octane	alembic	dioxide
carboy	osmium	amalgam	element
casein	oxygen	ammonia	essence
cerate	pectin	ampoule	eutropy
cerium	pepsin	aniline	exhaust
citric	petrol	antacid	ferment
cobalt	phenol	arsenic	formula
curium	poison	atrazin	gallium
decane	potash	balance	geogony
dilute	radium	bell|jar	geology
diplon	reflux	benzene	glucose
dry|ice	retort	bismuth	hafnium
erbium	ribose	bitumen	halogen
ethane	saline	boiling	holmium
filter	silica	bromide	hydrate
funnel	sinter	bromine	hydride
fusion	sodium	burette	hyperon
galena	spirit	cadmium	iridium
gas|jar	stable	caesium	isotope
gluten	starch	calomel	isotopy
halide	symbol	capsule	isotron
helium	theory	carbide	keratin
indium	thoron	chemism	krypton
inulin	toxoid	chemist	lacquer
iodide	tripod	citrate	lactate
iodine	vapour	coal|tar	lactose
isomer	xylose	colloid	lanolin
ketone	acetate	corrode	leucine
labile	acetone	crystal	lipoids
litmus	acetose	cuprite	lithium
lutein	acid|dye	cyanide	matrass
lysine	acidity	deposit	melanin
matter	acyclic	dextrin	mercury
methyl	aerosol	dialyse	metamer
natron	alchemy	dibasic	methane
niacin	alcohol	diluent	micelle

CHEMICAL SCIENCES

mixture	titrate	Bakelite	equation
muonium	toluene	basicity	ethylene
niobium	tritium	benzoate	europium
nitrate	uranide	biochemy	exhalant
nitride	uranium	bivalent	filtrate
nitrite	valence	carbonyl	fluoride
nonacid	valency	catalyst	fluorine
nuclide	vinegar	catalyse	formulae
osmosis	vitriol	charcoal	francium
oxalate	yttrium	chemical	gasoline
oxidant	zymurgy	chemurgy	gelatine
oxidase	acid|bath	chlorate	globulin
oxonium	acid|salt	chloride	glutelin
oxyacid	acid|test	chlorine	glutenin
pentose	actinism	chlorite	glycogen
peptide	actinium	chromate	honeydew
reagent	actinoid	chromium	hydrogen
rhenium	activate	cleveite	isomeric
rhodium	activity	cobalite	isoteric
science	additive	cohesion	isotopic
sebacic	agar,agar	collagen	kerosene
silicon	alcahest	compound	leaching
solvent	aldehyde	copperas	lecithin
spatula	alkahest	crucible	levulose
spireme	alkaline	cucurbit	litharge
spirits	amandine	cyanogen	lutetium
subacid	ammonium	dendrite	magnesia
sucrose	analogue	dextrose	marshgas
sulphur	analyser	dialysis	melamine
tarnish	analysis	dialytic	mercuric
terbium	analytic	dilution	miscible
terpene	antimony	diplogen	molecule
thermal	arsenate	divalent	monoxide
thorium	arsenide	docimasy	nicotine
thulium	asbestos	dye,stuff	nitrogen
tinfoil	astatine	emulsion	nobelium

nonmetal	titanium	chemurgic
oxidizer	tribasic	colloidal
pedology	trioxide	copolymer
pentosan	tungsten	cork|borer
peroxide	unstable	corrosion
phenolic	uric|acid	covalence
phosgene	vanadium	covalency
plastics	volatile	desiccant
platinum	absorbent	detergent
polonium	actinides	detonator
polyacid	alchemist	deuterium
quantity	allotropy	developer
reactant	americium	dimorphic
reaction	amino|acid	dispenser
reactive	anglesite	distiller
research	anhydride	elastomer
resinoid	apparatus	elemental
rheology	aqua|regia	emanation
rubidium	aspirator	erythrite
samarium	atmolysis	erythrose
scandium	atmometer	fulminate
sediment	autoclave	fungicide
selenium	barricade	galactose
silicate	basic|salt	germanium
silicone	berkelium	glucoside
solation	beryllium	glutinous
solution	bivalence	glycerine
spagyric	bivariant	histidine
sulphate	boric|acid	homocycle
sulphide	carbonate	hydrazine
sulphite	carbonize	hydrolist
tantalum	catalysis	hydrolyte
tartrate	catalytic	hydroxide
test|tube	celluloid	inhibitor
thallium	cellulose	isinglass
tincture	chemiatry	isocyclic

isomerism	synthetic	disulphide
lanthanum	teleology	dysprosium
magnesium	tellurite	elementary
malic|acid	tellurium	emulsifier
manganese	tetroxide	equivalent
metalloid	titration	estimation
metameric	univalent	eudiometer
neodymium	verdigris	experiment
neptunium	virginium	fibrinogen
nitration	viscosity	fluorotype
oxidation	ytterbium	formic|acid
palladium	zirconium	gadolinium
petroleum	alkalinity	gallic|acid
phosphate	alpha|helix	heavy|water
phosphide	amylaceous	high|octane
phosphite	antifreeze	homocyclic
photogene	antimatter	hydrolysis
plutonium	aqua|fortis	hydrolytic
polybasic	ballistite	hypothesis
polyester	biochemics	immiscible
polythene	biochemist	ion|counter
potassium	bisulphate	ionization
prolamine	bisulphide	laboratory
protamine	calcareous	lactic|acid
pyrolysis	calciferol	lead|glance
pyrometer	cellophane	metamerism
raffinose	chloroform	molybdenum
reservoir	chrome|alum	monovalent
ruthenium	citric|acid	neutralize
saccharin	coalescent	nitric|acid
saltpetre	cyanic|acid	nucleonium
scientist	decinormal	octavalent
still|room	decompound	oxalic|acid
strontium	denaturant	phlogiston
sulphacid	dichromate	phosphorus
synthesis	disulphate	photolysis

picric|acid	butyric|acid	niacinamide
promethium	calcination	opalescence
rare|earths	calibration	oxidization
reactivity	californium	oxygen|meter
resolution	calorimeter	pectization
saccharate	calorimetry	pentavalent
saccharose	carbonation	peptization
scientific	chloric|acid	phosphorous
sodium|lamp	chromic|acid	pitchblende
solubility	closed|chain	plasmolysis
sorbic|acid	cobalt|bloom	polymorphic
sulphation	constituent	polyvalence
suspension	contaminate	proteolysis
technetium	dehydration	prussic|acid
technology	dissolution	quantometer
trivalence	double|helix	quicksilver
tryptophan	endothermal	radiocarbon
univalence	evaporation	retort|stand
viscometer	filter|paper	rule|of|thumb
wash|bottle	fume|cabinet	sal|ammoniac
water|still	gas|detector	sal|volatile
Winchester	haloid|acids	sub|critical
yield|point	heptavalent	technocracy
zero|valent	heterocycle	tetravalent
accelerator	hydrocarbon	transuranic
acidulation	hydrogen|ion	tripod|stand
acrylic|acid	hydrogenoid	volatile|oil
agglomerate	impermeable	xanthophyll
arsenic|acid	interaction	acceleration
atomic|table	lanthanides	acid|solution
atomologist	lipoprotein	aspartic|acid
beaker|flask	litmus|paper	atomic|theory
benzene|ring	mendelevium	atomic|weight
benzoic|acid	mensuration	Avogadro's|law
bicarbonate	monovalence	barrier|cream
brittleness	neutralizer	bicarbonates

CHEMICAL SCIENCES

biochemistry
breathalyzer
bunsen|burner
burette|stand
carbolic|acid
carbonic|acid
chemical|bond
chemical|pump
chlorination
chlorous|acid
cobalt glance
constituents
deactivation
deionization
deliquescent
dissociation
distillation
effervescent
experimental
ferrous|oxide
flocculation
fluorocarbon
fluorography
fume|cupboard
geochemistry
glutamic|acid
glycoprotein
gram molecule
heterocyclic
hydrocarbons
hydrogen|atom
hydrostatics
iatrochemist
inactivation
ion|exchanger
liquefaction

liquid|oxygen
lysergic|acid
melting|point
mesomorphous
microbalance
microburette
microelement
minor|element
multivalence
muriatic|acid
nicotinamide
nitromethane
oil|of|vitriol
oxycellulose
oxychromatin
pangamic|acid
permanganate
permeability
photochemist
praseodymium
quadrivalent
radiochemist
radioelement
radioisotope
radionuclide
reactivation
spark|chamber
thermocouple
transuranian
zoochemistry
carbon|dioxide
carbonisation
chain|reaction
compatibility
corrosiveness
decomposition

demonstration	distilled water
diffusion tube	electrochemist
dissolubility	microchemistry
hydrochloride	nitroglycerine
hydrosulphide	petroleum jelly
hydrosulphite	phosphorescent
hydroxylamine	photochemistry
nitro compound	photosynthesis
nitrogen cycle	surgical spirit
periodic table	biogeochemistry
petrochemical	decarbonisation
precipitation	electrochemical
radioactivity	molecular weight
reducing agent	nitro derivative
sulphuric acid	phosphorescence
carbon monoxide	trinitrotoluene

Cinema and Television

TV	play	movie	movies
act	plot	odeon	rushes
BBC	role	oscar	screen
cue	shot	radio	script
fan	show	scene	serial
ITV	star	telly	series
set	unit	video	sit com
cast	actor	camera	studio
crew	cable	Ceefax	talkie
film	drama	cinema	TV show
hero	enact	comedy	actress
mike	extra	critic	cartoon
part	flick	make up	compere

feature	cameraman
film|set	character
flicker	direction
heroine	entertain
musical	exhibitor
network	film|actor
perform	film|extra
phone¡in	film|strip
pop|star	flash¡back
portray	goggle¡box
present	guest|star
produce	interview
sponsor	movie¡goer
tragedy	movie|show
trailer	movie|star
audience	performer
bioscope	photoplay
chat|show	programme
Cinerama	projector
comedian	recording
director	rehearsal
festival	soap|opera
film|club	spectacle
film|crew	title|role
film|star	voice¡over
fruit¡pie	commercial
newsreel	crowd|scene
pictures	home¡movies
premiere	horror|film
producer	horse|opera
quiz|show	microphone
tape¡deck	movie|actor
telecast	needle|time
telefilm	newscaster
blue¡movie	newsreader
broadcast	on|location

performing
production
screenplay
silent|film
television
the|critics
broadcaster
credit|title
documentary
echo|chamber
entertainer
feature|film
performance
picture|show
radio|caster
sound|effect
talking|film
academy|award
cinéma|vérité
clapperboard
film|festival
picture|house
scriptwriter
show|business
silver|screen
sound|effects
technicolour
Chinese|puzzle
cinematograph
cine|projector
clapperboards
closed|circuit
continuity|man
entertainment

global|village
motion|picture
motion|picture
Nouvelle|Vague
picture|palace
tape|recording
telerecording
television|set
videocassette
video|recorder
book|at|bedtime,|a
cinematography
continuity|girl
feature|picture
features|editor
moving|pictures
question|master
supporting|cast
supporting|film
supporting|part
supporting|role
television|play
Third|Programme
animated|cartoon
cable|television
cinematographer
cinematographic
documentary|film
French|subtitles
peak|viewing|time
situation|comedy
slapstick|comedy
spot|advertising

Cities

Baku	Berne	Paris	Boston	Madras
Bari	Bursa	Patna	Bremen	Madrid
Bonn	Cairo	Perth	Cracow	Málaga
Brno	Chiba	Poona	Dallas	Malang
Cork	Dacca	Quito	Dayton	Manila
Gifu	Davao	Rabat	Denver	Moscow
Giza	Delhi	Sakai	Dublin	Multan
Graz	Essen	Seoul	Dundee	Munich
Homs	Genoa	Sofia	Durban	Mysore
Hull	Gorky	Surat	El|Paso	Nagpur
Ipoh	Haifa	Tampa	Frunze	Nantes
Kano	Halle	Tokyo	Fukoka	Naples
Kiel	Hanoi	Tomsk	Fushun	Newark
Kiev	Izmir	Tunis	Gdansk	Odessa
Kobe	Kabul	Turin	Geneva	Oporto
Lima	Kazan	Aachen	Harbin	Ottawa
Lodz	Kyoto	Abadan	Havana	Oxford
Nice	Lagos	Aleppo	Ibadan	Peking
Omsk	La|Paz	Ankara	Indore	Penang
Oran	Leeds	Asmara	Jaipur	Poznan
Oslo	Lyons	Athens	Kanpur	Prague
Riga	Malmo	Austin	Khulna	Puebla
Rome	Mecca	Baroda	Kumasi	Quebec
Accra	Miami	Beirut	Lahore	Santos
Adana	Milan	Berlin	Lisbon	Shiraz
Amman	Mosul	Bilbao	London	St|Paul
Basle	Omaha	Bochum	Luanda	Sydney
Basra	Osaka	Bogota	Lübeck	Tabriz
Belem	Padua	Bombay	Lusaka	Taipei

6/8 LETTERS

Talinn
Toledo
Venice
Verona
Vienna
Warsaw
Zagreb
Zürich
Abidjan
Algiers
Antwerp
Atlanta
Baghdad
Bangkok
Barnaul
Belfast
Bologna
Brescia
Bristol
Buffalo
Caracas
Cardiff
Chengtu
Chicago
Cologne
Colombo
Córdoba
Corunna
Detroit
Donetsk
Dresden
Firenze
Foochow
Glasgow
Gwalior
Hamburg

Hanover
Houston
Irkutsk
Isfahan
Jakarta
Kalinin
Karachi
Kharkov
Kowloon
Kwangju
La|Plata
Leipzig
Lucknow
Managua
Memphis
Messina
Mombasa
Nairobi
Nanking
Oakland
Palermo
Phoenix
Rangoon
Rosario
San|Jose
San|Juan
Santa|Fe
Sapporo
Saratov
Seattle
Seville
Soochow
Stettin
St|Louis
Taranto
Tbilisi

Teheran
Tel|Aviv
Toronto
Trieste
Tripoli
Utrecht
Aberdeen
Adelaide
Amritsar
Auckland
Augsburg
Belgrade
Bordeaux
Bradford
Brasilia
Brisbane
Brussels
Budapest
Bulawayo
Cagliari
Calcutta
Campinas
Canberra
Capetown
Columbus
Coventry
Curitiba
Damascus
Dortmund
Duisburg
Edmonton
Florence
Gorlovka
Hague,|The
Haiphong
Hamilton

CITIES

Hangchow	Ahmedabad	Marrakesh
Helsinki	Allahabad	Melbourne
Honolulu	Amagasaki	Milwaukee
Istanbul	Amsterdam	Nuremberg
Katmandu	Archangel	Reykjavik
Katowice	Asahikawa	Rotterdam
Khartoum	Astrakhan	Salisbury
Kingston	Baltimore	Samarkand
Kinshasa	Bangalore	Saragossa
Kumamoto	Barcelona	Sheffield
Kweiyang	Brunswick	Singapore
Mandalay	Bucharest	Stockholm
Mannheim	Cambridge	Stuttgart
Montreal	Cartagena	Vancouver
Murmansk	Chengchow	Volgograd
Nagasaki	Chihuahua	Wuppertal
Peshawar	Cleveland	Addis\Ababa
Plymouth	Des\Moines	Alexandria
Portland	Edinburgh	Baton\Rouge
Port\Said	Fort\Worth	Birmingham
Pretoria	Frankfurt	Bratislava
Pyongang	Guayaquil	Canterbury
Richmond	Hamamatsu	Casablanca
Salonika	Hiroshima	Chittagong
San\Diego	Hyderabad	Cincinnati
Santiago	Jerusalem	Coimbatore
Sao\Paulo	Karlsruhe	Copenhagen
Sarajevo	Krasnodar	Düsseldorf
Shanghai	Kuibyshev	Gothenburg
Sholapur	Kwangchow	Jamshedpur
Srinagar	Las\Palmas	Kansas\City
Tashkent	Leicester	Krivoi\Roig
Tientsin	Leningrad	Los\Angeles
Toulouse	Liverpool	Louisville
Winnipeg	Magdeburg	Manchester
Yokohama	Maracaibo	Marseilles

Mexico City   Rostov on Don
Montevideo   San Salvador
New Orleans   Southampton
Nottingham   Vladivostok
Panama City   Barquisimeto
Pittsburgh   Bloemfontein
Portsmouth   Braunschweig
Rawalpindi   Indianapolis
Sacramento   Jacksonville
San Antonio   Johannesburg
Strasbourg   Magnitogorsk
Sunderland   Oklahoma City
Sverdlovsk   Philadelphia
Tananarive   Port au Prince
Valparaiso   Rio de Janeiro
Washington   Salt Lake City
Wellington   San Francisco
Baranquilla   Santo Dómingo
Buenos Aires   Stoke on Trent
Chelyabinsk   Gelsenkirchen
Dar es Salaam   Guatemala City
Guadalajara   Karl Marx Stadt
Kuala Lumpur   Port Elizabeth
Mar del Plata   Shihkiachwang
New York City   Wolverhampton
Novosibirsk   Dnepropetrovsk
Pondicherry

Clothes

| alb | bib | bob | bun | fez | fop |
| bag | boa | bra | cap | fob | fur |

CLOTHES

hat	drag	muff	warp	cymar	moire
hem	duck	mule	wear	dandy	motif
kid	elan	peak	weft	denim	mufti
mac	felt	poke	welt	derby	mules
nap	fold	pump	woof	dhoti	nappy
net	frog	rags	wool	drape	ninon
pin	gamp	ring	wrap	dress	nylon
rag	garb	robe	yarn	drill	Orlon
rig	gear	ruff	yoke	ducks	paint
sox	gilt	sack	A line	ephod	pants
tab	gore	saga	amice	fanon	pants
tag	gown	sari	aodai	fichu	parka
tie	haik	sark	apron	flare	patch
wig	heel	sash	array	flash	patte
zip	hood	seal	badge	frill	pique
Afro	hoop	seam	baize	frock	pixie
alba	hose	shoe	bands	gauze	plaid
bags	hyke	silk	bangs	getup	plait
band	hype	skip	batik	glove	pleat
bang	jean	slip	beard	grego	plume
bead	jupe	sock	beret	guimp	plush
belt	kepi	sole	blond	guise	point
bias	kilt	stud	blues	gunny	print
boot	knot	suit	boots	habit	pumps
brim	lace	talc	braid	jabot	purse
cape	lame	tick	busby	jeans	queue
clog	lawn	tile	chain	jupon	rayon
coat	list	toga	chaps	lapel	robes
coif	lock	togs	check	Levis	romal
comb	mask	torc	cloak	linen	rumal
cope	maud	tuck	clogs	lisle	sable
cord	maxi	tutu	cotta	lungi	sabot
cowl	mini	vamp	crape	lurex	sagum
cuff	mink	veil	crash	manta	satin
curl	mitt	vent	crepe	manto	scarf
dart	mode	vest	crown	model	serge

shako	V₁neck	brogan	denier	infula
shawl	voile	brogue	diaper	insole
sheer	waist	brolly	dickey	jacket
shift	wamus	buckle	dimity	jemima
shirt	watch	burlap	dirndl	jerkin
shoes	weave	buskin	dittos	jersey
simar	wigan	bustle	dolman	jumper
skein	woven	button	duffel	kaftan
skirt	achkan	byssus	ermine	kagool
smock	afghan	caftan	fabric	kimono
snood	alnage	calash	facial	kirtle
spats	alpaca	calico	facing	lappet
specs	angora	camise	faille	lining
stays	anklet	canvas	fallal	livery
stock	anorak	capote	fannel	locket
stole	armlet	casque	fascia	madras
stuff	attire	castor	fedora	magyar
style	basque	cestus	feeder	make₁up
suede	bauble	chimer	fillet	mantle
tabby	beaver	chintz	finery	mantua
tails	bertha	chiton	fox|fur	marcel
talma	biggin	choker	frills	melton
tammy	bikini	chopin	fringe	minium
terry	blazer	cilice	gaiter	mitten
thrum	blouse	cloche	galosh	mob|cap
tiara	boater	coatee	gamash	mohair
topee	bodice	collar	garter	moreen
toque	bodkin	collet	girdle	muslin
train	bolero	corset	goatee	nankin
tress	bonnet	cotton	greave	needle
trews	bootee	cravat	gusset	nylons
tulle	bouclé	crewel	hairdo	outfit
tunic	bowler	curler	hankie	panama
tweed	bow|tie	Dacron	hat|box	parure
twill	braces	damask	hatpin	patent
upper	briefs	dapper	helmet	peplos

CLOTHES

peplum	tabard	wimple	chaplet
peruke	talcum	woolly	chechia
pocket	tartan	zoster	chemise
pomade	tassle	Acrilan	cheviot
pompom	tettix	à|la|mode	chevron
poncho	thread	alamode	chiffon
pongee	tiepin	apparel	chignon
poplin	tights	armband	chimere
powder	tin|hat	armhole	chlamys
raglan	tippet	baboosh	chopine
rebato	tissue	baldric	civvies
reefer	toecap	bandana	clobber
revers	tongue	bandbox	clothes
ribbon	top|hat	bandeau	cockade
rigout	topper	bath|oil	compact
rochet	torque	batiste	corsage
roller	toupee	beading	costume
ruffle	tricot	belcher	couture
sacque	trilby	biretta	coxcomb
samite	trunks	bombast	crewcut
sandal	T|shirt	brocade	crochet
sarong	tucker	buckram	cuculla
sateen	turban	bunting	culotte
scarab	tussah	burdash	doeskin
semmit	tusser	burnous	doublet
serape	tuxedo	bycoket	drawers
sheath	tweeds	cagoule	dress|up
shoddy	ulster	calotte	droguet
shorts	unisex	cambric	drugget
shroud	uppers	capuche	elastic
ski|cap	velure	cassock	falsies
slacks	velvet	casuals	fashion
sleeve	waders	cat's|eye	feather
slip|on	wallet	cat|suit	felt|hat
sun|hat	wampus	chamois	ferrule
switch	whites	chapeau	fig|leaf

filibeg	leghorn	panache	singlet
fitting	leotard	pannier	skimmer
flannel	loafers	panties	slicker
flounce	long|bob	parasol	soft|hat
foulard	Mae|West	partlet	soutane
freckle	malines	pattern	spencer
frocked	maniple	pegtops	sporran
frogged	manteau	pelisse	stammel
fur|coat	manteel	pendant	stetson
fustian	mascara	percale	sun|suit
gaiters	Mechlin	perfume	surcoat
garment	modesty	peridot	surtout
gingham	modiste	periwig	swaddle
girasol	monocle	petasus	sweater
glasses	mozetta	pigskin	tabaret
grogram	mudpack	pigtail	taffeta
G|string	muffler	pillbox	taffety
guipure	nankeen	pin|curl	tarbush
gumboot	necktie	pith|hat	tatters
gym|slip	New|Look	porkpie	tatting
haircut	nightie	puttees	tea|gown
hairnet	oil|silk	pyjamas	textile
hairpin	oilskin	raiment	texture
handbag	organdy	ringlet	ticking
hatband	organza	rompers	tiffany
hemline	orphrey	rosette	tile|hat
hessian	outsize	rubbers	tonsure
high|hat	overall	rug|gown	top|boot
hip|boot	Oxfords	sacking	topcoat
homburg	padding	sagathy	top|hose
hosiery	paenula	sandals	topknot
jaconet	page|boy	sarafan	torchon
jaegers	paisley	selvage	tricorn
kilt|pin	pajamas	shampoo	trinket
layette	paletot	shingle	tunicle
leather	pallium	silk|hat	turn|ups

twinset	calyptra	elflocks	hairline
undress	camisole	ensemble	half,boot
uniform	capeline	Eton|crop	half,hose
veiling	capuchin	Eton|suit	hand,knit
velours	cardigan	eyeshade	hatguard
webbing	cashmere	face,lift	headband
wellies	Celanese	face,pack	headgear
worsted	chaperon	fair|isle	headwear
yashmak	chasuble	fastener	high|heel
aigrette	chenille	fatigues	himation
appliqué	cheverel	fillibeg	hipsters
Ascot|tie	ciclaton	fish,tail	homespun
babouche	cincture	flannels	hot|pants
Balmoral	cingulum	fob|watch	inch|tape
barathea	cloth|cap	fontange	jackboot
basquine	clothing	fool's|cap	Jacquard
bath|cube	coiffure	footwear	jodhpurs
bathrobe	cold|wave	frippery	kerchief
bearskin	corduroy	froufrou	kiss|curl
bedsocks	corselet	furbelow	knickers
birretta	cosmetic	fur|stole	knitwear
black|tie	creepers	galoshes	leggings
bloomers	cretonne	gamashes	leotards
boat|neck	crew|neck	gambados	lingerie
bobbinet	crush|hat	gambeson	lip|brush
body|suit	culottes	gauntlet	lip|rouge
bongrace	dalmatic	glad|rags	lip|salve
boot,lace	day|dress	gold|lamé	lipstick
bouffant	disguise	gossamer	mackinaw
braiding	dress,tie	grey|hair	manicure
brass,hat	drilling	gridelin	mantelet
breeches	drop|curl	guernsey	mantilla
brocatel	dunce|cap	gym|pants	material
buckskin	dust|coat	gym|shoes	moccasin
burberry	Dutch|cap	gym|tunic	moleskin
bustline	ear,muffs	hair|band	mourning

muscadin	raincoat	surplice
mustache	red|sable	swaddled
nail|file	reticule	swim|suit
nainsook	sandshoe	taglioni
near|silk	scanties	tail|coat
neckband	scapular	tapestry
neckline	sealskin	tarboosh
negligee	seamless	tarlatan
nightcap	Shantung	Terylene
nose|ring	shirring	Thai|silk
oilcloth	shirting	toilette
oilskins	shirt|pin	top|boots
opera|hat	shoehorn	trimming
overalls	shoelace	trot|cozy
overcoat	shoe|tree	trousers
pabouche	short|bob	tweezers
paduasoy	shot|silk	two|piece
pedicure	sideburn	umbrella
peignoir	side|vent	vestment
pelerine	siege|cap	wardrobe
perruque	ski|boots	war|paint
philabeg	ski|pants	whiskers
pinafore	skullcap	white|tie
play|suit	slipover	wig|block
plimsoll	slippers	woollens
pochette	smocking	wristlet
polka|dot	snap|brim	zoot|suit
polo|neck	sneakers	Alice|band
pomander	snub|nose	astrakhan
ponyskin	sombrero	baby|linen
pony|tail	spit|curl	balaclava
postiche	stickpin	baldachin
pullover	stocking	ball|dress
pure|silk	straw|hat	bath|salts
quilting	streamer	bed|jacket
rag|trade	subucula	billycock

blue|jeans
bobbin|net
bombasine
bowler|hat
brassiere
breast|pin
Breton|hat
broadloom
bush|shirt
calamanco
camel|coat
camel|hair
caparison
cap|in|hand
cap|sleeve
cassimere
chantilly
chevelure
China|silk
chinstrap
coat,frock
coat,tails
cocked|hat
cold|cream
comforter
corduroys
cosmetics
crinoline
Cuban|heel
cuff,links
décolleté
demob|suit
deodorant
djellabah
dog,collar
drainpipe

drape|suit
dress|coat
dress|ring
dress|suit
duffel|bag
dungarees
epaulette
eye|shadow
face|cream
false,face
farandine
filoselle
fingering
floss|silk
forage|cap
frock|coat
full|dress
full|skirt
gabardine
gaberdine
georgette
girandole
gold|watch
great|coat
Greek|lace
grenadine
grosgrain
hairbrush
hair|cloth
hairpiece
hair|shirt
hand|cream
headdress
headpiece
high|stock
hip|pocket

hoop|skirt
horsehair
housecoat
huckaback
in|fashion
Inverness
jockey|cap
Juliet|cap
kick|pleat
kid|gloves
kirby|grip
knee,socks
lambswool
linenette
loincloth
longcloth
longcoats
lorgnette
millinery
miniskirt
model|gown
moustache
muckender
mustachio
nauticals
neckcloth
neckpiece
nightgown
nightwear
nun's|habit
off|the|peg
overdress
overshoes
overskirt
Panama|hat
pantalets

Paris doll	ski jacket	whalebone
pea jacket	ski jumper	wrap round
peaked cap	skin tight	wristband
percaline	sloppy Joe	zucchetto
petersham	slouch hat	after shave
petticoat	snowshoes	all the rage
phillibeg	solitaire	ankle socks
pinstripe	sou'wester	astringent
pixie hood	sphendone	Balbriggan
plus fours	spun rayon	ballet shoe
point lace	steenkirk	bathing cap
polo shirt	stitching	beauty spot
pompadour	stockinet	Berlin wool
pourpoint	stomacher	black dress
press stud	strapless	bobbed hair
ready made	sun bonnet	bobbin lace
redingote	sun helmet	bobbysocks
Roman lace	swansdown	boiler suit
round neck	sweatband	boudoir cap
sack dress	swing curl	bovver boot
safety pin	tarpaulin	broadcloth
sailcloth	toilet bag	bubble bath
sailor hat	towelling	bush jacket
school cap	track suit	buttonhole
school hat	trousseau	button hook
scoop neck	tube dress	camel's hair
separates	undervest	cap and gown
sharkskin	underwear	chaparajos
sheepskin	urchin cut	chatelaine
shirt band	velveteen	chevesaile
shirt stud	victorine	chinchilla
shirt tail	waistband	claw hammer
shovel hat	waistcoat	coat hanger
shower cap	waistline	coat of mail
sideburns	war bonnet	collarette
siren suit	wedge heel	collar stud

CLOTHES

college|cap	Geneva|gown	persiennes
cossack|hat	grass|skirt	picture|hat
cotton|wool	habit,cloth	pillow|lace
court,dress	hair|ribbon	pin|cushion
court|shoes	half,kirtle	pith|helmet
covert,coat	halter|neck	plastic|mac
cummerbund	hand|lotion	poke|bonnet
curling|pin	headsquare	powder|puff
dentifrice	hook|and|eye	print|dress
deshabille	hop|sacking	puff|sleeve
dinner|gown	hugmetight	rabbitskin
dishabille	jersey|silk	riding|hood
double|chin	jersey|wool	romper|suit
drainpipes	lappet,head	roquelaure
dressing|up	life|jacket	rubber|sole
dressmaker	lounge|suit	sailor|suit
dress|shirt	lover's|knot	scalloping
duster|coat	mackintosh	scatter|pin
embroidery	maquillage	scratch,wig
emery|board	marcel|wave	seersucker
empire,line	masquerade	shaving|kit
Eton|collar	mess|jacket	shirtdress
Eton|jacket	monk's|cloth	shirt,frill
evening|bag	monk's|habit	shirtfront
eye|glasses	mousseline	shoe,buckle
face,powder	nail|polish	silhouette
false|teeth	needlecord	silver|lamé
fancy|dress	nightdress	ski|sweater
fascinator	nightshirt	sleeveless
fearnought	old|clothes	smock|frock
feather|boa	overblouse	smoking|cap
fitted|coat	Oxford|bags	solar|topee
flak|jacket	Oxford|ties	spectacles
foundation	pantaloons	sports|coat
fourchette	Paris|model	sport|shirt
fustanella	party|dress	sports|suit

sportswear	aiguillette	farthingale
square,neck	alexandrite	fine,feather
suede,shoes	barrel,dress	flannelette
Sunday,best	bathing,suit	flared,skirt
sunglasses	beauty,sleep	flying,panel
suspenders	bellbottoms	formal,dress
sweat,shirt	best,clothes	granny,dress
tailor,made	black,patent	grease,paint
terry,cloth	black,velvet	guipure,lace
the,cap,fits	Blucher,boot	hand,me,downs
threadbare	blue,clothes	Harris,tweed
tight,skirt	boiled,shirt	herringbone
toiletries	boutonniere	high,fashion
toilet,soap	boxer,shorts	hobble,skirt
toothbrush	button,shoes	Indian,shawl
toothpaste	campaign,hat	kilted,skirt
trench,coat	candy,stripe	lacing,shoes
turtle,neck	canvas,shoes	lawn,sleeves
underlinen	cap,and,bells	leatherette
underpants	casual,shoes	leg,of,mutton
undershirt	cheesecloth	leopardskin
underskirt	Chinese,silk	marquisette
upper,stock	clodhoppers	matinee,coat
vanity,case	cloth,of,gold	Mechlin,lace
virgin,knot	contact,lens	middy,blouse
wampum,belt	crash,helmet	morning,coat
watch,chain	cutaway,coat	morning,gown
watchstrap	dark,glasses	mortarboard
waterproof	décolletage	mutton,chops
Wellington	deerstalker	nail,varnish
widow's,peak	dinner,dress	neckerchief
Windsor,tie	dreadnought	needle,point
wing,collar	dress,length	orangestick
wrap,around	dressmaking	overgarment
wraprascal	dress,shield	Oxford,shoes
wrist,watch	evening,gown	panty,girdle

CLOTHES

Persian|lamb white|collar divided|skirt
Phrygian|cap widow's|weeds donkey|jacket
pilot|jacket windbreaker double|jersey
ready|to|wear windcheater dressing|case
regimentals Windsor|knot dressing|gown
riding|habit wooden|shoes dressing|room
school|dress work|clothes dress|uniform
set,in|sleeve woven|fabric dropped|waist
shaving|soap antigropelos duchesse|lace
shawl|collar apron|strings duffel|jacket
shell|jacket bathing|dress Easter|bonnet
shirt,button bespectacled eau,de,Cologne
shock,headed bib|and|tucker evening|cloak
shoe|leather bicycle|clips evening|dress
shoulder|bag birthday|suit evening|shoes
Spanish|comb bluestocking fashion|house
spatterdash body|stocking fashion|plate
stiff|collar brass|buttons fatigue|dress
subcingulum breast|pocket flaxen|haired
suede|gloves brilliantine football|boot
Sunday|black business|suit full|mourning
swagger|coat cap|of|liberty galligaskins
swallowtail cardinal's|hat glass|slipper
tailor|tacks cavalry|twill golden,haired
tam,o|shanter chastity|belt haberdashery
tennis|dress chesterfield hair|dressing
tennis|shoes chin|whiskers hair|restorer
toilet|water clothes|brush half|mourning
tooth|powder clothes,horse handkerchief
torchon|lace collar|and|tie haute|couture
trencher|cap college,scarf Hessian|boots
trouser|suit combinations hummel,bonnet
walking|shoe crepe,de,Chine if|the|cap|fits
wash|leather crewel|needle knee|breeches
watch,pocket curling|tongs knitting|wool
watered|silk dinner|jacket lightning|zip

lumber jacket
magyar|sleeve
monkey|jacket
morning|dress
mousquetaire
nail|clippers
nail|scissors
night|clothes
old,fashioned
out|of|fashion
Paisley|shawl
Paris|fashion
pedal,pushers
Penang|lawyer
plain|clothes
pressure,suit
Prince|Albert
Princess|line
raglan|sleeve
set|one's|cap|at
beauty|parlour
camel,hair|coat
carpet,slipper
casual|clothes
cocktail|dress
fashion|parade
hacking,jacket
Highland|dress
Inverness|cape
lavender|water
leather,jacket
made|to|measure
matinee|jacket
patent|leather
period|costume
quizzing|glass

shoulder|strap
smoking|jacket
sock,suspender
suspender,belt
underclothing
unfashionable
anti,perspirant
artificial|silk
chest|protector
cleansing|cream
clerical|collar
collar|attached
double,breasted
evening|clothes
fireman's|helmet
fully|fashioned
hobnailed|boots
mandarin|collar
off|the|shoulder
ostrich|feather
pair|of|slippers
pair|of|trousers
pyjama|trousers
riding,breeches
shooting,jacket
single,breasted
stocking|stitch
tartan|trousers
top,hat|and|tails
vanishing|cream
wedding,garment
winter|woollies
working|clothes
Balaclava|helmet
civilian|clothes
crease,resistant

foundation|cream
full,bottomed|wig
highland|costume
outdoor|clothing
pair|of|stockings
regulation|dress

sheepskin|jacket
shrink,resistant
swallow,tail|coat
swimming|costume
wellington|boots

Colours

dun	flame	cerise	emerald
red	green	cobalt	filemot
tan	helio	copper	gamboge
blue	henna	indigo	iron|red
buff	ivory	lustre	magenta
fawn	khaki	madder	new|blue
flam	lemon	maroon	old|blue
gold	lilac	modena	old|gold
grey	mauve	murrey	ruby|red
lake	ochre	orange	saffron
navy	peach	pastel	scarlet
pink	perse	purple	sea|blue
puce	rouge	reseda	sky|blue
rose	sepia	russet	tile|red
rust	taupe	sienna	ash,blond
sage	tawny	silver	baby|blue
saxe	umber	titian	blood|red
wine	white	violet	brunette
azure	albert	yellow	Burgundy
beige	annato	apricot	chestnut
black	auburn	carmine	dark|blue
brown	blonde	citrine	dove|grey
cream	bronze	crimson	dyestuff

eau de nil	madder red	Irish green
iron grey	moss green	madder blue
lavender	mouse grey	madder lake
mulberry	Naples red	madder pink
navy blue	Nile green	marine blue
off white	olive drab	olive brown
pea green	opera pink	olive green
poppy red	pearl grey	Oxford grey
primrose	raw sienna	Paris green
raw umber	royal blue	Persian red
red ochre	smoke grey	powder blue
sanguine	solferino	raven black
sap green	soot black	rose madder
sapphire	steel blue	salmon pink
saxe blue	steel grey	silver grey
sea green	tangerine	terra cotta
tincture	Turkey red	trypan blue
viridian	turquoise	bottle green
xanthein	vermilion	brown madder
azure blue	acid yellow	burnt orange
blue black	apple green	burnt sienna
burnt lake	aquamarine	cardinal red
burnt rose	Berlin blue	carmine lake
cameo pink	beryl green	chrome green
champagne	brown ochre	chrome lemon
cherry red	burnt umber	cobalt green
chrome red	Chinese red	crimson lake
claret red	cobalt blue	cyanine blue
duck green	direct blue	Dresden blue
Dutch pink	fast yellow	English pink
Indian red	flake white	flesh colour
jade green	French blue	hunting pink
leaf green	French grey	incarnadine
light blue	grass green	Italian blue
lime green	green ochre	Italian pink
livid pink	heliotrope	Japanese red

COLOURS

king's yellow

lemon yellow

Paris yellow

Persian blue

Persian blue

Prussian red

Russian jade

terra sienna

ultramarine

Venetian red

Vienna green

yellow ochre

air force blue

burnt carmine

canary yellow

cerulean blue

Chinese white

chrome orange

chrome yellow

electric blue

emerald green

golden yellow

gun metal grey

hyacinth blue

lavender blue

Lincoln green

madder orange

madder violet

madder yellow

midnight blue

orange madder

pastel colour

pillar box red

Prussian blue

quince yellow

sapphire blue

scarlet ochre

black and white

Cambridge blue

flame coloured

kaleidoscopic

lemon coloured

monochromatic

multicoloured

particoloured

peach coloured

pepper and salt

slate coloured

stone coloured

straw coloured

sulphur yellow

tortoise shell

cornflower blue

glowing colours

heather mixture

imperial purple

livery coloured

orange coloured

platinum blonde

primary colours

salmon coloured

strawberry roan

swaddling cloth

turquoise green

colour blindness

colouring matter

greenery yallery

rainbow coloured

secondary colour

Composers

Bax	Dukas	Bartók	Rubbra
Gay	Elgar	Brahms	Schutz
Suk	Fauré	Bridge	Searle
Adam	Field	Busoni	Tallis
Arne	Finzi	Coates	Varese
Bach	Gluck	Czerny	Wagner
Berg	Grieg	Daquin	Walton
Blow	Haydn	Delius	Webern
Byrd	Henze	Duparc	Wilbye
Cage	Holst	Dvořák	Albeniz
Ives	Ibert	Flotow	Allegri
Lalo	Lehár	Franck	Bellini
Nono	Liszt	Gliere	Bennett
Orff	Locke	Glinka	Berlioz
Wolf	Lully	Gounod	Borodin
Alwyn	Parry	Gretry	Britten
Auber	Ravel	Handel	Copland
Auric	Reger	Herold	Corelli
Balfe	Satie	Hummel	Creston
Berio	Sousa	Joplin	Debussy
Bizet	Spohr	Kodaly	Delibes
Bliss	Suppé	Lassus	Dowland
Bloch	Verdi	Ligeti	Duruflé
Boito	Weber	Mahler	Falla,de
Boyce	Weill	Moeran	Gibbons
Brian	Widor	Morley	Howells
Bruch	Alfven	Mozart	Ireland
Cilea	Arnold	Piston	Janáček
d'Indy	Barber	Rameau	Lambert

COMPOSERS

Litolff	Cimarosa	MacDowell
MacCunn	Clementi	Meyerbeer
Martinu	Couperin	Offenbach
Mathias	Gabrieli	Pachelbel
Medtner	Gershwin	Pergolesi
Menotti	Giordano	Prokoviev
Milhaud	Grainger	Scarlatti
Nielsen	Granados	Birtwistle
Poulenc	Honegger	Boccherini
Puccini	Ketelbey	Kabalevsky
Purcell	Korngold	Monteverdi
Quilter	Kriesler	Mussorgsky
Rodrigo	Mascagni	Palestrina
Rossini	Massenet	Penderecki
Roussel	Messiaen	Ponchielli
Salieri	Paganini	Praetorius
Schuman	Panufnik	Rawsthorne
Shankar	Respighi	Rubinstein
Smetana	Sarasate	Saint Saens
Stainer	Schubert	Schoenberg
Stamitz	Schumann	Stravinsky
Strauss	Scriabin	Villa Lobos
Tartini	Sibelius	Waldteufel
Thomson	Stanford	Wieniawski
Tippett	Sullivan	Williamson
Vivaldi	Taverner	Butterworth
Warlock	Telemann	Charpentier
Weelkes	Beethoven	Dittersdorf
Albinoni	Bernstein	Humperdinck
Benedict	Boellmann	Leoncavallo
Benjamin	Buxtehude	Lloyd Webber
Berkeley	Cherubini	Lutoslawski
Boughton	Donizetti	Mendelssohn
Bruckner	Glazounov	Rachmaninov
Chabrier	Hindemith	Stockhausen
Chausson	Hoddinott	Szymanowski

92

Tchaikovsky
Khachaturian
Shostakovich
Maxwell␣Davies

Rimsky␣Korsakov
Coleridge␣Taylor
Vaughan␣Williams

Computing

baud	deprogram
byte	mainframe
chip	programme
read	slide␣rule
Algol	alphameric
Basic	memory␣bank
Cobol	peripheral
input	throughput
micro	binary␣digit
adding	binary␣scale
binary	multi␣access
hacker	punched␣card
on␣line	punched␣tape
Fortran	programmable
gigabit	random␣access
off␣line	adding␣machine
program	microcomputer
bistable	shift␣register
computer	word␣processor
data␣bank	analog␣computer
database	data␣processing
hardware	microprocessor
print␣out	systems␣analyst
software	computerisation
terminal	computer␣science

COMPUTING

digital|computer   storage|capacity
electronic|brain   systems|analysis

Deadly Sins

envy   pride   accidie
lust   sloth   gluttony
anger   wrath   covetousness

Drink

ale	sake	bisque	shandy
bin	soup	borsch	sherry
gin	Toby	bottle	spirit
jug	wine	brandy	squash
nip	wino	carafe	tea bag
pop	booze	cassis	teacup
rum	broth	cellar	tipple
tea	cider	claret	whisky
tot	cocoa	coffee	absinth
tyg	cream	cognac	alcohol
urn	drain	eggnog	aniseed
vat	dregs	goblet	Bacardi
beer	drink	imbibe	beef tea
brew	gumbo	kirsch	beer mug
cafe	jorum	kumiss	bitters
cask	julep	kummel	borscht
coke	lager	liquid	bouquet
dram	Médoc	liquor	bourbon
flip	mocha	magnum	carouse
grog	punch	muscat	chianti
hock	quaff	nectar	cobbler
kola	stock	noggin	cordial
lees	stout	oxtail	curacao
mead	syrup	Pernod	custard
milk	toddy	porter	draught
must	treat	posset	dry wine
ouzo	vodka	potage	egg flip
port	water	rummer	gin fizz
sack	bibber	Scotch	iced tea

DRINK

limeade	Dubonnet	black|drop
liqueur	fruit|cup	cappucino
Madeira	gin|and|it	champagne
malmsey	gin|sling	clear|soup
martini	green|tea	Cointreau
Moselle	hangover	cold|drink
new|wine	highball	dishwater
philtre	hot|drink	doorframe
potable	hot|toddy	dry|sherry
red|wine	hydromel	firewater
sherbet	ice|water	ginger|ale
shoe|box	infusion	ginger|pop
sloe|gin	julienne	heavy|wine
spirits	lemonade	light|wine
spritza	libation	metheglin
tea|leaf	muscatel	milk|shake
tequila	nightcap	mint|julep
vintage	pink|lady	muscadine
wassail	port|wine	neat|drink
whiskey	potation	onion|soup
absinthe	rice|beer	orangeade
Adam's|ale	rice|soup	Rhine|wine
anisette	Riesling	rye|whisky
aperitif	root|beer	small|beer
armagnac	ruby|port	soda|water
audit|ale	rum|punch	soft|drink
beverage	Sauterne	still|wine
Bordeaux	schnapps	sweet|wine
bouillon	schooner	tawny|port
Burgundy	tantalus	tea|leaves
China|tea	tea|caddy	tiger|milk
cocktail	verjuice	white|wine
consommé	vermouth	yard|of|ale
daiquiri	Adam's|wine	Beaujolais
demijohn	appetiser	Bloody|Mary
Drambuie	aqua|vitae	buttermilk

café au lait
cappuccino
Chambertin
Chartreuse
fruit juice
ginger beer
grape juice
half bottle
Holland gin
iced coffee
intoxicant
Jamaica rum
lemon juice
liquid diet
love potion
malt whisky
malted milk
manzanilla
maraschino
minestrone
mixed drink
mock turtle
Mulled wine
Munich beer
on the rocks
Russian tea
slivowitza
soda syphon
stiff drink
stirrup cup
Tom Collins
tomato soup
tonic water
turtle soup
usquebaugh
Vichy water

whisky sour
amontillado
apple brandy
barley broth
barley water
beef extract
Benedictine
black coffee
brandy smash
chicken soup
coffee break
cooking wine
cowslip wine
draught beer
French wines
ginger punch
Irish coffee
orange juice
peach brandy
Scotch broth
strong drink
sweet sherry
tomato juice
vintage wine
white coffee
breathalyser
café espresso
Danzig brandy
hot chocolate
ice cream soda
Irish whiskey
mineral water
non alcoholic
Pilsener beer
sarsaparilla
spirit of wine

DRINK

supernaculum
apricot|brandy
brandy|and|soda
coffee|grounds
condensed|milk
cooking|sherry
creme|de|menthe
dandelion|wine
deoch|an|doruis
estate|bottled
gin|and|bitters
instant|coffee
liqueur|brandy
liquid|measure
mild|and|bitter
morning|coffee
prairie|oyster
round|of|drinks
Scotch|and|soda
sparkling|wine
whisky|and|soda
as|drunk|as|a|lord
bottle|of|brandy
bottle|of|claret

bottle|of|Scotch
bottle|of|whisky
champagne|lunch
cocktail|shaker
coffee|strainer
elderberry|wine
espresso|coffee
evaporated|milk
French|vermouth
John|barleycorn
lemonade|shandy
little|brown|jug
Napoleon|brandy
pineapple|juice
Scotch|and|water
beer|and|skittles
drop|of|good|stuff
gin|and|angostura
grapefruit|juice
green|Chartreuse
Italian|vermouth
one|over|the|eight
wines|and|spirits

Education

BA	ABC	ink	book	dean	fail
Dr	con	jot	co-ed	demy	form
go	den	pen	copy	desk	gown
IQ	dux	ambo	cram	exam	grad
MA	fag	blot	crib	fact	guru

head	flunk	browse	old|boy
lore	forum	bursar	optime
mark	fresh	campus	pandit
mode	gaudy	course	pedant
mods	gloss	creche	pencil
note	grade	debate	period
nous	grind	degree	peruse
oral	guide	docent	preach
pass	hadji	doctor	primer
prep	house	duenna	pundit
prof	imbue	eraser	reader
quad	khoja	examen	recite
quiz	kudos	fellow	rector
read	learn	finals	regius
roll	lines	genius	remove
sage	loach	grader	report
seat	lycee	grades	rubber
soph	major	gradus	savant
swat	merit	greats	school
swot	minor	ground	scroll
talk	paper	homily	senior
tech	poser	infant	sermon
term	prime	infuse	smalls
test	prize	inkpot	syndic
tyro	quill	jotter	taught
atlas	sizar	junior	teaser
board	slate	lector	theory
chair	spell	lesson	tripos
chalk	staff	lyceum	truant
class	study	manual	vellum
coach	teach	master	academy
dunce	tutor	matron	alumnus
ecole	usher	mentor	amateur
edify	alumna	mullah	boarder
essay	brains	munshi	bookish
final	brainy	novice	bookman

Braille	maestro	written	highbrow
brush|up	major|in	academic	homework
bursary	minor|in	aegrotat	humanism
coacher	monitor	agitprop	inceptor
college	nursery	aularian	informed
crammer	old|girl	beginner	inkstand
culture	oppidan	book|lore	instruct
dabbler	pandect	bookworm	Latinist
degrees	papyrus	classman	learning
diploma	passman	coaching	lecturer
dominie	pointer	commoner	lettered
Dunciad	precept	copybook	liripipe
egghead	prefect	cramming	liripoop
entrant	primary	cultural	literacy
erudite	problem	cultured	literate
examine	proctor	didactic	little|go
explain	qualify	disciple	memorize
expound	read|for	division	mistress
faculty	reading	dry|nurse	moralize
failure	satchel	educable	neophyte
fresher	scholar	educated	note|book
grammar	schools	educator	Oxbridge
great|go	seminar	elective	pansophy
grinder	student	emeritus	pass|mark
hearing	studier	examiner	pedagogy
honours	studies	exercise	pedantic
inkhorn	teacher	foolscap	pedantry
inkwell	teach|in	freshman	playtime
instill	the|arts	Gamaliel	polemics
learned	theatre	glossary	polyglot
learner	thinker	gownsman	pore|over
lectern	three|R's	graduand	postgrad
lecture	trainee	graduate	preacher
letters	tuition	guidance	punditry
lexicon	varsity	half|term	question
lowbrow	writing	harangue	read|up|on

redbrick	chalkdust	institute
research	chalk|talk	knowledge
revision	champaign	law|school
roll,cast	classmate	lucubrate
sciolist	classroom	masterate
semester	collegian	note|paper
seminary	cosmogony	novitiate
servitor	day|school	orography
spelling	dean|of|men	palaestra
studious	desk,bound	parchment
studying	didactics	pedagogic
teaching	diligence	pedagogue
textbook	direction	pensioner
training	discourse	play|group
treatise	doctorate	portioner
tutoring	dunce's|cap	precentor
tutelate	education	preceptor
tutorage	enlighten	prelector
tutoress	erudition	pre,school
tutorial	extempore	principal
vacation	fifth|form	professor
versed|in	final|year	proselyte
well,read	first|form	qualified
wordbook	first|year	receptive
wrangler	formalist	refresher
absey|book	gaudeamus	rough|note
alma|mater	gazetteer	scholarch
art|school	governess	scholarly
assistant	greenhorn	schoolboy
associate	Gymnasium	schooling
Athenaeum	homiletic	schoolish
booklover	honour|man	school|kid
brainwave	hortatory	school|lad
brainwork	ignoramus	schoolman
catechism	ingestion	sermonize
catechize	inspector	sixth|form

smatterer	curricular	memorandum
sophister	curriculum	middle|brow
sophomore	dame|school	Nobel|prize
staffroom	dictionary	past|master
star|pupil	dilettante	pedagogics
streaming	discipline	pedagogist
supplicat	dual|school	pensionnat
syndicate	educatress	Philistine
take|notes	eleven|plus	playground
teachable	escritoire	playschool
thesaurus	exposition	postmaster
third|form	extramural	preceptive
third|year	fellowship	prep|school
timetable	form|master	prize|idiot
tuitional	fourth|form	prolocutor
tutorhood	fraternity	propaganda
tutorship	free|period	quadrangle
undergrad	free|school	quadrivium
abiturient	graduation	quiz|master
academical	hard|lesson	readership
arithmetic	headmaster	report|card
bibliology	high|school	Sabbatical
bibliomane	humanities	scholastic
bibliosoph	illiterate	schoolbook
blackboard	illuminate	school|chum
brainchild	illuminati	schooldame
brain|storm	imposition	schoolgirl
cap|and|gown	inquisitor	schoolma'am
catechumen	instructed	schoolmaid
chautauqua	instructor	schoolmarm
classicism	intramural	schoolmate
classicist	junior|high	school|meal
college|boy	lead|pencil	school|miss
collegiate	lower|fifth	schoolroom
common|room	lower|sixth	scrutinize
coryphaeus	lower|third	second|form

second|head
second|year
self,taught
senior|high
shibboleth
smattering
specialist
specialize
sub,culture
supervisor
tenderfoot
university
upper|fifth
upper|sixth
upper|third
vocabulary
well,versed
widely|read
abecedarian
abecedarium
academician
arts|college
attainments
Bible|school
bibliolatry
bibliomania
bibliophile
board|school
bookishness
brain|teaser
bright|pupil
certificate
charm|school
class|fellow
coeducation
college,bred

college|girl
collegianer
crash|course
enlightened
examination
fellow|pupil
former|pupil
give|a|lesson
grade|school
head|teacher
house|master
inculcation
information
informative
institution
instruction
instructive
intelligent
invigilator
lecture|hall
lecture|room
lectureship
liberal|arts
literary|man
litterateur
moral|lesson
mortarboard
music|lesson
music|school
naval|school
night|school
omniscience
point|a|moral
polytechnic
preceptress
preparation

preparation
prizegiving
prizewinner
probationer
questionist
read|a|lesson
reading|desk
re,education
researchist
responsions
scholarship
School|Board
sharp|lesson
spelling|bee
student|body
teachership
teacher's|pet
teaching|aid
trade|school
upper|fourth
wide|reading
writing|desk
amphitheatre
aptitude|test
assimilation
baccalaureus
battle|of|wits
bibliomaniac
blue|stocking
book|learning
brain|twister
church|school
classicalist
College|Board
conservatory
disciplinary

disquisition
encyclopedia
exercise|book
exhibitioner
form|mistress
French|lesson
ground|school
headmistress
indoctrinate
infant|school
instructress
intellectual
intelligence
junior|school
kindergarten
learn|by|heart
make|the|grade
man|of|letters
master|of|arts
matter|of|fact
memorization
mental|labour
middle|school
naval|academy
normal|school
painting|book
parish|school
perscrutator
phrontistery
postgraduate
preselection
professorate
professorial
psychometric
pupil|teacher
riding|school

roll|of|honour
school|dinner
schoolfellow
schoolkeeper
schoolmaster
self|educated
senior|school
spelling|book
summer|school
Sunday|school
teach|a|lesson
training|slip
underteacher
writing|table
academic|dress
advanced|level
baccalaureate
Berkeleianism
careers|master
charity|school
coeducational
comprehension
comprehensive
concentration
conceptualism
conceptualist
contemplation
contemplative
contradiction
educationally
encyclopaedia
enlightenment
faculty|of|arts
grammar|school
home|economics
honours|degree

infant|prodigy	existentialist
learning|curve	high|technology
matriculation	honorary|degree
metaphysician	honorary|fellow
misunderstand	intelligentsia
moment|of|truth	lending|library
non|collegiate	loaded|question
nursery|school	metempsychosis
ordinary|level	misinstruction
parrot|fashion	moral|certainty
philosophical	multiple|choice
primary|school	multiracialism
private|school	Open|University
professorship	parapsychology
psychoanalyst	postmastership
Rhodes|scholar	predestination
scholasticism	psychoanalysis
school|leaving	sandwich|course
school|prefect	schoolmistress
schoolteacher	senior|wrangler
social|science	speech|training
speech|therapy	vice|chancellor
undergraduate	a|little|learning
understanding	analytical|logic
vice|president	Aristotelianism
vice|principal	audio|visual|aids
vicious|circle	careers|mistress
word|blindness	combination|room
approved|school	domestic|economy
beg|the|question	domestic|science
boarding|school	epistemological
Cuisenaire|rods	extra|curricular
educationalist	finishing|school
encyclopaedist	first|principles
epistemologist	higher|education
existentialism	horns|of|a|dilemma

lateral|thinking	regius|professor
logical|analysis	schoolboy|howler
moral|philosophy	school|inspector
open|scholarship	secondary|modern
oral|examination	secondary|school
pathetic|fallacy	tertiary|college
psychometrician	training|college
refresher|course	

First Names

Abe	Guy	Net	Tim	Bart	Elma
Ada	Ian	Nye	Tom	Bert	Elsa
Alf	Ina	Pam	Una	Bess	Emma
Amy	Isa	Pat	Val	Beth	Enid
Ann	Jan	Peg	Vic	Bill	Eric
Bab	Jim	Pen	Viv	Cara	Evan
Bea	Joe	Pip	Wal	Carl	Ewan
Bel	Joy	Pru	Zoe	Chad	Fred
Ben	Kay	Rab	Abel	Ciss	Gail
Bob	Kim	Rae	Abie	Clem	Gene
Dan	Kit	Ray	Adam	Cleo	Gill
Don	Len	Reg	Alan	Dave	Gina
Dot	Leo	Rex	Aldo	Dawn	Gwen
Ena	Liz	Roy	Ally	Dick	Gwyn
Eva	Lyn	Sal	Alma	Dirk	Hope
Eve	Max	Sam	Amos	Dora	Hugh
Fay	May	Sid	Andy	Drew	Hugo
Flo	Meg	Sis	Anna	Duke	Iain
Gay	Nan	Sue	Anne	Earl	Iona
Ger	Nat	Tam	Avis	Edna	Iris
Gus	Ned	Ted	Babs	Ella	Ivan

Ivor	Nell	Aaron	Cecil	Effie	Hetty
Jack	Nick	Abbie	Celia	Elias	Hilda
Jake	Nina	Adele	Chloe	Eliot	Hiram
Jane	Nita	Aggie	Chris	Elise	Honor
Jean	Noel	Agnes	Clara	Eliza	Inigo
Jeff	Olaf	Aidan	Clare	Ellen	Irene
Jess	Olga	Ailie	Cliff	Ellis	Isaac
Jill	Oona	Ailsa	Clive	Elmer	Jacky
Joan	Owen	Alfie	Colin	Elsie	Jacob
Jock	Paul	Algie	Coral	Emily	James
John	Pete	Alice	Corin	Enoch	Jamie
Josh	Phil	Aline	Cyril	Ernie	Janet
Judy	Rene	Alvin	Cyrus	Errol	Janey
June	Rhys	Angus	Daisy	Ethel	Jason
Karl	Rick	Anita	Danny	Faith	Jayne
Kate	Rita	Annie	Darby	Fanny	Jenny
Leah	Rolf	April	D'Arcy	Felix	Jerry
Lena	Rory	Avril	David	Fiona	Jesse
Leon	Rosa	Barry	Davie	Fleur	Jimmy
Lily	Rose	Basil	Delia	Flora	Josie
Lisa	Ross	Becca	Denis	Frank	Joyce
Lois	Ruby	Bella	Derek	Freda	Julie
Lola	Ruth	Benny	Diana	Garry	Karen
Lucy	Ryan	Berry	Diane	Garth	Keith
Luke	Sara	Beryl	Dilys	Gavin	Kevin
Lynn	Saul	Betsy	Dinah	Geoff	Kitty
Mark	Sean	Betty	Dodie	Gerda	Lance
Mary	Stan	Biddy	Dolly	Giles	Laura
Matt	Tess	Boris	Donna	Ginny	Leila
Maud	Theo	Brian	Doris	Grace	Lenny
Mick	Toby	Bruce	Dylan	Greta	Leona
Mike	Tony	Bruno	Eamon	Harry	Lewis
Muir	Vera	Caleb	Eddie	Hazel	Libby
Myra	Walt	Carla	Edgar	Helen	Linda
Neal	Will	Carol	Edith	Helga	Lindy
Neil	Yves	Cathy	Edwin	Henry	Lloyd

FIRST NAMES

Lorna	Niall	Tania	Audrey	Dugald
Louis	Nicky	Tanya	Aurora	Dulcie
Lucia	Nicol	Tatum	Austin	Duncan
Lydia	Nigel	Terry	Aylwin	Dustin
Lynne	Norma	Tilly	Barney	Dwight
Mabel	Orson	Tracy	Bertha	Easter
Madge	Oscar	Vicky	Billie	Edmund
Maeve	Paddy	Vince	Blaise	Edward
Magda	Patty	Viola	Bobbie	Edwina
Mamie	Paula	Wanda	Brenda	Egbert
Manny	Pearl	Wayne	Bryony	Eileen
Marge	Peggy	Wendy	Calvin	Eilidh
Margo	Penny	Adrian	Carmen	Elaine
Maria	Perce	Agatha	Carole	Elinor
Marie	Percy	Aileen	Carrie	Elisha
Mario	Perry	Albert	Caspar	Elvira
Marty	Peter	Aldous	Cedric	Emilia
Maude	Polly	Alexis	Cherry	Ernest
Mavis	Ralph	Alfred	Cheryl	Esmond
Merle	Rhoda	Alicia	Claire	Esther
Miles	Rhona	Alison	Claude	Eugene
Milly	Robin	Althea	Connor	Eunice
Mitzi	Rodge	Amanda	Conrad	Evadne
Moira	Roger	Amelia	Damian	Evelyn
Molly	Rufus	Andrea	Daniel	Fergus
Morag	Sadie	Andrew	Daphne	Gareth
Moray	Sally	Angela	Darsey	Gaston
Morna	Sandy	Antony	Davina	George
Moses	Sarah	Arabel	Debbie	Gerald
Myles	Sarah	Archie	Denise	Gerard
Myrna	Simon	Arline	Dermot	Gertie
Nancy	Sonia	Arnold	Dianne	Gideon
Nanny	Steve	Arthur	Donald	Gladys
Naomi	Susan	Astrid	Doreen	Gloria
Nelly	Susie	Athene	Dougal	Gordon
Netty	Sybil	Aubrey	Dudley	Graham

6 LETTERS

Gregor	Judith	Mervyn	Robert
Gretel	Julian	Michel	Robina
Gwenda	Juliet	Mickey	Rodney
Hamish	Julius	Minnie	Roland
Hannah	Justin	Miriam	Ronald
Harold	Kenelm	Monica	Rowena
Harvey	Kirsty	Morgan	Roxana
Hattie	Larrie	Morrie	Rupert
Hector	Laurie	Morris	Sabina
Hester	Lesley	Morven	Salome
Hilary	Leslie	Muriel	Samuel
Horace	Lester	Murray	Sandra
Howard	Lilian	Myrtle	Selina
Hubert	Lionel	Nadine	Selwyn
Hunter	Lolita	Nathan	Serena
Imogen	Lottie	Nessie	Sharon
Ingram	Louisa	Nettie	Sheena
Ingrid	Louise	Nicola	Sheila
Irving	Lucius	Nicole	Sidney
Isabel	Luther	Noelle	Silvia
Isaiah	Maggie	Norman	Sophia
Isobel	Magnus	Norris	Sophie
Isolde	Maisie	Odette	Stella
Israel	Manuel	Oliver	Steven
Jackie	Marcia	Oonagh	Stuart
Janice	Marcus	Oriana	Sydney
Jasper	Margie	Osbert	Sylvia
Jemima	Marian	Oswald	Tamsin
Jeremy	Marion	Pamela	Thelma
Jerome	Marius	Petrus	Thomas
Jessie	Martha	Petula	Trevor
Joanna	Martin	Philip	Tricia
Joanne	Maxine	Phoebe	Trixie
Joseph	Melvin	Rachel	Trudie
Joshua	Melvyn	Regina	Ursula
Josiah	Merlin	Reuben	Verity

FIRST NAMES

Victor	Brendan	Fenella	Lucinda
Violet	Bridget	Florrie	Malcolm
Vivian	Bronwen	Flossie	Margery
Vivien	Cameron	Frances	Marilyn
Wallis	Camilla	Francis	Martina
Walter	Candida	Gabriel	Martine
Warner	Carlton	Geordie	Matilda
Warren	Carolyn	Geraint	Matthew
Wesley	Cecilia	Gilbert	Maureen
Wilbur	Celeste	Gillian	Maurice
Willie	Charity	Giselle	Maxwell
Willis	Charles	Godfrey	Melanie
Winnie	Charlie	Gregory	Melissa
Yehudi	Chrissy	Gwyneth	Michael
Yvette	Christy	Harriet	Mildred
Yvonne	Clarice	Heather	Mirabel
Abigail	Claudia	Herbert	Miranda
Abraham	Clement	Horatio	Modesty
Adriana	Clemmie	Jeffrey	Montagu
Alfreda	Corinna	Jessica	Murdoch
Alister	Cynthia	Jocelyn	Myfanwy
Ambrose	Deborah	Juliana	Natalie
Annabel	Deirdre	Justine	Natasha
Annette	Desmond	Katrina	Neville
Anthony	Diarmid	Kenneth	Nicolas
Antonia	Dolores	Kirstie	Obadiah
Ariadne	Dominic	Lachlan	Ophelia
Aurelia	Dorothy	Lavinia	Ottilie
Baldwin	Douglas	Leonard	Patrick
Barbara	Eleanor	Leonora	Pauline
Barnaby	Elspeth	Leopold	Perdita
Belinda	Emanuel	Letitia	Petrina
Bernard	Erasmus	Lillian	Phyllis
Bernice	Estella	Lindsey	Queenie
Bertram	Eugenia	Linette	Quentin
Blanche	Ezekiel	Lucille	Raphael

Raymond	Alastair	Florence
Rebecca	Aloysius	Francine
Richard	Angeline	Geoffrey
Roberta	Arabella	Georgina
Rosalie	Augustus	Gertrude
Rudolph	Barnabas	Hercules
Rudyard	Beatrice	Hermione
Russell	Benedict	Humphrey
Sabrina	Benjamin	Iseabail
Shelagh	Bertrand	Jeanette
Shelley	Beverley	Jennifer
Shirley	Carlotta	Jonathan
Siobhan	Carolina	Kathleen
Solomon	Caroline	Lancelot
Spencer	Cathleen	Laurence
Stanley	Catriona	Lawrence
Stephen	Charlton	Llewelyn
Stewart	Charmian	Lorraine
Susanna	Clarence	Madeline
Suzanne	Claribel	Magdalen
Terence	Clarissa	Margaret
Theresa	Claudius	Marianne
Timothy	Clemence	Marigold
Valerie	Clifford	Marjorie
Vanessa	Collette	Matthias
Vaughan	Cordelia	Meredith
Vincent	Cressida	Michelle
Wallace	Cuthbert	Montague
Wilfred	Danielle	Morrison
William	Dominica	Mortimer
Windsor	Dorothea	Nicholas
Winston	Drusilla	Octavius
Wyndham	Ebenezer	Odysseus
Yolande	Euphemia	Patience
Adrienne	Farquhar	Patricia
Alasdair	Felicity	Penelope

FIRST NAMES

Percival	Christine
Perpetua	Constance
Philippa	Cornelius
Primrose	Elizabeth
Prudence	Esmeralda
Prunella	Ethelbert
Reginald	Ferdinand
Roderick	Francesca
Rosalind	Frederica
Rosamund	Frederick
Rosemary	Genevieve
Samantha	Geraldine
Scarlett	Gwendolyn
Sherlock	Henrietta
Silvanus	Jacquetta
Sinclair	Josephine
Somerset	Katharine
Theodora	Madeleine
Theodore	Magdalene
Veronica	Marmaduke
Victoria	Millicent
Violette	Mirabelle
Virginia	Nathaniel
Winifred	Nicolette
Alexander	Peregrine
Alexandra	Priscilla
Alphonsus	Rosabella
Anastasia	Sebastian
Annabella	Sempronia
Archibald	Seraphina
Augustine	Siegfried
Cassandra	Stephanie
Catherine	Sylvester
Charlotte	Veronique
Christian	Antoinette
Christina	Bernadette

Christabel	Marguerite	Wilhelmina
Christiana	Maximilian	Bartholomew
Clementine	Montgomery	Christopher
Jacqueline	Petronella	Constantine

Fish

bib	goby	cohog	skate	cockle
cod	hake	dorse	smelt	comber
dab	huso	fluke	smolt	conger
eel	kelt	gaper	snook	cottus
fin	keta	gaper	spawn	cuttle
gar	luce	genus	sprat	darter
hag	opah	guppy	squid	dorado
ide	parr	hydra	sting	ellops
ray	pike	lance	tench	fogash
roe	pout	murex	trout	garvie
barb	rudd	murry	tunny	grilse
bass	scad	ormer	umber	groper
blay	scup	perch	whelk	gurnet
carp	shad	pinna	alevin	kipper
char	sole	pogge	angler	launce
chub	tail	polyp	barbel	limpet
chum	tope	porgy	beluga	maigre
clam	tuna	prawn	bester	marlin
claw	basse	roach	bowfin	meagre
coho	blain	roker	burbot	medusa
crab	bleak	saury	Cancer	megrim
dace	bream	scale	caplin	merman
dory	brill	shark	caribe	milter
fish	cobia	shell	cheven	minnow
gill	cohoe	shoal	chevin	mud eel

FISH

mullet	tarpon	herring	sea,cock
murena	tautog	hogfish	sea,dace
murine	triton	homelyn	sea,hare
murray	turbot	jawfish	sea,pike
murrey	twaite	jewfish	sea,slug
mussel	urchin	lamprey	sea,star
nekton	weever	lobster	sea,wife
ostrea	wrasse	mahseer	sea,wolf
oyster	abalone	merling	sea,worm
partan	abalone	mermaid	sockeye
pholas	acaleph	mollusc	spawner
pirana	alewife	mollusk	sun,fish
pisces	anchovy	mudfish	tiddler
plaice	aquatic	muraena	titling
pollan	benthos	mytilus	toheroa
puffer	bergylt	oarfish	torpedo
quahog	bivalve	octopod	trepang
redeye	bluecap	octopus	whiting
redfin	bummalo	osseter	anguilla
remora	capelin	pellock	band|fish
robalo	catfish	piddock	blue,back
salmon	cichlid	piranha	bluefish
sea,bat	codfish	piscine	bonefish
sea,cat	codling	pomfret	brisling
sea,ear	cyclops	pompano	bullhead
sea,eel	dogfish	redfish	calamary
sea,fox	eel,pout	rock,cod	carapace
sea,hog	finnock	sand,eel	coalfish
sea,pen	flipper	sardine	congo|eel
sea,pig	garfish	sawfish	crawfish
serran	gar,pike	scallop	crayfish
shiner	grouper	scomber	deal|fish
shrimp	gudgeon	sculpin	dragonet
sponge	gurnard	sea,bass	eagle,ray
squama	haddock	sea,bear	earshell
sucker	halibut	sea,calf	filefish

firebird	sailfish	conger|eel
fishpond	salmonid	crossfish
fish|tank	sandling	devil,fish
flatfish	sand,sole	dog,salmon
flounder	sea,acorn	dorsal,fin
fox,shark	sea,adder	Dover|sole
frog,fish	sea,beast	fishgarth
game|fish	sea,bream	fish,louse
goatfish	sea,devil	gaspereau
goldfish	sea,eagle	gastropod
grayling	sea,hound	ghost|crab
hornbeak	sea,lemon	globe|fish
John|Dory	sea,lungs	goldfinny
king,crab	sea,perch	goldsinny
kingfish	sea,robin	green,bone
land,crab	sea,snail	horny,head
lemon|dab	sea,trout	ichthyoid
lion|fish	sparling	jellyfish
lump,fish	spawning	lake|trout
lungfish	starfish	langouste
mackerel	sting,ray	lemon|sole
man,eater	sturgeon	pike,perch
man,of,war	tentacle	pilot|fish
menhaden	tuna|fish	porbeagle
monkfish	univalve	razorfish
nauplius	wallfish	red|mullet
physalia	weakfish	rock,perch
pickerel	wolf,fish	round|clam
pilchard	angel|fish	royal,fish
pipefish	barracuda	sandpride
plankton	black|bass	scaldfish
red,belly	blackfish	schnapper
rock,cook	blindfish	sea,nettle
rock,fish	blue|shark	sea,salmon
rockling	brandling	sea,sleeve
rose,fish	bull,trout	sea,urchin

FISH

selachian
shellfish
solenette
stonefish
surmullet
swordfish
sword tail
thornback
trachinus
troutling
trunkfish
water flea
whitebait
white bass
whitefish
widow bird
acorn shell
archer fish
bêche-de-mer
bitterling
Bombay duck
bottle fish
brook trout
brown trout
butterfish
candlefish
coelacanth
crustacean
cuttle fish
demoiselle
fish ladder
hammer fish
hellbender
hermit crab
kabeljauer
lancet fish

lumpsucker
mossbunker
mud skipper
paddlefish
parrot fish
periwinkle
purple fish
rabbit fish
red herring
ribbon fish
rock salmon
rock turbot
salamander
sand dollar
sand launce
sand sucker
sea poacher
sea surgeon
shovelhead
silverfish
spider crab
spotted ray
squeteague
tiger shark
vinegar eel
whale shark
bellows fish
brine shrimp
calling crab
channel bass
Dolly Varden
electric eel
flying squid
golden trout
heart urchin
hippocampus

lantern fish
laterigrade
lophobranch
muskellunge
pearl oyster
pelican fish
piranha fish
piscatorial
salmon trout
sea cucumber
sea hedgehog
sea scorpion
soldier crab
spawning bed
stickleback
striped bass
sucking fish
trumpet fish
whiting pout
basking shark
branchiopoda
fighting fish
golden salmon
goldfish bowl
ground feeder
ichthyopsida
kettle of fish
man of war fish
mantis shrimp
miller's thumb
paradise fish
rainbow trout
scorpion fish
sea butterfly
sea porcupine
sentinel crab

12/15 LETTERS

sergeant‚fish	white|herring
silver|salmon	findon|haddock
spring|keeper	finnan|haddock
swimming|crab	horse|mackerel
trachypterus	ichthyologist
tropical|fish	spermaceti|whale
trout|nursery	

Flowers

bed	aster	sprig	florid
bud	bloom	stalk	flower
lei	calyx	stock	garden
sow	clump	style	growth
arum	daisy	thorn	hen‚bit
bulb	dwale	tulip	hybrid
corm	flora	viola	lupine
cyme	graft	yulan	maguey
flag	hardy	althea	mallow
geum	lotus	annual	mimosa
irid	malva	anther	nectar
iris	mould	azalea	orchid
lily	ocrea	border	orchis
pink	oxlip	carpel	pistil
poke	pansy	cistus	pollen
posy	peony	corona	raceme
rosa	petal	corymb	rosery
seed	phlox	cosmos	runner
spur	poppy	crocus	salvia
stem	sepal	dahlia	scilla
wort	shoot	exotic	silene
agave	spray	floret	smilax

FLOWERS

spadix
spathe
stamen
stigma
sucker
violet
wreath
yarrow
zinnia
aconite
althaea
alyssum
anemone
begonia
blawort
blossom
bouquet
burgeon
campion
chaplet
clarkia
climber
corolla
corsage
cowslip
cutting
day|lily
dog,rose
erodium
figwort
fuchsia
garland
gentian
godetia
jasmine
jonquil

kingcup
leafage
leaflet
lily|pad
lobelia
may,lily
mimulus
mullein
nemesia
nigella
nosegay
panicle
papaver
pedicel
petiole
petunia
primula
pruning
ragweed
ragwort
rambler
rampion
red|rose
rockery
rosebay
rosebud
roselle
saffron
sea,pink
seed|pod
setwall
spiraea
sub|rosa
tagetes
tea|rose
thyrsus

verbena
verdant
verdure
weed|out
amaranth
anthesis
arum|lily
auricula
bear's|ear
biennial
bird's,eye
bluebell
buddleia
camellia
camomile
catchfly
chinampa
clematis
corn,flag
cyclamen
daffodil
dianthus
dog,daisy
epicalyx
feverfew
floweret
foxglove
gardenia
geranium
gladioli
gloxinia
goat's,rue
greenery
harebell
hawkweed
henequen

hot,house	wood,sage	full|bloom
hyacinth	Aaron's|rod	gelsemium
japonica	amarantus	gladiolus
larkspur	amaryllis	golden|rod
lily|pond	aquilegia	gynophore
marigold	bear's,foot	half,hardy
maybloom	bedded|out	hellebore
moss|rose	bulb|field	herb|Paris
musk,rose	buttercup	hollyhock
myosotis	calendula	home|grown
offshoot	campanula	lady,smock
peduncle	candytuft	mayflower
perianth	capitulum	moon|daisy
petalody	carnation	naked|lady
pond|lily	celandine	narcissus
primrose	China,rose	nelumbium
red|poppy	cineraria	perennial
rock|rose	clove,pink	perpetual
rose|bush	colchicum	pimpernel
roseroot	coltsfoot	pollen,sac
scabiosa	columbine	pollinate
scabious	composite	poppy,head
sea,heath	coreopsis	pyrethrum
seedcase	cotyledon	remontant
seedling	culver,key	richardia
seminary	dandelion	root,prune
snowdrop	digitalis	rootstock
stapelia	dog,violet	rose,elder
sun,drops	dry|garden	saxifrage
sweetpea	duck's|foot	seed|plant
trillium	edelweiss	snowflake
veronica	eglantine	speedwell
wild|rose	flowerage	sunflower
wistaria	flower|bed	tiger|lily
woodbind	flowering	wake,robin
woodbine	flower,pot	water,flag

water‚lily
wax|flower
white|wood
window‚box
wolf's|bane
amaranthus
anthophore
belladonna
bellflower
bluebottle
burnet‚rose
buttonhole
carpophore
China|aster
cinquefoil
compositae
corncockle
cornflower
crane's|bill
cuckoo‚pint
cut|flowers
daisy|chain
damask|rose
delphinium
Dutch|tulip
field|poppy
fleur‚de‚lis
floral|leaf
floribunda
flower‚head
flower‚show
frangipani
fritillary
garden|city
gelder|rose
German|iris

goldi|locks
gypsophila
heart's‚ease
helianthus
heliotrope
herbaceous
Indian|pink
Indian|poke
Indian|shot
king's‚spear
lady's‚smock
maiden|pink
marguerite
marshlocks
mayblossom
mignonette
mock|orange
nasturtium
nightshade
opium|poppy
orange|lily
ox‚eye|daisy
passiflora
periwinkle
pillar|rose
poinsettia
polyanthus
ranunculus
red|jasmine
rock‚garden
rock‚violet
roof‚garden
rose‚mallow
sarracenia
Scotch|rose
snapdragon

stavesacre
stork's|bill
sweet‚briar
sweet‚brier
wallflower
water|elder
water|lemon
wild‚flower
willow‚herb
wood‚sorrel
yellow‚root
yellow‚weed
yellow‚wort
Aaron's|beard
antirrhinum
bear's‚breech
boutonniere
cabbage‚rose
calceolaria
convallaria
convolvulus
dusty‚miller
everlasting
forget‚me‚not
garden‚glass
gillyflower
guelder|rose
hardy|annual
honeysuckle
Indian|cress
lady's‚mantle
London|pride
loosestrife
love‚in‚a‚mist
Madonna|lily
meadow‚sweet

Nancy|pretty
night,flower
orange|grass
Parma|violet
phyllomania
plum,blossom
pollen|grain
pollination
propagation
ragged|robin
rambler|rose
red,hot|poker
rose,campion
stephanotis
St|John's|wort
tiger|flower
water|garden
white|bottle
wild|flowers
wood|anemone
Adam's|flannel
alpine|flower
apple|blossom
autumn,crocus
bog,pimpernel
bridal|wreath
Carolina|pink
century,plant
corn,marigold
cuckoo,flower
fennel|flower
flower|border
flower,delice
flower,de,luce
flower|garden
flower|of|Jove

fresh|flowers
Iceland|poppy
lady's,slipper
monkey,flower
morning|glory
old|man's|beard
orange,flower
pasque|flower
peach,blossom
rambling|rose
rhododendron
rose|of|Sharon
Shirley|poppy
snow,in,summer
Solomon's|seal
St|Peter's|wort
sunken|garden
sweet|alyssum
sweet|William
virgin's|bower
water|flowers
wild|hyacinth
bougainvillea
cherry|blossom
Christmas|rose
chrysanthemum
eschscholtzia
Flanders|poppy
floricultural
marsh|marigold
meadow|saffron
orange|blossom
passion|flower
traveller's|joy
bladder|campion
bunch|of|flowers

FLOWERS

Canterbury|bell   shepherd's|purse
floriculturist   butterfly,orchis
lords|and|ladies   evening,primrose
love,in,idleness   lily,of,the,valley
love,in,idleness   Michaelmas,daisy
night,flowering   woody|nightshade
shepherd's|glass

Food

bin	cafe	lamb	stew	crust	lunch
bun	cake	lard	suet	curds	manna
can	chop	loaf	tart	curry	mince
egg	chow	loin	tuck	dicer	offal
fry	curd	malt	tuna	dough	pasta
ham	deli	mash	veal	feast	pasty
ice	diet	meal	whet	flank	patty
jam	dine	meat	whey	fudge	pecan
leg	dish	menu	wing	gigot	pilaf
nut	duck	nosh	yolk	goody	pilaw
oil	duff	olio	zest	goose	pizza
ort	eats	olla	àdemi	gorge	poach
pie	Edam	pate	aspic	Gouda	purée
poi	fare	peel	bacon	gravy	quail
roe	feed	pork	bread	grill	roast
sup	flan	puff	bully	gruel	round
wok	food	rare	candy	honey	salmi
beef	fool	rock	capon	icing	sauce
bite	fowl	roll	cheer	jelly	sauté
boil	game	rump	chips	joint	scone
bolt	grub	rusk	chuck	kebab	scrag
bran	hash	salt	crumb	liver	shank

slops	course	mutton	trifle
snack	croute	noodle	tucker
spice	cutlet	nougat	tuck‚in
steak	dainty	nutmeg	turbot
sugar	dining	omelet	turkey
sweet	dinner	oxtail	umbles
swill	dragee	paella	viande
table	eat‚out	panada	viands
T‚bone	eclair	parkin	waffle
toast	edible	pastry	walnut
torte	egg‚box	peanut	albumen
treat	entree	pepper	aliment
tripe	flitch	pickle	anchovy
vegan	fodder	picnic	bannock
wafer	fondue	pilaff	banquet
addled	forage	quiche	banting
almond	frappe	ragout	Bath‚bun
banger	fridge	rasher	biscuit
batter	gammon	ration	boiling
blintz	gateau	recipe	brisket
bonbon	giblet	relish	brittle
breast	grouse	repast	broiler
brunch	hot‚dog	saddle	cake‚mix
buffet	hot‚pot	salami	calorie
butter	humbug	salmon	candies
cachou	jam‚jar	sponge	caramel
canape	jam‚pot	spread	catchup
cashew	jujube	sundae	caviare
catsup	junket	supper	cayenne
caviar	kernel	sweets	charqui
cheese	kidney	tamale	chicken
cockle	kipper	tamara	chowder
collop	leaven	tiffin	chutney
comfit	morsel	titbit	commons
cookie	mousse	toffee	compote
cornet	muffin	tongue	cookery

cooking	matzoth	strudel	date|roll
cracker	meat|pie	tabasco	déjeuner
crumpet	mustard	teacake	delicacy
cuisine	nurture	treacle	doggy|bag
cupcake	oatcake	truffle	doughnut
deep|fry	pabulum	vanilla	dressing
dine|out	pancake	venison	dried|egg
edibles	paprika	vinegar	dripping
egg,yolk	parfait	vitamin	duckling
epicure	pikelet	wine|gum	dumpling
essence	pimento	yoghurt	egg,shell
fig|roll	poisson	acid|drop	egg,white
fondant	popcorn	a|la|carte	Emmental
fritter	popover	allspice	escalope
game|pie	pork|pie	ambrosia	escargot
gelatin	pottage	angelica	flan|case
giblets	poultry	antepast	flapjack
glucose	praline	ante,room	flesh|pot
glutton	pretzel	appetite	fried|egg
gnocchi	protein	apple|pie	frosting
goulash	pudding	baked|egg	fruit,gum
gourmet	ratafia	barbecue	gelatine
granish	rations	betel|nut	grilling
grocery	ravioli	bull's|eye	hard|tack
Gruyère	risotto	caneloni	hazelnut
gumdrop	rissole	chapatty	ice|cream
helping	rum|baba	chop|suey	kedgeree
hot|cake	sardine	chow|mein	licorice
ice|cube	sausage	cinnamon	loin|chop
ingesta	saveloy	clambake	lollipop
jam|roll	savoury	cold|meat	luncheon
jam|tart	seafood	conserve	macaroni
ketchup	seltzer	coq|au|vin	macaroon
knuckle	sirloin	cross|bun	main|dish
lardoon	soufflé	croutons	marinade
lozenge	soupçon	crudités	marinate

marzipan	soy|sauce	butter|pat
meat|ball	stockpot	calf's|head
meat|loaf	stuffing	Camembert
meat|roll	supplies	cashew|nut
meat|stew	syllabub	charlotte
meringue	take|away	club|steak
mince|pie	tamarind	cochineal
molasses	tarragon	colcannon
moussaka	teabread	collation
mushroom	tea|break	condiment
olive|oil	tortilla	confiture
omelette	trotters	cough|drop
pastille	turnover	crackling
pastrami	viaticum	cream|cake
pemmican	victuals	cream|horn
pheasant	water|ice	cream|puff
pigs|feet	wishbone	croissant
pig|swill	yoghourt	croquette
plum|cake	zwieback	croustade
pope's|eye	acid|drops	dark|bread
pork|chop	addled|egg	dried|eggs
porridge	aitchbone	drop|scone
pot|roast	angel|cake	drumstick
preserve	antipasto	egg|powder
quenelle	arrowroot	elevenses
rock|cake	banquette	entremets
rock|salt	barmbrack	epicurean
roly|poly	bean|feast	epulation
rye|bread	beefsteak	foodstuff
salt|beef	beer|glass	forcemeat
salt|pork	bite|to|eat	foretaste
sandwich	boiled|egg	fricassee
scrag|end	Brazil|nut	fried|rice
scramble	breakfast	fried|sole
shoulder	bubble|gum	fruit|cake
side|dish	bully|beef	galantine

gravy|soup
groceries
groundnut
guest|room
half|a|loaf
hamburger
humble|pie
Irish|stew
jelly|baby
lamb|chops
lamb|fries
layer|cake
left|overs
leg|of|lamb
liquorice
loaf|sugar
lump|sugar
macedoine
marchpane
margarine
marmalade
meat|paste
mincemeat
mint|sauce
monkey|nut
nutriment
patty|cake
peanut|bar
petit|four
phosphate
picnic|ham
piping|hot
pistachio
pot|pourri
pound|cake
preserves

provender
provision
rabbit|pie
red|pepper
rice|paper
roast|beef
rock|candy
Roquefort
rump|steak
Scotch|egg
seasoning
shortcake
short|ribs
soda|bread
soda|scone
spaghetti
spareribs
spearmint
spun|sugar
sugar|lump
sweet|corn
sweetmeat
Swiss|roll
tasty|dish
tipsy|cake
vol|au|vent
wheat|germ
white|meat
wild|honey
apple|cover
apple|sauce
aristology
baked|beans
Bath|oliver
bill|of|fare
blancmange

blue|cheese
boiled|fish
boiled|meat
Bombay|duck
bon|appetit
brandy|snap
breadcrumb
bread|sauce
bread|stick
Brie|cheese
brown|sugar
calf's|brain
candy|floss
caper|sauce
cooking|fat
cooking|oil
corned|beef
corned|meat
cornflakes
custard|pie
daily|bread
Danish|blue
devil's|food
dill|pickle
dinner|roll
dog|biscuit
double|loin
dropped|egg
Edam|cheese
fatted|calf
flank|steak
food|supply
fork|supper
frangipane
French|cake
fresh|cream

fricandeau	provisions	Vienna|loaf
frozen|food	puff|pastry	Vienna|roll
garlic|salt	regalement	water|icing
ginger|snap	rolled|lamb	white|bread
Gorgonzola	rolled|pork	white|sauce
ham|and|eggs	round|steak	zabaglione
hearty|meal	royal|icing	almond|icing
hickory|nut	saccharine	almond|paste
honey|crisp	salmagundi	banana|split
hot|and|cold	sea|biscuit	barley|sugar
icing|sugar	shallow|fry	beef|sausage
ingredient	sheep's|head	black|butter
jardinière	shirred|egg	black|pepper
jugged|hare	shish|kebab	bonne|bouche
lamb|cutlet	shortbread	brandy|sauce
light|lunch	shortcrust	breadcrumbs
liverwurst	silverside	burnt|almond
maple|syrup	Simnel|cake	caster|sugar
marble|cake	sour|pickle	Castile|soap
marrow|bone	spatchcock	chicken|feed
mayonnaise	sponge|cake	chilli|sauce
meal|ticket	spotted|dog	clam|chowder
Melba|toast	square|meal	clove|pepper
mint|humbug	staple|diet	comestibles
mortadella	stroganoff	cottage|loaf
mozzarella	stuffed|egg	cover|charge
mutton|chop	sucking|pig	cream|cheese
pastry|case	sugar|candy	curry|powder
pâtisserie	sugar|mouse	custard|tart
peach|melba	sweetbread	devilled|egg
peppermint	sweet|stuff	devilled|ham
piccalilli	table|d'hôte	dinner|party
pickled|egg	tea|biscuit	double|cream
plat|du|jour	tenderloin	dressed|crab
poached|egg	veal|cutlet	Dutch|cheese
potted|meat	vermicelli	Eve's|pudding

festal|board
fillet|steak
flank|mutton
frankfurter
French|bread
French|toast
fresh|butter
gammon|steak
gingerbread
Gouda|cheese
green|pepper
griddlecake
ground|spice
health|foods
Hollandaise
hors|d'oeuvre
hot|cross|bun
hot|luncheon
ice|lollipop
invalid|fare
iron|rations
jam|turnover
jellied|eels
leg|of|mutton
light|repast
link|sausage
loaf|of|bread
Madeira|cake
marshmallow
milk|pudding
morning|roll
olla,podrida
parson's|nose
petits|fours
pig's|trotter
plum|pudding

poached|fish
pork|sausage
potato|crisp
potato|salad
preparation
pressed|beef
refreshment
rice|pudding
roast|grouse
roast|potato
room|service
sausage|roll
self,service
ship|biscuit
side|of|bacon
single|cream
sliced|bread
smörgasbord
spotted|Dick
staff|of|life
suet|pudding
sweet|almond
sweet|pepper
sweet|pickle
Swiss|cheese
tagliatelle
toffee|apple
tomato|sauce
tossed|salad
treacle|tart
Vienna|steak
wedding|cake
Welsh|rabbit
wheaten|loaf
white|pepper
white|potato

afternoon|tea
apple|fritter
apple|strudel
bacon|and|eggs
bakewell|tart
birthday|cake
bitter|almond
black|pudding
blood|pudding
bouquet|garni
breast|of|lamb
breast|of|veal
brewer's|yeast
butcher's|meat
butterscotch
caraway|seeds
cheeseburger
chilli|pepper
chitterlings
chocolate|box
choice|morsel
cinnamon|ball
clotted|cream
club|sandwich
Cornish|pasty
coupe|Jacques
crust|of|bread
curds|and|whey
custard|sauce
Danish|pastry
delicatessen
fillet|of|sole
finnan|haddie
fish|and|chips
fish|dressing
Forfar|bridie

128

French|pastry
grated|cheese
grilled|steak
ground|almond
ground|ginger
ground|pepper
Hamburg|steak
hasty|pudding
haute|cuisine
ice|cream|cone
Leyden|cheese
luncheon|meat
mulligan|stew
peanut|butter
pease|pudding
pickled|onion
pig's|knuckles
pistachio|nut
planked|steak
pork|and|beans
potato|crisps
pumpernickel
Russian|salad
sage|and|onion
salted|peanut
scrambled|egg
sherry|trifle
short|commons
sirloin|steak
smoked|salmon
sponge|finger
streaky|bacon
sweet|and|sour
tabasco|sauce
tartare|sauce
vegetable|oil

Waldorf|salad
water|biscuit
Welsh|rarebit
whipped|cream
apple|crumble
apple|dumpling
apple|fritters
apple|turnover
barbecue|sauce
bouillabaisse
bread|and|water
breakfast|food
burnt|offering
buttered|toast
cayenne|pepper
chateaubriand
cheddar|cheese
cheese|biscuit
Christmas|cake
confectionery
contamination
cottage|cheese
custard|powder
Edinburgh|rock
finnan|haddock
food|poisoning
French|mustard
fruit|cocktail
lemon|meringue
meals|on|wheels
meat|and|two|veg
mess|of|pottage
milk|chocolate
minced|collops
Neapolitan|ice
pease|porridge

pickled|walnut	mock|turtle|soup
rasher|of|bacon	nutritiousness
roll|and|butter	Parmesan|cheese
salad|dressing	pate|de|fois|gras
scrambled|eggs	peppermint|drop
smoked|sausage	pickled|herring
soused|herring	plaice|and|chips
starch|reduced	plain|chocolate
stilton|cheese	polyunsaturate
strawberry|ice	pontefract|cake
strawberry|jam	saddle|of|mutton
sugar|and|spice	sausage|and|mash
summer|pudding	Scotch|woodcock
toad|in|the|hole	steak|and|kidney
transport|cafe	tapioca|pudding
veal|and|ham|pie	tea|and|biscuits
vegetable|dish	treacle|pudding
apple|charlotte	tripe|and|onions
banana|fritters	Turkish|delight
bangers|and|mash	vegetable|curry
bar|of|chocolate	vegetable|salad
bread|and|butter	vegetarian|dish
bread|and|cheese	Worcester|sauce
bread|and|scrape	box|of|chocolates
cabinet|pudding	breakfast|cereal
Canterbury|lamb	bubble|and|squeak
charlotte|russe	Camembert|cheese
cheese|sandwich	chicken|Maryland
Cheshire|cheese	chocolate|eclair
college|pudding	chocolate|sundae
curried|chicken	convenience|food
French|dressing	cooked|breakfast
gooseberry|fool	Devonshire|cream
hearty|appetite	French|breakfast
ice|cream|sundae	fricassee|of|veal
macaroni|cheese	grilled|sausages

grilled|tomatoes   redcurrant|jelly
orange|marmalade   roly|poly|pudding
peaches|and|cream   sausage|and|chips
peppermint|cream   sausages|and|mash
ploughman's|lunch   Wiener|schnitzel

Foreign Words and Phrases

ami	ca|ira	tutti	emptor
jeu	canto	usine	en|fête
mot	corno	abattu	fi|donc
à|bas	desto	abrege	flèche
abbé	dolce	agrege	giusto
doge	domus	allons	grazia
gene	école	aperçu	ibidem
in|re	étude	à|terre	in|vivo
lied	grave	aubade	legato
vivo	largo	au|fait	Lieder
ab|ovo	lento	au|fond	maison
addio	lycée	avanti	mañana
à|deux	mores	avenir	nobile
ad|hoc	obiit	bel|air	ottava
adios	per|se	bêtise	palais
ad|lib	plaza	bon|mot	posada
ad|rem	pleno	bon|ton	presto
adsum	Reich	Cortes	rubato
à|gogo	salle	crible	sempre
aidos	segno	da|capo	subito
apage	segue	dégagé	tenuto
arras	sordo	déja|vu	torero
assai	tacet	de|jure	troppo
buffo	torte	der|Tag	vivace

FOREIGN WORDS AND PHRASES

acharne	chanson	peccavi	au|revoir
ad|astra	château	pension	autobahn
ad|finem	chez|moi	pesante	aux|armes
ad|litem	clavier	piacere	à|volonté
à|droite	codetta	plafond	banlieue
ad|vivum	comedia	pomposo	bel|canto
affaire	con|brio	pro|rata	bien|être
affiche	con|moto	qui|vive	bona|fide
agaçant	couloir	ragazza	bout|rime
à|gauche	cui|bono	Rathaus	chez|nous
agitato	d'accord	Rigsdag	col|legno
à|jamais	danseur	Riksdag	con|amore
à|la|mode	ébauche	ripieno	con|fuoco
alcaide	en|prise	rondeau	coryphée
alcalde	en|route	rondino	cum|laude
al|conto	ex|aequo	rosalia	dal|segno
altesse	fagotto	roulade	danseuse
animato	farceur	Schloss	déjeuner
a|priori	fermata	sine|die	démarche
à|quatre	friture	sordino	Deus|vult
attacca	furioso	sub|rosa	dies|irae
au|mieux	Gestalt	tant|pis	distrait
Auslese	giocoso	vibrato	doloroso
bas|bleu	gouache	abat|jour	duettino
battuta	haut|ton	abatvoix	enceinte
berceau	ich|dien	abat|voix	entresol
bonjour	in|utero	ad|summum	estancia
bonsoir	in|vacuo	agaçerie	et|cetera
bourrée	in|vitro	agrément	excerpta
bravura	Ländler	à|la|carte	ex|gratia
calando	laus|Deo	alta|moda	faubourg
cantina	Märchen	apéritif	Fine|Gael
canzona	morceau	a|piacere	gendarme
canzone	morendo	après|ski	grand|mal
caramba	palazzo	à|quoi|bon	hacienda
chambre	pas|seul	au|gratin	hic|jacet

idée|fixe	ad|valorem	coup|d'état
leggiero	a|fortiori	das|heisst
maestoso	alla|breve	dei|gratia
maggiore	alma|mater	de|rigueur
mala|fide	âme|perdue	dolce|vita
mal|de|mer	Anschluss	en|famille
mandamus	antipasto	en|passant
mea|culpa	à|outrance	et|tu,|Brute
moderato	arc|en|ciel	flute|a|bec
mon|repos	aria|buffa	Folketing
mot|juste	assez|bien	gemütlich
ostinato	au|courant	glissando
par|avion	au|naturel	grandioso
parlando	au|secours	grand|prix
parlante	Ausgleich	haut|monde
pro|forma	autopista	inter|alia
raisonné	autoroute	ipse|dixit
rara|avis	bal|masque	ipso|facto
ritenuto	beaux|arts	Landsting
sayonara	beaux|yeux	Leitmotiv
scordato	bel|esprit	Mardi|Gras
semplice	belle|amie	meden|agan
serenata	ben|venuto	mezza|voce
Sobranje	bête|noire	nisi|prius
spianato	bon|marché	obbligato
staccato	bon|vivant	objet|d'art
sub|poena	bon|viveur	pari|passu
trouvère	bon|voyage	pas|de|deux
una|corda	Bundesrat	passepied
Vorspiel	Bundestag	per|capita
à|bon|droit	buona|sera	per|contra
ab|origine	cantabile	petit|four
a|cappella	carpe|diem	piacevole
ad|hominem	cauchemar	piangendo
ad|libitum	cave|canem	Politburo
ad|nauseam	centumvir	pro|patria

pro|re|nata	bêche|de|mer	perdendosi
ricercare	ben|trovato	pied|à|terre
rus|in|urbe	billet|doux	plat|du|jour
scherzoso	bon|appetit	ponticello
sforzando	buon|giorno	prima|facie
siciliana	café|au|lait	Prix|unique
sine|prole	camino|real	pro|hac|vice
smerzando	canto|fermo	quid|pro|quo
solfeggio	canzonetta	recitativo
sostenuto	certiorari	ritardando
sotto|voce	cinquepace	ritornelle
spiritoso	confiserie	ritornello
sub|judice	con|sordini	scherzando
sub|specie	con|spirito	scordatura
succès|fou	cordon|bleu	seguidilla
tant|mieux	danke|schön	semper|idem
taoiseach	Deo|gratias	sens|unique
tête|à|tête	Deo|volente	sine|qua|non
tout|à|fait	dernier|cri	stringendo
tout|court	Eisteddfod	sui|generis
vers|libre	feuilleton	table|d'hôte
Volkslied	Fianna|Fáil	terra|firma
vox|humana	fortepiano	thé|dansant
à|bon|marché	Gesundheit	Tiergarten
absente|reo	in|excelsis	tout|de|même
ad|absurdum	in|extremis	tremolando
affettuoso	jardinière	ultra|vires
aficionado	jus|commune	urbi|et|orbi
alla|Franca	jus|gentium	villanella
allargando	Lebensraum	accelerando
anno|Domini	magnum|opus	ad|avizandum
art|nouveau	mezzo|forte	ad|infinitum
au|pis|aller	mezzo|piano	aetatis|suae
autostrada	nom|de|plume	aide|mémoire
avant|garde	opera|buffa	alla|tedesca
bar|mitzvah	ottava|rima	allez|vous|en

alto relievo	hors d'oeuvre	ante meridiem
amor patriae	in medias res	appassionata
amour propre	in principio	appoggiatura
à nos moutons	lèse majesté	à quatre mains
a posteriori	lignum vitae	arrière garde
Arcades ambo	litterateur	ave atque vale
arrivederci	mise en scène	ballon d'essai
au contraire	motu proprio	basso relievo
avec plaisir	musica ficta	basso rilievo
à votre santé	ne plus ultra	buenas noches
belle époque	nihil obstat	carte blanche
bien entendu	nom de guerre	cause célèbre
bonne bouche	nous verrons	caveat emptor
boutonnière	obiter dicta	compos mentis
capriccioso	objet trouvé	Concertstück
carte du jour	opera bouffe	conseil d'état
cavo relievo	papier mâché	contra mundum
che sera sera	pas de quatre	crème caramel
comme il faut	pax vobiscum	degringolade
concertante	politbureau	Donnerwetter
contrapunto	raison d'être	doppelganger
contredanse	rallentando	eppur si muove
coram populo	savoir faire	experto crede
crème brûlée	Schottische	fait accompli
Dail Eireann	smörgasbord	ferae naturae
decrescendo	summum bonum	feu d'artifice
degringoler	tempo giusto	force majeure
de haut en bas	tempus fugit	Gesellschaft
de profundis	tempus fugit	glockenspiel
ex hypothesi	tertium quid	Habeas corpus
ex post facto	tout le monde	hasta la vista
femme fatale	und so weiter	haute couture
fieri facias	vivacissimo	haute cuisine
fin de siècle	acciaccatura	homme du monde
fritto misto	amicus curiae	honoris causa
hasta mañana	ancien régime	hors concours

hors|de|combat
hotel|de|ville
laissez‚faire
lapsus|calami
lite|pendente
mezzo‚relievo
modus|vivendi
nolens|volens
obiter|dictum
opéra|comique
piobaireachd
pollice|verso
pons|asinorum
porte‚cochère
porte‚monnaie
quelque|chose
rien|ne|va|plus
salle|à|manger
sauve|qui|peut
s'il|vous|plait
terminus|a|quo
Zigeunerlied
ab|urbe|condita
aggiornamento
à|la|bonne|heure
à|propos|de|rien
ariston|metron
arrière‚pensée
avant‚gardiste
avis|au|lecteur
basso|profondo
Champs|Élysées
cogito|ergo|sum
corps|de|ballet
corpus|delicti
couleur|de|rose

crème|de|menthe
croix|de|guerre
cum|grano|salis
deux|ex|machina
éminence|grise
exempli|gratia
ex|proprio|motu
faites|vos|jeux
fête|champêtre
force|de|frappe
in|vino|veritas
laissez‚passer
lapsus|linguae
magna|cum|laude
mirabile|dictu
modus|operandi
multum|in|parvo
noli‚me‚tangere
nolle|prosequi
Nouvelle|Vague
nulli|secundus
palais|de|danse
poisson|d'avril
quartier|latin
Schadenfreude
succès|d'estime
summa|cum|laude
très|au|sérieux
a|minori|ad|majus
annus|mirabilis
auf|Wiedersehen
bureau|de|change
ceteris|paribus
crème|de|la|crème
Deuxième|Bureau
dis|aliter|visum

divide|et|impera
dolce|far|niente
double|entendre
ejusdem|generis
enfant|terrible
et|in|Arcadia|ego
facile|princeps
hapax|legomenon
homme|d'affaires
in|loco|parentis
ipsissima|verba
maxima|cum|laude
ne|obliviscaris
obiit|sine|prole
petit|bourgeois

terminus|ad|quem
terra|incognita
tertius|gaudens
valet|de|chambre
ad|misericordiam
amende|honorable
à|propos|de|bottes
argumentum|ad|rem
cherchez|la|femme
cordon|sanitaire
crime|passionnel
gaudeamus|igitur
mutatis|mutandis
persona|non|grata
rem|acu|tetigisti

French Revolutionary Calendar

Nivose	Dohnanyi	Pluviose
Cavalli	Fervidor	Prairial
Floreal	Frimaire	Fructidor
Ventose	Germinal	Thermidor
Brumaire	Messidor	Vendemière

Fruit

cob	anise	achene	pomelo
fig	apple	acinus	punica
fir	areca	almond	quince
haw	berry	ananas	raisin
hip	cacao	banana	rennet
hop	cocoa	cashew	rocket
nut	drupe	cherry	russet
pip	fruit	citron	savory
uva	gourd	citrus	squash
yam	graft	cobnut	tomato
aloe	grape	damson	unripe
core	guava	doghip	vinery
crab	gumbo	durian	apricot
date	hazel	kernel	avocado
gean	lemon	litchi	blossom
hull	mango	locust	bramble
lime	melon	lovage	brinjal
okra	olive	lychee	buckeye
pear	orris	mammee	capsule
peel	papaw	medlar	catawba
pepo	peach	muscat	coconut
pina	pecan	nutmeg	colanut
pith	pinon	orange	cumquat
plum	prune	papaya	currant
pome	shell	pawpaw	dessert
rind	shoot	peanut	dikanut
ripe	stalk	pippin	eggplum
seed	stipe	pollen	filbert
sloe	stone	pomato	grapery

138

harvest	chestnut	vine|leaf
kola|nut	citrange	vineyard
kumquat	cocoanut	alligator
lettuce	coco|palm	apple|tree
malmsey	cow|berry	baneberry
morello	date|plum	blaeberry
orchard	dewberry	blueberry
palm|nut	dogberry	Brazil|nut
pimento	earthnut	candle|nut
plumcot	endocarp	cashew|nut
putamen	follicle	cherimoya
rhubarb	fructose	coco|de|mer
rose|hip	hagberry	corozo|nut
ruddock	hazelnut	crab|apple
ruellia	hot|house	cranberry
salsify	locoweed	fruit|tree
sea|kale	mad|apple	grapevine
seed|pod	mandarin	greengage
sorosis	May|apple	groundnut
soursop	mulberry	grugru|nut
succory	muscatel	home|grown
sultana	musk|pear	in|blossom
tangelo	musk|plum	Indian|fig
vintage	nutshell	jackfruit
aesculus	oak|apple	jenneting
apple|pip	oleaster	jequirity
autocarp	orangery	Juneberry
beechnut	peachery	king|apple
beetroot	pericarp	kiwi|fruit
bergamot	pimiento	lemon|peel
betel|nut	prunello	love|apple
bilberry	sainfoin	manzanita
bromelia	self|heal	melocoton
calabash	shaddock	monkey|nut
capparis	sloebush	muscadine
caprifig	tiger|nut	muskmelon

FRUIT

nectarine
nux|vomica
orange|pip
persimmon
physic|nut
pineapple
pistachio
poison|nut
raspberry
salad|herb
sapodilla
succulent
sugar|plum
tangerine
wild|grape
wild|olive
banana|skin
bird|cherry
blackberry
blackheart
breadfruit
cantaloupe
chokeberry
conference
dried|fruit
elderberry
French|plum
fruit|salad
gooseberry
granadilla
grapefruit
hickory|nut
holly|berry
Idaean|vine
loganberry
mangosteen

orange|peel
peach|bloom
peppercorn
prayer|bead
Punic|apple
red|currant
rowan|berry
sand|cherry
strawberry
sugar|apple
watermelon
wild|cherry
an|apple|a|day
anchovy|pear
avocado|pear
bittersweet
boysenberry
bramble|bush
candleberry
chokecherry
citrus|fruit
eating|apple
goldenberry
hesperidium
huckleberry
Indian|berry
Jaffa|orange
mammee|apple
navel|orange
phyllomania
pomegranate
pompelmoose
prickly|pear
quince|jelly
suwarrow|nut
sweet|cherry

tutti frutti
American aloe
apple of Sodom
blackcurrant
bottled fruit
cherry laurel
cooking apple
custard apple
Dead Sea apple
Dead Sea fruit
ground cherry
mulberry bush
passion fruit
Persian berry
Persian melon
pistachio nut

sassafras nut
seaside grape
service berry
Victoria plum
white currant
whortleberry
alligator pear
bunch of grapes
honeydew melon
raspberry cane
Ribston pippin
Seville orange
conference pear
gooseberry bush
mandarin orange

Furniture

bar	door	chair	shelf	galley
bed	hall	chest	stool	garage
cot	loft	couch	study	garret
den	nook	decor	suite	larder
mat	oven	diner	table	lounge
pad	rack	divan	tapis	lowboy
pew	safe	duvet	alcove	luxury
rug	seat	lobby	bureau	mirror
ambo	sofa	piano	carpet	pantry
bath	ambry	porch	carver	remove
bunk	arras	press	castor	rocker
crib	attic	quilt	closet	ruelle
desk	blind	salon	day bed	screen

FURNITURE

serdab	ballroom	club|chair
settee	banister	cookhouse
settle	barstool	cubby|hole
teapoy	basement	davenport
veneer	bedstead	deck|chair
almirah	bookcase	double|bed
antique	chair|bed	drum|table
armoire	chair|leg	easy|chair
bedroom	corridor	footstool
bibelot	hatstand	furniture
boudoir	jalousie	garden|hut
boxroom	love|seat	glory|hole
bunk|bed	mess|hall	grillroom
buttery	outhouse	guest|room
canteen	pembroke	hallstand
car|port	playroom	high|chair
chamber	scullery	household
charpoy	stairway	house|room
commode	table|leg	inglenook
curtain	table|top	leaf|table
dinette	tea|table	lunchroom
dresser	upstairs	maid's|room
epergne	vargueno	marquetry
furnish	wall|safe	mezzanine
kitchen	wardrobe	music|room
landing	woodshed	parquetry
library	apartment	pierglass
nursery	bed|settee	pier|table
ottoman	bookshelf	refectory
parlour	brasserie	rice|paper
picture	bric|a|brac	sideboard
tallboy	cane|chair	side|table
tearoom	card|table	spare|room
whatnot	carpeting	sun|lounge
armchair	carpet|rod	top|drawer
back|door	cloakroom	washstand

wing|chair	fireside|rug
balustrade	fold,away|bed
bucket|seat	furnishings
chiffonier	garden|chair
coal,cellar	Heppelwhite
dining|hall	kitchenette
dining|room	laundry|room
downstairs	morning|room
dumb|waiter	player|piano
escritoire	reading|lamp
featherbed	roll,top|desk
folding|bed	sitting|room
four,poster	studio|couch
garden|shed	summer,house
lumber|room	swivel|chair
music|stool	utility|room
passageway	wicker|chair
piano|stool	writing,desk
public|room	bedside|table
rumpus|room	chaise|longue
scatter|rug	chesterfield
secretaire	console,table
sun|parlour	contour|chair
swing|chair	dressing|room
upholstery	Dutch|dresser
Victoriana	emergency|bed
wicker,work	fitted|carpet
wine|cellar	gate,leg|table
basket|chair	inner|sanctum
below|stairs	ironing|table
bookshelves	kitchen|table
cabriole|leg	kneehold|desk
Chippendale	library|table
coffee|table	nest|of|tables
dining|table	regency|chair
drawing|room	reproduction

FURNITURE

rocking|chair
sheepskin|rug
spare|bedroom
trestle|table
upright|piano
Welsh|dresser
writing|table
dressing|table
Louis|quatorze
Persian|carpet
reception|room
revolving|door
room|with|a|view
skirting|board
umbrella|stand
wash|hand|basin

airing|cupboard
breakfast|table
central|heating
chest|of|drawers
French|polisher
kitchen|cabinet
kitchen|dresser
venetian|carpet
Axminster|carpet
cocktail|cabinet
dining|room|table
furniture|polish
gate|legged|table
occasional|table
soft|furnishings
tables|and|chairs

Geography

air	fen	pap	arid	calm	duct
ait	fog	pit	bank	cape	dune
alp	gap	ria	beck	cave	dust
bed	gas	rip	belt	city	dyke
ben	GMT	sea	berg	clay	east
bog	har	sod	bill	crag	eyot
cay	jet	wad	bolt	dale	fall
col	jut	wax	bomb	damp	fell
cwm	map	wet	bore	dawn	firn
dam	mud	adit	brae	deep	floe
dew	nip	apex	burn	dell	flow
dip	oil	arch	bush	dirt	flux
eye	orb	area	calf	down	fold

fork	moss	spot	bourn	dunes	joint
foss	mull	spur	brash	dwarf	karoo
gang	naze	tarn	broad	eagre	knoll
gill	neck	till	broch	earth	kopje
glen	ness	tilt	brogh	emery	kraal
grit	neve	town	brook	erode	lapse
hade	node	trap	brush	esker	layer
hail	ooze	vale	burgh	ether	levee
halo	park	vane	butte	falls	level
haze	pass	veld	campo	fault	llano
head	peak	void	canal	fauna	local
high	peat	wadi	canon	fiord	locus
hill	plat	wane	chain	firth	loess
holm	plat	ward	chalk	fjord	lough
home	pond	warm	chart	flats	magma
hook	pool	wash	chase	flint	marge
isle	purl	weir	chasm	flood	marly
kame	race	well	chine	flora	marsh
khor	rack	west	cliff	fluor	mould
lake	rias	wold	clime	focus	mount
land	rift	zoic	close	frith	mouth
lias	rill	zone	coast	froth	nodes
lieu	ring	abysm	coomb	gelid	north
limb	sand	abyss	crack	geode	Notus
lime	scar	adobe	craig	geoid	oasis
linn	scud	amber	creek	ghyll	oxⱼbow
loam	seam	ambit	crust	glare	ozone
loch	seat	argil	cycle	globe	place
lord	sial	atlas	deeps	gorge	plain
mere	sill	azure	delta	grail	plash
mesa	silt	bayou	ditch	grove	playa
midi	sima	beach	downs	gully	plaza
mild	site	bedew	drift	heath	point
mire	slag	bleak	drink	humus	polar
mist	soil	bluff	dross	inlet	range
moor	spit	boggy	druse	islet	rapid

reach	urban	deluge	lagoon	runlet
realm	vault	depths	layers	runnel
Reich	veldt	desert	levant	rustic
ridge	waste	dew|bow	locale	saddle
right	weald	dingle	lochan	salina
river	wilds	dolmen	lunate	sarsen
rural	wilds	domain	map|out	schist
salse	world	efflux	margin	season
sault	alpine	Empire	marshy	sector
scale	arctic	Eocene	massif	shadow
scarp	autumn	eothen	menhir	sierra
scaur	barrow	ethnic	mirage	sinter
scree	border	Europa	morass	skerry
serac	bottom	facies	nation	slough
shade	branch	famine	native	slurry
shaft	broads	feeder	nebula	solano
sheer	brough	flurry	Orient	source
shelf	burrow	geodes	outlet	sphere
shire	canopy	geyser	pampas	splash
slope	canton	gravel	parish	spring
slush	canyon	groove	pebble	steppe
smoke	cavern	grotto	period	strata
solum	circle	ground	placer	strath
sough	cirque	gulley	plains	stream
south	clayey	hamlet	plasma	strial
spate	clunch	hiatus	plenum	suburb
stack	colony	hiemal	polder	summer
state	colure	hollow	puddle	summit
stria	common	Ice|age	quaggy	sun|dog
surge	corral	icecap	rapids	swampy
swale	corrie	icicle	ravine	tremor
swamp	coulee	influx	region	trench
swirl	county	inland	riding	tropic
table	course	island	rillet	trough
talus	crater	jungle	ripple	tundra
tract	defile	karroo	rubble	tunnel

turnip	crevice	meander	tideway
upland	crystal	mill|run	topical
valley	culvert	Miocene	topsoil
vernal	debacle	mofette	torrent
vortex	demesne	mundane	trickle
welkin	diurnal	Neogene	tropics
wester	dog|days	pot|hole	uplands
window	freshet	prairie	village
winter	full|sun	proctor	volcano
zenith	geodesy	profile	West|end
zephyr	geogony	quarter	worldly
alluvia	geology	quietus	affluent
almanac	glacial	radiant	alluvial
azimuth	glacier	rivulet	alluvion
barrens	habitat	road|map	alluvium
bedding	hachure	salband	altitude
bone|bed	harbour	salt|pan	anabatic
bottoms	hillock	savanna	autumnal
boulder	hilltop	section	bearings
breaker	horizon	settled	bone,cave
caldera	hummock	shingle	boom|town
capture	iceberg	sky|line	boondock
cascade	ice|cave	snow|bed	borehole
chimney	icefall	snow|cap	boundary
clachan	ice|floe	souther	brooklet
cluster	ice|pack	station	calciole
commune	ice|raft	stratum	Cambrian
compass	incline	stretch	catacomb
conduit	insular	subsoil	cataract
conflux	isobase	suburbs	causeway
contour	isthmus	sunbeam	cleavage
corcass	kingdom	sundown	coal|mine
couloir	lakelet	surface	confines
country	land|ice	terrain	corridor
country	lowland	the|line	crevasse
crannog	machair	thermal	darkling

GEOGRAPHY

darkness	indigent	overhang
date|line	interior	photomap
detritus	irrigate	pinnacle
diluvium	isostasy	plateaux
district	Jurassic	Pliocene
dominion	lakeland	polar|cap
downtown	land|form	position
drainage	land|mass	precinct
dustbowl	landslip	prospect
easterly	latitude	province
effluent	lava,flow	purlieus
Eolithic	left|bank	quagmire
epifocal	lenticle	ring,dyke
eruption	levanter	riparian
exposure	Lewisian	river|bed
fold,axis	littoral	riverine
foreland	location	rotation
fountain	lodestar	sabulose
fracture	lowlands	salt|lake
frontier	mainland	sandbank
fumarole	Menevian	sand|dune
granules	Mesozoic	sandhill
headland	millpool	sandspit
headrace	millrace	seaboard
hibernal	monolith	sea|level
hick|town	monticle	seashore
highland	moorland	sediment
hillside	mountain	seedtime
homeland	Nearctic	shallows
Huronian	Near|East	Silurian
hypogene	New|World	snowball
hypogeum	Occident	snowland
ice|blink	Old|World	snow,line
ice|field	on|the|map	spectrum
ice|sheet	ordnance	stagnant
indented	overfold	Stone|Age

suburban	cisalpine	intrusion
syncline	city|state	isoclinal
tailrace	cliff|face	Kainozoic
telluric	coalfield	lake|basin
Tertiary	coastland	landscape
tide|gate	coastline	landslide
tide|race	concourse	loadstone
time|zone	continent	longitude
township	cornbrash	low|ground
Triassic	cosmology	macrocosm
undertow	curvature	maelstrom
undulate	dead|water	magnitude
upheaval	detrition	mare's|tail
vicinity	down|under	marshland
warm|cell	earth|wave	mattamore
warm|wave	epicentre	midstream
water|gap	esplanade	Neolithic
westerly	estuaries	north|east
Wild|West	estuarine	northerly
workings	everglade	north|pole
zastruga	evolution	North|star
adumbrate	exosphere	north|west
affluence	foliation	obsequent
anabranch	foothills	off|the|map
antarctic	foreshore	Oligocene
anticline	geography	parallels
antipodes	ghost|town	peneplain
Armorican	glacieret	peninsula
avalanche	green|belt	phacolith
backwater	highlands	phenomena
backwoods	Holarctic	polar|axis
billabong	homotaxis	pozzolana
Bronze|Age	hour|angle	precipice
brushland	hypogaeum	quicklime
canicular	ice|action	rainwater
catchment	inner|city	refluence

relief map	tidal flow	campestral
reservoir	tidal flux	chalkdowns
right bank	tide gauge	chersonese
riverhead	tidewater	cismontane
riverside	tornadoes	colatitude
rock basis	tributary	confluence
salt marsh	underfoot	consequent
sand dunes	unsettled	contortion
satellite	upcountry	contour map
Secondary	volcanoes	cordillera
sheer drop	vulcanism	cosmic dust
shoreline	wasteland	demography
situation	waterfall	denudation
snowdrift	water flow	deposition
snow field	water hole	depression
snowfield	watershed	dreikanter
snowscape	waterside	drosometer
solfatara	whirlpool	druid stone
solstices	wide world	earthlight
south east	wind blown	earthquake
southerly	aerography	earthshine
south land	aerosphere	embankment
south pole	air current	ephemerist
south west	arable land	equatorial
statehood	arid desert	escarpment
streamlet	atmosphere	excavation
streamway	barysphere	fatherland
subregion	bathometer	fieldstone
summer day	body of land	floatstone
surveying	borderland	fore shocks
survey map	borderline	fossilized
tableland	Boreal zone	foundation
tectonics	bottom land	freshwater
temperate	bradyseism	geographer
territory	breakwater	geophysics
tidal bore	Caledonian	ground mass

hard winter	oppressive	subtropics
headstream	Ordovician	summertide
headwaters	orogenesis	summertime
hemisphere	outline map	terra firma
high ground	overshadow	theodolite
hinterland	overthrust	topography
homosphere	Palaeogene	torrid zone
hot springs	Palaeozoic	trade route
hour circle	phenomenon	tramontana
hypocentre	plot of land	undercliff
ice crystal	population	undulation
insularity	potamology	vegetation
inundation	promontory	visibility
irrigation	rain forest	waterflood
jet streams	rift valley	water front
lacustrine	river basin	water gauge
landlocked	rock bottom	waterspout
large scale	rock desert	water table
latent heat	rock pillar	weathering
mappemonde	rock series	wilderness
map reading	rupestrian	wintertide
market town	seismic map	wintertime
meteor dust	seismology	archipelago
metropolis	serpentine	Austral zone
micrometer	settlement	back country
midchannel	small scale	barrier lake
Middle East	springtime	bathysphere
millstream	stalactite	bottom glade
morphology	stalagmite	boulder clay
motherland	steep slope	buffer state
narrow seas	still water	capital city
native land	stratiform	cartography
native soil	subsequent	cataclastic
natural gas	subsidence	chorography
no man's land	substratum	circumpolar
old country	subterrene	climate zone

climatology	land|surface	troposphere
colorimetry	lone|prairie	true|horizon
Continental	monticolous	ultra|violet
convergence	mountaintop	underground
coral|island	mural|circle	under|the|sun
counterflux	nationality	universally
counter|glow	native|heath	vulcanicity
countryside	native|lands	vulcanology
country|town	open|country	warm|springs
crag|and|tail	Palaearctic	watercourse
drusy|cavity	passage|beds	water|pocket
dust|counter	pile|dweller	whereabouts
earth|pillar	polar|circle	white|cliffs
earth's|crust	polar|region	wind|erosion
earth|tremor	Pre-Cambrian	alluvial|flat
environment	prominences	arctic|circle
equinoctial	raised|beach	artesian|well
exploration	raw|material	barren|ground
fata|Morgana	reclamation	biogeography
frontal|wave	rising|coast	Black|country
frozen|north	river|course	cartographer
fulmination	river|system	commonwealth
grain|of|sand	river|valley	compass|point
great|circle	seismic|zone	conglomerate
harvest|time	seismograph	cross|bedding
ice|movement	spelaeology	elevated|area
ichnography	stony|ground	evaporimeter
ignis|fatuus	submergence	false|bedding
impermeable	subtropical	false|horizon
indentation	swallow|hole	field|of|force
isogeotherm	terrestrial	fountainhead
katabothron	thrust|plane	frozen|tundra
Kelvin|scale	torridonian	geanticlinal
lake|dweller	transalpine	geochemistry
land|feature	transandine	geographical
land|measure	transmarine	geomagnetism

geosynclinal	subterranean
geotectonics	transleithan
glacial drift	transmundane
glacial epoch	transoceanic
glaciologist	tropical heat
granular snow	tropical zone
jack o' lantern	unconformity
Lake District	undercurrent
lake dwelling	variable zone
law of gravity	volcanic cone
magnetic axis	volcanic rock
magnetic pole	will o' the wisp
main sequence	zoogeography
marginal land	above sea level
mean sea level	active volcano
metamorphism	cardinal point
metasomatism	cardinal point
midcontinent	catchment area
mountain pass	drainage basin
mountain peak	east north east
municipality	east south east
neighbouring	Latin American
oceanography	Mediterranean
one horse town	mountain chain
otherworldly	North Atlantic
palaeobotany	north easterly
Palaeolithic	north eastward
parcel of land	north westerly
polarization	north westward
principality	seismographer
rising ground	seismological
running water	south easterly
semi diameter	south eastward
sinking coast	south westerly
stratigraphy	south westward
subcontinent	temperate zone

transatlantic
arrondissement
cartographical
compass|bearing
compass|reading
ethnologically
geographically
north‚eastwards
north‚north‚east
north‚north‚west
north‚westwards
Ordnance|Survey

south‚eastwards
south‚south‚east
south‚south‚west
south‚westwards
Antarctic|Circle
biogeographical
north‚eastwardly
north‚westwardly
south‚eastwardly
south‚westwardly
topographically

Government

CD	HMS	brig	imam	poll	tana
MP	nob	bull	Inca	pomp	toft
PC	red	camp	jack	rack	Tory
PM	rex	clan	king	raja	tsar
UN	rod	czar	lady	rani	visa
act	SOS	dame	left	rank	vote
aga	tax	deed	levy	rent	ward
beg	UDI	demo	mace	rota	Whig
bey	UNO	diet	memo	rule	whip
bug	wet	dove	mute	sack	aegis
CID	ally	duke	nick	seal	agent
con	alod	duty	OHMS	seat	agora
dip	axis	earl	oyes	serf	alias
don	beat	emir	oyez	shah	amban
dot	bill	fief	pact	soke	baron
FBI	bloc	file	peer	sway	begum
Fed	bond	hawk	pink	tail	blimp

5/6 LETTERS

board	junto	sheik	debate	nonage
bonds	laird	slate	depute	notice
booty	liege	staff	deputy	nuncio
boule	lobby	thane	despot	office
bulla	major	tribe	digest	orator
burgh	manor	truce	domain	ordeal
cabal	mayor	trust	durbar	papacy
caste	minor	usurp	dynast	parage
cause	Mogul	voter	empire	patrol
chair	nabob	Whigs	eparch	patron
chief	nawab	agenda	exarch	pledge
civic	Neddy	aristo	Fabian	pogrom
class	negus	asylum	faggot	policy
co,opt	noble	ballot	fasces	polity
corps	noose	bandit	Fuhrer	powwow
count	panel	barony	gentry	prince
crown	party	brevet	holder	puisne
curia	pasha	bureau	homage	puppet
deeds	plebs	Caesar	induna	quorum
divan	poach	caliph	junker	ransom
doyen	polls	caliph	Kaiser	rapine
draft	Porte	caucus	keeper	rating
duchy	posse	censor	knight	recess
edict	power	census	leader	record
elder	proof	clause	legate	reform
elect	proxy	clique	Majlis	regent
elite	queen	coheir	master	regime
fence	rajah	colony	mayhem	reward
filch	rally	con,man	mikado	sachem
forum	realm	consul	milady	satrap
frame	rebel	copper	milord	sconce
front	regal	cordon	moiety	senate
graft	reign	Cortes	motion	shogun
guard	royal	county	mutiny	sircar
guild	ruler	curfew	Nazism	sirdar
junta	ruler	daimio	NIBMAR	socage

155

soviet	cacique	enclave	neutral
speech	canvass	esquire	New|Deal
squire	capital	faction	officer
status	Capitol	Fascism	pageant
sultan	captain	Fascist	patriot
summit	captive	federal	peerage
syndic	Chamber	general	peeress
throne	charter	Gestapo	pension
ticket	closure	grandee	Pharaoh
tocsin	colonel	harmost	pillage
Tories	command	hidalgo	plunder
treaty	Commons	his|nibs	poacher
truant	compact	hot|seat	podesta
Tyburn	con|game	infanta	politic
tyrant	consort	khedive	praetor
umpire	coronet	Knesset	precept
vassal	corsair	Kremlin	prefect
vizier	council	land|tax	Premier
voting	counsel	leftist	primary
warden	czarina	libelee	process
yeoman	deed|box	Liberal	protest
abstain	diarchy	lording	proviso
adjourn	dictate	majesty	purview
admiral	D|notice	mandate	radical
adviser	dowager	marquis	reality
Aga|Khan	duarchy	Marxism	recount
amnesty	duchess	Marxist	red|tape
anarchy	dukedom	measure	referee
annuity	dyarchy	mediate	refugee
armiger	dynasty	militia	regency
autarky	earldom	minutes	regimen
band|aid	elector	mob|rule	returns
baronet	embargo	mobsman	Rigsdag
biparty	embassy	mobster	Riksdag
borough	emperor	monarch	royal|et
cabinet	empress	mormaor	royalty

7/8 LETTERS

sacking	argument	diadochi	kingship
samurai	arrogate	dictator	ladyship
sceptre	aspirant	diplomat	left|wing
senator	assassin	division	legation
settler	Assembly	doctrine	lobbying
shyster	assessor	dominion	lobbyist
soapbox	atheling	don't|know	lordship
Speaker	autarchy	election	loyalist
spy|ring	autonomy	embezzle	maharani
station	averment	Fine|Gael	majority
statist	balloter	flatfoot	mandarin
steward	bankrupt	freehold	marauder
sultana	baronage	free|vote	margrave
Sun|King	baroness	fugitive	martinet
support	Bastille	Gaullist	mayoress
supremo	bicamera	gendarme	mem|sahib
swear|in	Black|Rod	genocide	Minister
sworn|in	brass|hat	governor	ministry
tallage	campaign	grilling	minority
Templar	caudillo	guardian	monarchy
toisech	ceremony	gynarchy	monition
torture	chairman	hanger|on	movement
Toryism	chambers	heckling	narratio
tsarina	champion	hegemony	navicert
uniform	chartism	heirloom	nihilism
Vatican	citation	henchman	nobility
viceroy	civilian	heritage	nobleman
villain	claw|back	highness	nonvoter
villein	Conclave	home|rule	official
abdicate	congress	hustings	oligarch
abrogate	countess	imperial	overlord
accolade	danegeld	in|camera	overrule
activism	dead|hand	incivism	pacifism
alienate	delegate	Jingoism	palatine
alliance	demagogy	John|Bull	partisan
archduke	Democrat	jointure	party|man

157

passport	thearchy	bodyguard
patentee	the|chair	bolshevik
Pentagon	top|brass	bourgeois
platform	town|hall	brain,wash
politico	treasury	buccaneer
politics	triarchy	Bundesrat
polygamy	ultraist	Bundestag
preamble	Uncle|Sam	caliphate
princess	upper|ten	candidate
protocol	vendetta	capitular
puissant	verbatim	captaincy
put,up|job	vice,king	catchpole
question	viscount	centumvir
quisling	wardmote	chain,gang
reformer	Whiggism	chieftain
regicide	Wool|Sack	Chief|Whip
regnancy	abduction	class|rule
reigning	absconder	coalition
republic	accession	collegian
royalist	accessory	colonelcy
sabotage	actionist	Cominform
saboteur	Admiralty	Comintern
Salic|law	alarm|bell	commander
sanction	amendment	committee
security	anarchist	communism
seigneur	annulment	communist
shanghai	apartheid	complaint
Sobranje	Areopagus	concordat
solatium	authority	constable
splinter	autocracy	consulate
Stormont	back|bench	cosmocrat
suffrage	bailiwick	coup|d'etat
summitry	ballot|box	custodian
suzerain	black|book	Dalai|Lama
tanaiste	blood,feud	death|blow
taxation	blue|blood	demagogue

democracy	Landsting	presidium
desertion	lend₁lease	pretender
desperado	liege|lord	princedom
diplomacy	life|owner	princelet
dogmatist	logroller	privateer
enactment	LordMayor	procedure
espionage	maharajah	programme
exchequer	maharanee	protector
exciseman	major|domo	publicist
executive	majorship	put|in|suit
ex|officio	manifesto	queenship
extremist	mayoralty	quittance
feudalism	menshevik	red₁tapism
feudatory	mobocracy	registrar
fire|alarm	moral|code	remainder
first|lady	next|of|kin	represent
first|lord	oligarchy	right|wing
Folketing	Ombudsman	sanctions
formality	pageantry	sanhedrin
franchise	palsgrave	secretary
frithgild	paramount	selectman
generalcy	party|line	seneschal
grand|duke	party|whip	sheriffry
Grand|Turk	patriarch	socialism
high|birth	patrician	socialist
impartial	patronage	sovereign
imperator	pendragon	statement
incognito	plutocrat	statesman
incumbent	Politburo	straw|poll
influence	political	straw|vote
Iron|Guard	portfolio	supporter
kingcraft	potentate	synedrion
kingmaker	power|game	taoiseach
Labourite	precedent	terrorism
landgrave	prescript	tetrarchy
landslide	president	theocracy

think|tank
tidal|wave
top|secret
treasurer
viscounty
waldgrave
walkabout
abdication
absolutism
aggression
allegiance
ambassador
annexation
arbitrator
aristarchy
aristocrat
autonomous
bureaucrat
Big|Brother
bill|of|sale
birthright
Black|Shirt
blood|royal
blue|murder
brevet|rank
by|election
Caesarship
campaigner
canvassing
capitalist
capitulary
cashiering
casual|ward
censorship
centralism
chancellor

Chauvinism
chrematist
city|father
civil|death
classified
commandant
commissary
commission
common|weal
communiqué
conversion
coronation
corruption
councillor
councilman
counsellor
department
dispatches
dotted|line
doubletalk
duumvirate
electorate
encyclical
Falangists
federation
Fianna|Fáil
figurehead
filibuster
fiscal|year
forfeiture
front|bench
full|pardon
Gallup|poll
gas|chamber
government
Grand|Mufti

grass|roots
Green|Paper
handshaker
harman|beck
hatchet|man
heteronomy
hold|office
Home|Office
imposition
inducement
in|jeopardy
Inner|House
invocation
king's|peace
knighthood
land|pirate
leadership
left|winger
legitimacy
Liberalism
lieutenant
logrolling
lower|house
mace|bearer
machinator
Magna|Carta
maiden|name
major|party
man|of|straw
margravine
marquisate
matriarchy
memorandum
metrocracy
metropolis
militarism

minor|party	queencraft	trade|union
mitigation	ransacking	underworld
morganatic	ration|book	upper|class
mouthpiece	real|estate	upper|crust
muckraking	referendum	upper|house
mugwumpery	reform|bill	vigilantes
neutralism	refutation	voters|roll
neutrality	regulation	White|House
noble|birth	reparation	White|Paper
noblewoman	Republican	adjournment
no|man's|land	resolution	agrarianism
nomination	revolution	appointment
ochlocracy	right|of|way	archduchess
on|the|fence	ringleader	aristocracy
Ostpolitik	sanctioned	authorities
Outer|House	search|form	backbencher
palatinate	separation	black|and|tan
parliament	settlement	body|politic
party|liner	single|vote	buffer|state
patriarchy	speed|limit	bureaucracy
plebiscite	Square|Deal	burgomaster
plundering	stadholder	Butskellism
plural|vote	statecraft	candidature
pocket|veto	Statehouse	capital|city
politician	statistics	casting|vote
Post|Office	statute|cap	chairperson
power|happy	strategist	chamberlain
pray|a|tales	straw|voter	civil|rights
presidency	succession	civvy|street
princeling	suffragist	co|existence
procession	suspension	colonelship
protection	suzerainty	colonialism
proveditor	the|Commons	condominium
pursuivant	the|Royal|we	confederate
quarantine	third|reich	congressman
quarter|day	throne|room	constituent

GOVERNMENT

corporation	investiture	public enemy
crowned head	Iron Curtain	public works
crown prince	Kellogg pact	queen mother
Dail Eireann	king's speech	rate capping
declaration	Labour party	reactionary
diplomatics	lieutenancy	rear admiral
disarmament	limited veto	right to vote
dissolution	Machiavelli	right winger
divine right	maintenance	Royal Assent
doctrinaire	marchioness	royal family
duty officer	meritocracy	royal palace
electioneer	ministerial	royal pardon
empanelment	mudslinging	royal person
ergatocracy	nationalism	rubber stamp
fifth column	Nationalrat	rule of thumb
functionary	negotiation	ruling class
generalship	nonpartisan	safe conduct
gentlewoman	null and void	sansculotte
geopolitics	officialdom	secretariat
gerrymander	officialism	senatorship
good offices	Papal Nuncio	ship of state
grand vizier	partisanism	shore patrol
gynecocracy	partnership	show of hands
head of state	party member	sovereignty
heir general	peace treaty	speech maker
high sheriff	policy maker	squirearchy
high society	politbureau	stateswoman
high steward	powermonger	statute book
House of Keys	power of veto	stratocracy
hunger march	prerogative	suffragette
imperialist	proceedings	summit talks
independent	procuration	sympathizer
in duplicate	progressive	syndicalism
inner circle	Prohibition	Tammany Hall
institution	proletariat	technocracy
intercessor	protest vote	traffic duty

mean|tide
millpond
neap|tide
ocean|bed
offshore
rough|sea
sandbank
sand|reef
seaboard
sea|floor
seascape
seashore
sounding
tidal|rip
choppy|sea
coastline
coral|reef
flood|tide
high|water
marigraph
quicksand
salt|water
sea|breeze
sea|margin
seven|seas
tidal|wave
choppiness
ebb|and|flow
heavy|swell

sea|breezes
spring|tide
arm|of|the|sea
deep|blue|sea
echo|sounder
ground|swell
hydrography
hydrosphere
neritic|zone
ocean|depths
wave|erosion
white|horses
drift|current
oceanography
opposite|tide
the|seven|seas
tidal|current
fall|overboard
high|water|mark
master|mariner
ship's|register
starboard|side
circumnavigate
herring|fishery
starboard|watch
any|port|in|a|storm
circumnavigable
circumnavigator

Mathematics

pi	trig	prism	Euclid
add	unit	radii	eureka
arc	zero	radix	factor
cos	acute	ratio	figure
cot	angle	rhomb	finite
nil	bevel	rider	fluent
sec	chord	ruler	heptad
sin	conic	solid	loglog
sum	cosec	table	matrix
tan	count	tenth	minute
apex	cubed	tithe	moduli
axes	cubic	triad	nonary
axis	curve	value	nought
cone	datum	X rays	number
cosh	digit	abacus	oblong
cube	equal	adding	octant
cusp	field	alidad	pentad
data	graph	apogee	radian
half	helix	binary	radius
line	index	binate	secant
lune	lemma	bisect	sector
node	locus	circle	senary
plot	minus	cosine	series
plus	octad	cosinh	sphere
root	octet	cuboid	square
sine	plane	cyclic	tables
sinh	point	degree	tetrad
sums	power	denary	trigon
surd	prime	divide	ungula

vector	minuend	analogue
versin	modulus	argument
vertex	nonuple	binomial
volume	nothing	brackets
abaxial	null|set	calculus
algebra	numeral	cardinal
alidade	numeric	centrode
aliquot	oblique	centroid
analogy	octagon	centuple
angular	octuple	constant
bearing	ordinal	cosecant
bracket	per|cent	cube|root
compass	polygon	cubiform
complex	problem	cylinder
counter	product	decimate
cubical	pyramid	diagonal
cycloid	quinary	diameter
decagon	radiant	dihedral
decimal	rhombic	dividers
diagram	rhombus	division
digital	scalene	dynamics
divided	segment	empty|set
divisor	sextant	exponent
ellipse	squared	figurate
figures	tabular	fluxions
flexure	tangent	formulae
fluxion	ternary	fraction
formula	ternion	function
fulcrum	theorem	geometer
hexagon	totient	geometry
indices	trapeze	gradient
inertia	unitary	helicoid
integer	accuracy	heptagon
isochor	addition	hexagram
isotype	algorism	infinity
lattice	aliquant	integral

MATHEMATICS

isogonic	velocity	octagonal
mantissa	vicenary	parameter
matrices	vinculum	perimeter
monomial	aggregate	polygonal
multiple	algebraic	pyramidal
multiply	algorithm	quadruple
negative	bipyramid	quintuple
nonenary	callipers	reckoning
numerary	chiliagon	rectangle
octonary	cochleate	reduction
one₁sided	compasses	re₁entrant
parabola	cotangent	rhombical
parallel	curvature	set|square
pentagon	decagonal	slide|rule
prismoid	dimension	summation
quadrant	directrix	tabulator
quadrate	duodenary	tetragram
quantity	eccentric	trapezium
quotient	ellipsoid	trapezoid
rational	equipoise	trinomial
repetend	Euclidean	algebraist
rhomboid	figure|out	arithmetic
septimal	fluxional	asymmetric
septuple	hemicycle	biquadrate
sequence	hexagonal	calculator
sextuple	histogram	cancellate
spheroid	hyperbola	centesimal
subtract	increment	complement
sum|total	inversion	concentric
tetragon	isosceles	co₁ordinate
totitive	logarithm	cross₁staff
triangle	mechanics	decahedron
trigonal	Newtonian	difference
trochoid	numbering	duodecimal
variable	numerator	elongation
variance	numerical	estimation

fractional	subtrahend	mirror|image
half|circle	tetragonal	mixed|number
hemisphere	triangular	Napier's|rods
heptagonal	trilateral	number|field
hexahedral	triplicate	obtuse|angle
hexahedron	unilateral	pentahedral
hexangular	versed|sine	pentahedron
holohedral	aliquot|part	permutation
hypotenuse	binary|digit	prime|factor
irrational	binary|scale	prime|number
mathematic	bipartition	progression
multiplier	biquadratic	proposition
numeration	calculation	rectangular
octahedral	coefficient	reflex|angle
octahedron	combination	right|angled
orthogonal	comptometer	right|angles
pantograph	computation	round|number
pentagonal	coordinates	rule|of|three
percentage	cubic|system	sesquialter
polyhedral	denominator	simple|curve
polyhedron	directrices	solution|set
protractor	dodecagonal	submultiple
quadrangle	enumeration	subtraction
quadratrix	equidistant	tetrahedron
quadrature	equilibrium	trapezoidal
quadricone	equilateral	whole|number
quadriform	heptahedron	arithmograph
quaternary	holohedrism	arithmometer
reciprocal	icosahedron	chiliahedron
relativity	integration	combinations
rhomboidal	latus|rectum	common|factor
right|angle	locus|vector	conic|section
semicircle	logarithmic	critical|path
square|root	mathematics	decimal|point
statistics	mensuration	differential
subalgebra	metaphysics	dodecahedron

eccentricity
geometrician
hyperalgebra
line|geometry
long|division
metric|system
mixed|decimal
multiangular
multilateral
multiplicand
Napier's|bones
oblique|angle
open|sentence
orthorhombic
Platonic|body
pons|asinorum
quadrangular
quadrinomial
rhombohedron
serial|number
straight|line
substitution
tally|counter
tetrahedroid
trigonometry
vernier|scale
antilogarithm
apportionment
approximately
approximation
arithmetician
associativity
beyond|measure
circumference
commutability
complementary

complex|number
computational
concentricity
corresponding
differentiate
dihedral|angle
disproportion
exponentially
exterior|angle
geometrically
geometric|mean
golden|section
hydrodynamics
indeterminate
interior|angle
irrationality
mathematician
parallelogram
perfect|number
perpendicular
Platonic|solid
quadratic|mean
quadrilateral
quantum|number
ready|reckoner
short|division
standard|error
statistically
alphanumerical
arithmetically
asymmetrically
asymptotically
axis|of|symmetry
cardinal|number
common|multiple
decimalisation

head for figures
infinite number
linear equation
mathematically
miscalculation
multiplication
multiplicative
natural numbers
paralellopiped
proper fraction
rational number
transformation
two dimensional

vulgar fraction
decimal notation
differentiation
Fibonacci series
golden rectangle
identity element
imaginary number
proportionately
pure mathematics
square the circle
trigonometrical
unknown quantity

Measurement

amp	volt	plumb	chiliad
BTU	watt	score	compass
cab	angle	therm	decibel
erg	curie	third	geodesy
ohm	cycle	ampere	gilbert
rad	dozen	armful	hundred
rem	farad	calory	kiloton
atom	fermi	degree	lambert
BThU	gauge	kilerg	maximum
dyne	gross	megohm	maxwell
iota	henry	minute	minimum
mole	hertz	myriad	modicum
norm	joule	photon	neutron
phon	level	proton	pelorus
phot	lumen	radian	poundal
size	meter	second	quarter

MEASUREMENT

rontgen	kilocycle	hypsometer
sextant	manometer	micrometer
sixfold	megacurie	multicurie
tenfold	megacycle	nitrometer
twofold	minometer	odorimetry
umpteen	nonillion	ombrometer
vernier	osmometer	pantometer
zillion	pedometer	piezometer
angstrom	pinchbeck	planimeter
electron	potometer	planimetry
fivefold	pyrometer	protractor
fourfold	set|square	pyknometer
fraction	sevenfold	radiometer
gas|meter	slide|rule	radiometry
kilovolt	surveying	Rutherford
kilowatt	telemeter	spirometer
magneton	telemetry	tachometer
megavolt	threefold	tachymetry
megawatt	umpteenth	theodolite
microbar	vicesimal	tintometer
milliard	vigesimal	twelvefold
molecule	anemometer	viscometer
ninefold	audiometer	voltameter
odometer	bathometer	volt|ampere
particle	brinometer	actinometer
roentgen	Centigrade	baker's|dozen
standard	clinometer	calibration
thousand	cyclometer	calorimeter
viameter	densimeter	calorimetry
watt|hour	depth|gauge	candle|power
astrolabe	Fahrenheit	chronometry
barometer	goniometer	dynamometer
eightfold	goniometry	gradiometer
geodesist	gravimeter	mensuration
graticule	heliometer	polarimeter
hodometer	hygrometer	polarimetry

quantometer
salinometer
spirit|level
thermal|unit
thermometer
undecennary
undecennial
cathetometer
decimal|point
declinometer
electrometer
electronvolt
extensometer
golden|guinea
inclinometer
kilowatt|hour
magnetometer
metric|system
microohmeter
millirontgen
psychrometer

respirometer
spectrometer
thousandfold
alcoholometer
alcoholometry
anticlockwise
common|measure
dead|reckoning
made|to|measure
measuring|tape
quadruplicate
tablespoonful
as|the|crow|flies
commensuration
counterbalance
counter|measure
mismeasurement
third|dimension
antepenultimate
drop|in|the|bucket
fourth|dimension

Medicine

Dr	bed	ENT	hip	oil	sty
GP	cup	eye	ill	pep	tea
MD	cut	fat	jaw	pox	tic
MO	doc	fit	lab	pus	toe
os	DTs	flu	LDS	rib	vet
TB	ear	gas	leg	rub	wan
ail	ECG	gum	lip	sac	wen
arm	EEG	gut	LSD	spa	abed

MEDICINE

ache	face	lint	shin	aorta	croup
acne	fade	lips	shot	atomy	dagga
ague	fall	lisp	sick	aural	dandy
AIDS	flux	lobe	skin	bathe	death
back	foot	lung	slim	baths	decay
bald	gall	maim	sole	belch	digit
balm	game	malt	sore	birth	dizzy
band	gash	mask	spot	blain	donor
bile	germ	mole	stab	bleed	drain
body	gout	mute	stye	blind	drill
boil	grip	nail	swab	blood	drops
bone	guts	nape	tent	bolus	dying
bubo	hair	nape	turn	bomoh	edema
burn	halt	neck	ulna	borax	elbow
burp	hand	noma	umbo	botch	ether
calf	harm	nose	vein	bowel	faint
case	head	numb	vena	brace	femur
cast	heal	oral	wale	brain	fever
cell	heel	otic	wall	brash	fibre
chin	hemp	pain	ward	break	flesh
clot	hips	pale	wart	build	flush
cold	home	palm	weal	bulla	fossa
coma	hurt	pang	welt	bursa	frame
corn	hypo	pest	wilt	canal	fugue
cure	ilia	pill	wits	catch	Galen
cusp	iris	plug	womb	chafe	gauze
cyst	iron	pock	X-ray	cheek	gland
daze	itch	pons	yawn	chest	gonad
deaf	junk	pore	yaws	chest	gored
diet	kibe	rash	acute	clava	gouty
dope	kink	rest	agony	colic	graft
dose	knee	ribs	algid	colon	graze
drip	lame	roof	alive	conch	gripe
drug	lens	root	ancon	cough	gumma
duct	limb	scab	ankle	cramp	gyrus
dumb	limp	scar	anvil	crick	heart

helix	opium	sound	virus	binder
herbs	organ	spasm	vomer	biopsy
hilum	ovary	spine	vomit	blanch
hives	palsy	stall	waist	bowels
hyoid	panel	sting	wheal	bracer
ictus	pinna	stupe	whelk	breast
ileum	plate	sweat	wince	breath
ilium	polio	swoon	wound	bruise
incus	polyp	tabes	wreck	bulimy
inion	probe	tabid	wrist	bunion
inlay	psora	taint	aching	caecum
jerks	pulse	talus	addict	caligo
joint	pupil	teeth	ailing	callus
jowls	purge	thigh	albino	cancer
lance	quack	throb	alexia	canker
lazar	rabid	throe	amytal	caries
leech	ramus	thumb	anemia	carpus
leper	raphe	tibia	anemic	cavity
liver	renal	tired	angina	cervix
local	rheum	tonic	anoint	chafed
locum	salts	tooth	antrum	chiasm
lungs	salve	torso	apnoea	choler
lymph	scalp	trace	areola	chorea
lysis	seedy	tract	armpit	clavus
mamma	senna	treat	arnica	clinic
medic	serum	trunk	artery	clonus
medic	shell	tummy	asthma	coccyx
miasm	shock	ulcer	ataxia	codein
molar	sight	ulnar	atocia	coelom
mouth	sinew	uncus	attack	comedo
mumps	sinus	unfit	aurist	concha
nasal	skull	urine	axilla	corium
navel	sleep	uvula	balsam	cornea
nerve	sling	vagus	bedpan	corpse
nevus	smart	valve	benign	cortex
nurse	sopor	villi	biceps	coryza

costal	fungus	lotion	peptic	septic
cowpox	gargle	lumber	phlegm	serous
crisis	goitre	lunula	phobia	sicken
crusta	gripes	maimed	physic	sickly
crutch	grippe	malady	pimple	simple
cuboid	growth	marrow	plague	sister
cuneus	gullet	matron	plasma	slough
damage	hallux	measly	pleura	sneeze
dartre	hammer	meatus	plexus	spatum
deadly	healer	medico	poison	spinal
defect	health	medius	poorly	spleen
demise	hearty	megrim	potion	splint
dengue	hernia	member	ptisan	spotty
dental	heroin	meninx	puncta	sprain
dermis	humour	mentum	pyemia	squint
doctor	immune	miasma	queasy	stapes
dorsum	infirm	midrib	quinsy	stasis
dosage	injury	mongol	rabies	stigma
dossil	inpain	morbid	rachis	stitch
dropsy	instep	mucous	radial	strium
eczema	insula	muscle	ranula	stroke
elixir	intern	mutism	reflex	struma
embryo	iodine	myopic	relief	stupor
emetic	kidney	naevus	remedy	stylet
engram	labial	nasion	retina	suffer
eschar	labour	nausea	rhesus	suture
eyelid	laidup	needle	rictus	tablet
fascia	lambda	neuron	robust	tampon
fester	lancet	nipple	roller	tarsus
fibula	lappet	oculus	sacrum	temple
figure	larynx	opiate	saliva	tender
fillip	lavage	osteal	scrape	tendon
finger	lesion	palate	scurvy	tetter
foetus	lichen	pallor	seeing	thorax
fornix	lipoma	papule	senses	throat
fundus	lobule	pelvis	sepsis	throes

thrush	airsick	calcium	decease
thymus	alcohol	calomel	decline
ticker	allergy	camphor	deltoid
tingle	allheal	cannula	dentist
tisane	ampulla	capsule	derange
tissue	anaemia	carcass	disease
tongue	anaemic	cardiac	draught
tragus	analyst	carious	earache
tremor	anatomy	carrier	eardrum
trepan	anodyne	carsick	ear|lobe
trocar	antacid	cascara	earshot
troche	antigen	catarrh	epithem
tumour	aphasia	cautery	erosion
twinge	aphonia	chalone	ethmoid
unwell	apraxia	chancre	eyeball
ureter	arcanum	chemist	eyebrow
vector	aspirin	chiasma	eyewash
vesica	assuage	cholera	failing
vessel	atebrin	chorion	fantasy
villus	atrophy	choroid	fatigue
viscus	auricle	chronic	febrile
vitals	autopsy	ciliary	feel|ill
vomica	bacilli	cocaine	feeling
voyeur	bandage	cochlea	femoral
weaken	bedfast	colicky	fibroid
weakly	bedsore	colitis	fidgets
wrench	bilious	condyle	filling
writhe	bismuth	cordial	fimbria
xyster	bladder	coroner	fistula
zygoma	blister	cranium	flushed
abdomen	booster	cricoid	foramen
abscess	bow|legs	cripple	forceps
acidity	bromide	cupping	forearm
aconite	bubonic	cure,all	frailty
adrenal	bulimia	cuticle	freckle
ailment	cadaver	deathly	frontal

game|leg	linctus	panacea	rubeola
gastric	lockjaw	papilla	run,down
glasses	lozenge	paresis	rupture
gumboil	lumbago	parotid	saccule
haggard	malaise	passage	sarcoma
hashish	malaria	pass|out	scabies
heal,all	malleus	patella	scalpel
healing	massage	patient	scapula
healthy	masseur	pessary	scratch
hearing	mastoid	phalanx	seasick
hipbone	maxilla	pharynx	seconal
history	measles	pigment	section
hormone	medical	pill,box	seizure
hospice	medulla	pinkeye	seltzer
hot|bath	menthol	placebo	sensory
humerus	microbe	plaster	sick|bay
hygiene	midwife	pledget	sickbed
icterus	milk|leg	podagra	sinking
illness	mixture	pterion	skin|man
incisor	myringa	punctum	soother
innards	nail|bed	pustule	spastic
insides	nervous	putamen	spitoon
insulin	nostril	pyaemia	springs
invalid	nostrum	pylorus	stammer
ischium	obesity	pyramid	sterile
jawbone	occiput	pyretic	sternum
jejunum	oculist	pyrexia	stirrup
jugular	omentum	quassia	stomach
kneecap	operate	quinine	stutter
kneepan	orbital	regimen	sublime
laid|low	orderly	relapse	sulphur
lanolin	organic	removal	sun|bath
lazaret	osseous	reviver	sun|lamp
lentigo	ossicle	ribcage	surgeon
leprosy	otology	rickets	symptom
leprous	ovaries	rubella	syncope

syntone	vitamin	backache	collapse
syntony	whitlow	backbone	comatose
syringe	witless	bacteria	compress
tactile	zymotic	baldness	confined
taenial	abnormal	barbital	contract
take|ill	abortion	beriberi	coronary
talipes	abrasion	bicuspid	critical
tampion	accident	bifocals	crutches
tapetum	acidosis	bile|duct	curative
tear|bag	acromion	bistoury	cyanosis
tetanus	adenoids	black|eye	cynanche
theatre	adhesion	black|out	dandruff
theriac	agar|agar	bleeding	deathbed
thermae	agraphia	blind|eye	debility
thyroid	albinism	blockage	decrepit
toenail	allergic	brachial	delicate
tonsils	allopath	break|out	delirium
tormina	alopecia	bulletin	delivery
toxemia	amputate	caffeine	dentures
trachea	analysis	cannabis	diabetes
travail	anatomic	carditis	diagnose
triceps	antibody	casualty	digestif
trional	antidote	cataract	diplegia
typhoid	aperient	catching	disabled
unction	apoplexy	catheter	diseased
unguent	aposteme	cathexis	disgorge
unsound	appendix	cephalic	disorder
urethra	appetite	cerebral	dispense
utricle	arteries	cervical	diuretic
vaccine	Asian|flu	choleric	dog|tired
vapours	asphyxia	cicatrix	dosology
variola	assuager	clavicle	dressing
veronal	asthenia	clinical	drop|dead
verruca	atropine	club|foot	druggist
vertigo	autacoid	cockeyed	drumhead
viscera	bacillus	cold|sore	ductless

duodenum	glycerin	lethargy	ointment
ecraseur	grandmal	leukemia	olive oil
edgebone	hair ball	ligament	operator
embolism	handicap	ligature	otoscope
emulsion	hard drug	lincture	overdose
enceinte	hay fever	liniment	pancreas
engramma	headache	lip salve	pandemia
entrails	heat lamp	lobotomy	papillae
epidemic	heat spot	lordosis	parasite
epilepsy	heel bone	love drug	parietal
epiploon	hemostat	malarial	paroxysm
eruption	hip joint	maldemer	pectoral
erythema	holotony	mandible	peduncle
etiology	homesick	marasmus	pellagra
excision	hospital	masseter	perspire
exit dose	hot flush	masseuse	petit mal
exposure	houseman	maturant	phalange
eye drops	immunity	medicate	pharmacy
eye patch	impetigo	medicine	philtrum
eyesalve	impotent	membrane	phthisis
eyesight	incision	midbrain	physical
eye tooth	infected	migraine	physique
face lift	inflamed	morphine	pia mater
first aid	inhalant	muscular	pick me up
flat feet	inner ear	mycology	pisiform
follicle	insomnia	naked eye	placenta
forehead	internal	narcosis	pleurisy
fracture	iron lung	narcotic	podagric
freak out	irritant	necrosis	podiatry
frenulum	jaundice	nembutal	posology
fumigant	languish	neoplasm	poultice
furuncle	laudanum	neuritis	practice
gallipot	laudanum	nosogeny	pregnant
ganglion	lavement	nosology	premolar
gangrene	laxative	novocain	prenatal
glaucoma	lenitive	numbness	procaine

prostate	skin|dose	trachoma
pulmonic	smallpox	traction
pump|room	smarting	trephine
purblind	soft|drug	true|skin
pus|basin	somatist	tubercle
pyorrhea	soothing	tumerous
reaction	soreness	tympanum
receptor	sore|spot	ulcerous
Red|Cross	specimen	unciform
remedial	speculum	uroscopy
resident	sphenoid	vaccinia
rest|cure	sphygmus	valerian
ringworm	splenium	variolar
roborant	stinging	vascular
salivary	stitches	vaseline
sanatory	striatum	vena|cava
scaphoid	subacute	venotomy
scarring	sudarium	vertebra
sciatica	sufferer	vesicant
scrofula	surgical	vitality
secretin	swelling	vomiting
sedation	take|sick	wall|eyed
sedative	tear|drop	wandered
senility	tear|duct	weakling
serology	teething	wet|nurse
shinbone	temporal	admission
shingles	teratoma	adrenalin
shoulder	thalamus	aitchbone
sick|abed	the|bends	alcoholic
sickling	thin|skin	alkalizer
sickness	thoracic	alleviate
sickroom	thyroxin	allopathy
sinapism	tingling	amaurosis
skeletal	tocogony	ambulance
skeleton	tocology	analeptic
skin|deep	toponymy	analgesia

analgesic	callipers	cough|drop
anamnesis	callosity	crash|diet
anklebone	calmative	cretinism
ankylosis	calvities	cross|eyed
antenatal	cankerous	cuneiform
antihelix	carbuncle	curvature
antiserum	carcinoma	dead|faint
antitoxin	cartilage	dead|tired
arthritis	caruncula	defective
aspirator	case|sheet	delirious
assuasive	castor|oil	demulcent
audiology	catalepsy	dentistry
auriscopy	cataplasm	depth|dose
bacterium	cataplexy	diagnosis
bandaging	catatonia	diaphragm
barbitone	catatonic	diarrhoea
bath|chair	catch|cold	diathermy
bedridden	catharsis	dichotomy
bellyache	cathartic	diet|sheet
birthmark	cauterize	digitalis
blackhead	cheekbone	discharge
blindness	chilblain	dispenser
blind|spot	chin|cough	distemper
blood|bank	chiropody	dizzy|turn
blood|bank	cicatrice	dosimeter
blood|test	cirrhosis	dosimetry
blue|blood	claustrum	drain|tube
body|odour	cleansing	dropsical
boric|acid	collyrium	dura|mater
bow|legged	complaint	dysentery
brain|cell	condition	dyspepsia
breakdown	conscious	dyspeptic
broken|arm	contagion	dystrophy
broken|leg	contusion	echolalia
Caesarean	corpuscle	electuary
calenture	cortisone	emaciated

embrocate
emergency
emollient
endocrine
endolymph
energumen
ephedrine
epidermis
epileptic
epiphyses
esotropia
exotropia
extremity
eye|doctor
eyelashes
faith|cure
fallopian
fallotomy
false|ribs
febrifuge
febrility
festering
fetishism
fever|heat
fever|ward
flatulent
fore|brain
frostbite
fumigator
fungosity
funny|bone
gastritis
gathering
geriatric
germicide
give|birth

gladiolus
glandular
glycerine
halitosis
hammer|toe
hamstring
heartbeat
heartburn
histamine
homeopath
horehound
hunchback
idiopathy
ill|health
impatient
incubator
incurable
infection
infirmary
infirmity
influenza
ingestion
inhalator
injection
injection
inoculate
in|plaster
invalided
iron|pills
iron|tonic
isolation
jail|fever
king's|evil
knee|joint
labyrinth
lachrymal

lazaretto
leucocyte
life|force
long|sight
lymphatic
malar|bone
malignant
malleolus
manubrium
marihuana
marijuana
maternity
maxillary
medicated
medicinal
mesentery
mesocolon
middle|ear
midwifery
milk|teeth
mongolism
morbidity
mortified
mouthwash
nappy|rash
narcotics
nasal|duct
nauseated
near|sight
nebulizer
neophobia
nephritis
nerve|cell
neuralgia
neurology
neuropath

noncompos
nutrition
nux|vomica
nystagmus
occipital
off|colour
officinal
olfactory
on|the|mend
operation
optic|disc
optometry
osteology
osteopath
otologist
pacemaker
paralysis
paregoric
parotitis
pathology
perilymph
pertussis
pesthouse
phagocyte
phalanges
phlebitis
phrenetic
physician
pin|and|web
pituitary
pneumeter
pneumonia
poisoning
pollution
precuneus
premature

prescribe
prognosis
prophasis
psoriasis
pulmonary
purgative
purifying
quadratus
rachidial
radiogram
radiology
resection
sartorius
sassafras
sauna|bath
sclerosis
sclerotic
sebaceous
secretion
seediness
semi|lunar
sensorium
sinusitis
skingraft
soporific
spare|part
splay|feet
squeamish
squinting
sterilize
stiff|dose
stiff|neck
stillborn
stimulant
stretcher
subsultus

sudorific
suffering
sunstroke
suppurant
sweat|bath
syntectic
taste|buds
tear|gland
tegmentum
thanatoid
therapist
thighbone
thyrotomy
toothache
toothpick
trapezium
trapezius
treatment
tricuspid
tummy|ache
umbilical
umbilicus
unguentum
unhealthy
urticaria
vaccinate
varicella
varicosis
venectomy
ventricle
vermifuge
vertibrae
vestibule
vulnerary
washed|out
waste|away

water|cure
wax|glands
wellbeing
wristbone
xeroderma
X-ray|plate
zoophobia
zooplasty
abirritant
abreaction
acetabulum
acrophobia
Adam's|apple
aerophobia
affliction
afterbirth
algophobia
alimentary
amputation
anesthesia
ankle|joint
antibiotic
antipoison
antisepsis
antiseptic
antitragus
apoplectic
apothecary
applicator
astragalus
barium|meal
batophobia
belladonna
Black|Death
blood|count
blood|donor

blood|group
bloodstain
bloody|flux
bonesetter
brain|fever
breastbone
breathless
broken|bone
broken|dose
broken|nose
bronchitis
buccinator
canker|rash
castration
catalepsis
catholicon
cerebellum
chickenpox
chloroform
chromosome
cibophobia
collarbone
commissure
common|cold
compulsion
concussion
consultant
contagious
convalesce
convulsion
corn|doctor
corrective
cotton|wool
cough|syrup
cyclothyme
cynophobia

cystectomy
cystoscope
dandy|fever
danger|list
deathwatch
dentifrice
dermatitis
dim|sighted
diphtheria
dipsomania
dirty|nurse
disability
discomfort
disfigured
dispensary
dizzy|spell
doraphobia
draw|breath
drop|serene
drug|addict
ear|trumpet
ectodermal
elbow|joint
emaciation
embonpoint
embryology
emplastrum
enclampsia
entodermal
epispastic
epithelium
Epsom|salts
ergophobia
erotomania
eructation
euthanasia

253

extraction	indisposed	metatarsus
faith|curer	infectious	microscope
false|teeth	inhibition	monophobia
farsighted	insolation	mutilation
feebleness	inspirator	nail|matrix
fever|pitch	instrument	narcissist
fibrositis	interferon	nauseation
fine|fettle	internship	nerve|fibre
fingernail	intestines	nettle|rash
five|senses	invalidate	neuropathy
flatulence	invalidism	night|float
fonticulus	invalidity	night|nurse
foot|doctor	irritation	nosophobia
gallstones	kill|or|cure	obstetrics
gamophobia	kiss|of|life	odontogeny
gastrotomy	knock|knees	oesophagus
geriatrics	laboratory	optic|nerve
gripe|water	laceration	optic|tract
haunch|bone	laparotomy	orthopraxy
healing|art	laryngitis	orthoscope
health|farm	lassa|fever	ossiferous
hearing|aid	last|breath	osteoblast
heatstroke	lazar|house	osteoclast
hemaglobin	leechcraft	osteopathy
hematology	lethal|dose	out|of|sorts
hemiplegia	loss|of|life	outpatient
hemisphere	lymph|gland	overweight
hemophilia	main|stream	oxygen|mask
hemophobia	medical|man	oxygen|tank
homeopathy	medicament	oxygen|tent
hot|springs	medicaster	padded|cell
hypodermic	medication	paediatric
hypodermis	meningitis	painkiller
idiopathic	mesogaster	palliative
immunology	metabolism	paraphasia
Indian|hemp	metacarpus	paraplegia

paronychia	resistance	strychnine
pathognomy	respirator	sublingual
pediatrics	rheumatics	suprarenal
pediatrist	root,sheath	sweat|gland
penicillin	rude|health	teratology
periosteum	salivation	thrombosis
peritoneal	salt,cellar	tonic|spasm
peritoneum	sanatorium	toothpaste
pestilence	sanitarian	toponymics
pharmacist	saucer|eyes	tourniquet
phenacetin	scarlatina	toxicology
phlebotomy	scrofulous	transplant
physiology	semeiology	traumatism
pigeon,toed	semeiotics	trochanter
pineal|body	sense|organ	truth|serum
plague|spot	septicemia	tumescence
podiatrist	serologist	ulceration
polychrest	short|sight	urinalysis
polyclinic	sick|as|a|dog	varicotomy
poor|health	sickliness	vesicotomy
post,mortem	sixth|sense	veterinary
premaxilla	soft|palate	Vichy|water
presbyopia	somatology	vital|force
prevention	sore|throat	vital|spark
preventive	specialist	vocal|cords
prognostic	spectacles	wheel|chair
protective	sphacelate	witch|hazel
public|ward	spinal|cord	wonder|drug
pyretology	spirograph	xenophobia
radiograph	spirometer	yellow|jack
radiometer	splanchnic	yellow|spot
radioscopy	squint|eyes	abnormality
radium|bath	staff|nurse	abortionist
ray|therapy	sterilizer	airsickness
recuperate	strabismus	amphetamine
regression	strict|diet	anaesthesia

anaesthetic	conjunctiva	gerontology
an|apple|a|day	consumption	gild|the|pill
antifebrile	consumptive	gnawing|pain
antipyretic	contact|lens	gold|therapy
aphrodisiac	convolution	granule|cell
application	convulsions	growing|pain
arteriotomy	corn|plaster	gynaecology
astigmatism	decrepitude	haemorrhage
auscultator	deep|therapy	handicapped
bactericide	deobstruent	healthiness
barbiturate	dermaplasty	health|salts
basket|cells	dermatology	heart|attack
blood|stream	diagnostics	hebephrenia
blood|stroke	diaphoretic	hectic|fever
blood|vessel	dislocation	hectic|flush
booster|dose	dull|sighted	heteropathy
breaking|out	eccrinology	Hippocratic
caesarotomy	Elastoplast	hormonology
canine|tooth	elixir|vitae	horse|doctor
cardiograph	embrocation	hospital|bed
carminative	endocardium	hospitalize
car|sickness	examination	hydrophobia
case|history	exoskeleton	indigestion
cephalalgia	expectorant	inoculation
chemiatrist	extremities	internal|ear
chiroplasty	face|lifting	intravenous
chiropodist	facial|nerve	ipecacuanha
chiropraxis	famine|fever	irradiation
choroid|coat	fatty|tissue	isodose|line
circulation	fibre|optics	jugular|vein
cleft|palate	fingerstall	kidney|basin
coconscious	floating|rib	laparoscopy
cod|liver|oil	fluoroscope	laughing|gas
cold|therapy	fomentation	locum|tenens
colour|blind	gall|bladder	long|sighted
confinement	gastrectomy	lycanthropy

malfunction	physiognomy	temperature
median nerve	plaster cast	therapeutic
medicine man	prickly heat	thermometer
miracle drug	private ward	the sniffles
miscarriage	probationer	tonsillitis
mitral valve	prognostics	tooth powder
mortal wound	prophylaxis	transfusion
musculature	quack remedy	trench fever
nasopharynx	quacksalver	trench mouth
naturopathy	rabbit fever	tumefaction
nearsighted	radiography	Turkish bath
nerve ending	radiologist	unconscious
nerve supply	radiopraxis	vaccination
neurologist	radiothermy	venesection
neuroplasty	respiration	warm springs
neutralizer	restorative	water canker
nursing home	rheumaticky	wisdom tooth
nyctophobia	rhinoplasty	X-ray machine
observation	rigor mortis	X-ray therapy
obstruction	roentgen ray	yellow fever
obtometrist	running nose	aero embolism
orthodontia	sal ammoniac	alexipharmic
orthopaedic	sal volatile	alpha blocker
orthopedics	schizoidism	anaesthetist
orthopedist	seasickness	anthropotomy
palpitation	senile decay	appendectomy
Pandora's box	skin disease	appendicitis
parathyroid	solar plexus	aquapuncture
parturition	stethoscope	at death's door
pathologist	stirrup bone	athlete's foot
pelvic colon	stomach ache	auscultation
peptic ulcer	stomach pump	bacteriology
pericardium	stomatology	balm of Gilead
peristaltic	sudden death	bill of health
peritonitis	suppuration	bismuth salts
pharyngitis	surgeon's saw	black and blue

bloodletting	gastric|juice	neurasthenia
breath|of|life	gastroplasty	obstetrician
casualty|ward	geriatrician	optic|chiasma
central|canal	grinding|pain	orthodiagram
chemotherapy	gynecologist	orthodontics
chiropractic	hair|follicle	orthodontist
chiropractor	hair|restorer	orthopaedics
cold|compress	health|resort	orthopaedist
come|down|with	heart|disease	ossification
complication	heart|failure	palpitations
conditioning	hydropathist	parasitology
constipation	hydrotherapy	parietal|bone
consultation	hypertension	parotid|gland
convalescent	hysterectomy	pediatrician
coronary|vein	iatrochemist	pelvic|girdle
cough|mixture	iatrophysics	perspiration
countervenom	immunization	pestilential
court|plaster	immunologist	pharmaceutic
critical|list	inflammation	pharmacology
curietherapy	integral|dose	pharmacopeia
debilitation	intoxication	phlebotomist
dietotherapy	island|of|Reil	phototherapy
disinfectant	knock|out|drop	pigmentation
electrolysis	laser|surgery	prescription
elixir|of|life	light|therapy	preventative
emergency|bed	lock|hospital	prophylactic
encephalitis	lose|one's|head	psychrometer
endoskeleton	lose|strength	purblindness
faith|healing	loss|of|memory	radiosurgery
fallen|arches	major|surgery	radiotherapy
family|doctor	malnutrition	radiotherapy
felinophobia	mammary|gland	reflex|action
fever|blister	minor|surgery	rehabilitate
feverishness	morbid|growth	resectoscope
formaldehyde	muscle|fibres	respirometer
friar's|balsam	natural|death	resuscitator

robust health
rubber gloves
scarlet fever
serum therapy
sesamoid bone
shaking palsy
shock therapy
shooting pain
shortsighted
simple reflex
sleep inducer
sleeping pill
sleepwalking
slimming diet
solar therapy
somnambulism
sphygmograph
sphygmometer
spinal column
spotted fever
stabbing pain
straitjacket
streptomycin
student nurse
St Vitus dance
subcutaneous
surgical boot
suture needle
therapeutics
therapeutist
thyroid gland
tonsillotomy
trained nurse
tranquillize
tuberculosis
turn a deaf ear

varicose vein
violent death
vitreous body
water blister
word deafness
zinc ointment
actinotherapy
adenoidectomy
anaphrodisiac
anastigmatism
anticoagulant
antihistamine
antiscorbutic
bacteriolysin
bacteriolysis
bacteriolytic
bacteriophage
blood pressure
brainsickness
bubonic plague
cardiac arrest
cardiographer
cauterisation
confined to bed
contraception
contraceptive
convalescence
dental surgery
dentist's chair
dermatologist
diagnostician
Down's syndrome
encephalogram
endocrinology
fertility drug
fever hospital

field dressing
field hospital
food poisoning
gentian violet
German measles
group practice
gynaecologist
haematologist
healthfulness
health service
health visitor
heat treatment
homoeopathist
indisposition
intensive care
kidney machine
medicine chest
paediatrician
pharmaceutics
pharmaceutist
pharmacopoeia
physicianship
physiognomist
physiotherapy
poliomyelitis
psychotherapy
second opinion
smelling salts
styptic pencil
tonsillectomy
tranquilliser
whooping cough
X ray apparatus
antaphrodisiac
anticonvulsant
antilymphocyte

antiseptically
appendicectomy
blood poisoning
breathlessness
Bright's disease
carcinogenesis
carcinological
cardiovascular
conjunctivitis
consulting room
contagiousness
cross infection
cystic fibrosis
dangerously ill
encephalograph
family planning
hole in the heart
housemaid's knee
house physician
infectiousness
medical officer
medical student
medicine bottle
milk of magnesia
national health
night blindness
operating table
pasteurisation
pharmaceutical
pharmacologist
phenobarbitone
pins and needles
plastic surgeon
plastic surgery
pneumoconiosis
rheumatic fever

surgical|spirit
travel|sickness
ankylostomiasis
anorexia|nervosa
antenatal|clinic
aversion|therapy
blackwater|fever
cerebrovascular
clearing|station
cottage|hospital
counter,irritant
delirium|tremens
dental|treatment

dressing|station
falling|sickness
gastroenteritis
general|practice
Hippocratic|oath
manic,depressive
morning|sickness
physiotherapist
psychotherapist
sleeping|draught
sticking|plaster
third|degree|burn

Meteorology

ice	wind	rainy	dry|air
icy	blast	sleet	flatus
low	blowy	storm	fogbow
blow	chill	sunny	freeze
cold	clime	windy	haboob
gale	cloud	Aeolus	hot|air
gust	Eurus	aurora	hot|day
haar	foggy	boreal	isobar
heat	front	Boreas	isohel
hoar	frost	breeze	nimbus
rain	gusty	breezy	red|sky
rime	hoary	brumal	samiel
smog	humid	chilly	serein
snow	misty	cirrus	simoom
thaw	muggy	cloudy	squall
warm	rains	degree	stormy

.

stuffy	squally	fresh|air
sultry	subzero	haziness
trades	sweltry	head|wind
aeolian	tempest	heat|haze
air|mass	the|blue	heatwave
aureola	thunder	heavy|sky
backing	tornado	high|wind
blue|sky	typhoon	humidity
bluster	veering	ice|storm
chinook	warm|air	isobront
clement	washout	isocheim
climate	weather	isocryme
cold|air	Beaufort	isothere
cumulus	black|ice	isotherm
current	blizzard	libeccio
cyclone	blow|over	low|cloud
drizzle	clear|day	moderate
drought	clear|sky	occluded
element	climatic	overcast
freshen	cloud|cap	pressure
gregale	cold|snap	rain|belt
grey|sky	cold|wave	rain|drop
ice|cold	cold|wind	rainfall
icy|wind	cyclonic	rainy|day
ill|wind	dew|point	scorcher
isohyet	doldrums	snowfall
khamsin	downpour	sunburst
mistral	east|wind	sunlight
monsoon	elements	sunshine
nebulae	Favonius	west|wind
pea|soup	favonian	wind|belt
rainbow	fireball	wind|cock
raining	firebolt	wind|cone
showery	fohn|wind	wind|vane
sirocco	forecast	anemology
sizzler	freezing	anemostat

barometer
baroscope
below|zero
blue|skies
bourasque
brilliant
cloud|bank
cloud|over
cold|front
cold|spell
corposant
dust|devil
dust|storm
fogginess
frostbite
gale|force
hailstone
hailstorm
hard|frost
harmattan
heavy|rain
high|cloud
hoar|frost
hurricane
inclement
Jack|Frost
lapse|rate
levin|bolt
lightning
London|fog
midday|sun
mild|spell
mistiness
nephology
nimbosity
nor'easter

north|wind
nor'wester
occlusion
overcloud
rain|cloud
rain|gauge
rainspout
rainstorm
rime|frost
sand|blast
sand|devil
sandspout
sandstorm
snowflake
snowstorm
snow|under
sou'easter
south|wind
sou'wester
trade|wind
turbulent
warm|front
weak|front
whirlwind
williwaws
wind|gauge
windiness
windscale
wind|speed
windstorm
windswept
anemometer
antitrades
atmosphere
black|frost
Cape|doctor

clear|skies
cloud|atlas
cloudburst
cloudiness
coastal|fog
cool|breeze
driven|snow
drying|wind
Euroclydon
frontal|low
gentle|wind
glaciation
hailstones
hot|weather
hyetograph
hyetometer
hygrometer
insolation
nebulosity
nubilation
ombrometer
powder|snow
radiosonde
sharp|frost
snow|flurry
snow|squall
stormblast
storm|cloud
storm|track
strong|wind
summer|heat
turbulence
weather|eye
weatherman
weather|map
wet|weather

wind sleeve	southwester
anticyclone	spell of rain
arctic front	storm centre
cats and dogs	temperature
cirrus cloud	tempestuous
cold weather	thermograph
driving rain	thermometer
evening mist	thunderball
flaming June	thunderbolt
fresh breeze	thunderclap
frigid zones	thunderpeal
frontal zone	weathercock
frozen stiff	weathervane
frozen water	bitterly cold
gale warning	blow up a storm
ground frost	cirro cumulus
harvest moon	cirro stratus
hunter's moon	cumulo cirrus
hydrometeor	cumulo nimbus
hyperborean	cumulus cloud
light breeze	etesian winds
lowering sky	freezing cold
low pressure	high pressure
mackerel sky	Indian summer
meteorology	keraunograph
monsoon wind	macroclimate
northeaster	meteorograph
northwester	microclimate
pluviometer	migratory low
pouring rain	moderate wind
precipitate	nephelometer
rainy season	offshore wind
sheet of rain	piercing wind
snow blanket	pressure belt
snow crystal	pressure wave
southeaster	rainy weather

snow|blizzard
thundercloud
thunderstorm
volcanic|wind
weather|chart
weather|gauge
weatherglass
wind|velocity
Beaufort|scale
climatography
climatologist
cumulostratus
electric|storm
meteorologist
thunder|shower
weather|report

weather|symbol
aurora|borealis
further|outlook
meteorological
roaring|forties
sheet|lightning
weather|prophet
weather|station
bolt|from|the|blue
forked|lightning
prevailing|winds
rain|cats|and|dogs
summer|lightning
tropical|climate
weather|forecast

Military Leaders

Lee	Alfred	Patton	Fairfax
Byng	Attila	Petain	Raleigh
Foch	Balboa	Pompey	Saladin
Haig	Beatty	Raglan	Sherman
Slim	Caesar	Rodney	Tirpitz
Blake	Cortes	Rommel	Wallace
Clive	Franco	Rupert	Wingate
Dayan	Gordon	Wavell	Agricola
Drake	Halsey	Allenby	Aurelian
Keyes	Ireton	Blucher	Burgoyne
Moore	Jervis	Bradley	Cardigan
Tromp	Moltke	Doenitz	Crockett
Wolfe	Nelson	Dowding	Cromwell

MILITARY LEADERS

Hannibal
Jellicoe
Lawrence
Leonidas
Montcalm
Montrose
Napoleon
Pershing
Potemkin
Runstedt
Stilwell
Woodward
Alexander
Bonaparte
Glendower
Grenville
Hasdrubal
Joan|of|Arc
Kitchener

MacArthur
Montezuma
Trenchard
Abercromby
Alanbrooke
Belisarius
Caractacus
Clausewitz
Cornwallis
Eisenhower
Kublai|Khan
Montgomery
Wellington
Charlemagne
Collingwood
Genghis|Khan
Marlborough
Mountbatten
Chiang|kai|Shek

Minerals

gem	lode	tufa	fluor	steel
ore	marl	tuff	gault	stone
tin	mica	vein	ingot	topaz
coal	onyx	zinc	magma	wacke
clay	opal	agate	metal	basalt
gold	rock	alloy	ochre	bronze
iron	ruby	beryl	shale	cerium
jade	salt	borax	slack	chrome
lava	spar	coral	slate	cobalt
lead	talc	flint	sleet	copper

6/8 LETTERS

erbium	azurite	mineral	diggings
flinty	bauxite	niobium	dolerite
Flysch	biotite	olivine	dolomite
gabbro	bornite	peridot	epsomite
galena	breccia	pig|iron	europium
gangue	cadmium	pyrites	euxenite
garnet	calcite	realgar	feldspar
gneiss	calcium	rhenium	fineness
gypsum	cat's|eye	sulphur	fire|opal
indium	chuckie	terbium	fluorite
iolite	citrine	thorium	gemstone
jargon	diabase	thulium	girasole
jasper	diamond	tin|mine	gold|dust
kaolin	diorite	tripoli	gold|mine
maltha	emerald	uranium	gold|rush
marble	epidote	wolfram	graphite
molten	felspar	yttrium	gritrock
morion	gallium	zeolite	hematite
nickel	girasol	zincite	idocrase
oroide	gothite	amethyst	ilmenite
osmium	granite	amygdule	inkstone
pewter	hafnium	antimony	iron|clay
pumice	holmium	argonite	lazurite
pyrite	hyalite	asbestos	limonite
quarry	igneous	autunite	liparite
quartz	iridium	basanite	lutecium
radium	iron|ore	brookite	metallic
rutile	iron|pan	cast|iron	monazite
scoria	jacinth	chlorite	mudstone
silica	jargoon	chromite	mylonite
silver	kerogen	chromium	nephrite
spinel	kyanite	cinnabar	obsidian
zircon	lignite	corundum	platinum
adamant	lithium	cryolite	plumbago
apatite	lithoid	dendrite	polonium
asphalt	mercury	dibstone	porphyry

MINERALS

pumicite	brimstone	marlstone
pyroxene	burrstone	metalloid
rhyolite	cairngorm	microlite
rock|salt	carbuncle	milkstone
rubidium	carnelian	mispickel
samarium	carnotite	moonstone
sapphire	china|clay	morganite
sardonyx	diatomite	neodymium
scandium	dripstone	ozocerite
selenite	elaterite	palladium
siderite	flagstone	pegmatite
smelting	fluorspar	periclase
steatite	fool's|gold	petroleum
stibnite	freestone	petrology
sunstone	gemmology	petrology
tantalum	germanium	phenolite
thallium	goldstone	plutonium
tinstone	granulite	quartzite
titanium	gritstone	rhodonite
trachyte	haematite	ruthenium
traprock	ironstone	sandstone
tungsten	jackstone	scheelite
vanadium	jadestone	semimetal
volcanic	kaolinite	slabstone
xenolith	laccolite	soapstone
alabaster	laccolith	spodumene
aluminium	lanthanum	strontium
americium	lapideous	tellurium
amphibole	limestone	turquoise
anglesite	lithology	uraninite
aragonite	magnesite	vulcanite
argentite	magnesium	wulfenite
base|metal	magnetite	ytterbium
beryllium	malachite	zirconium
blacklead	manganese	adamantine
brilliant	marcasite	adder|stone

268

aquamarine	rare metals
aventurine	rose quartz
bloodstone	sheet metal
brownstone	silver mine
chalcedony	slingstone
chalkstone	smokestone
chessylite	snakestone
chrysolite	spinel ruby
clinkstone	stinkstone
common salt	technetium
copper mine	touchstone
drakestone	tourmaline
dysprosium	wolframite
eaglestone	alexandrite
gadolinium	cassiterite
glauconite	chrysoberyl
globulites	chrysoprase
graptolite	clinochlore
greenstone	country rock
heliotrope	earth metals
hornblende	gravelstone
leadglance	hatchettite
lithomarge	igneous rock
meerschaum	iron pyrites
metallurgy	lapis lazuli
mica schist	layer of rock
mineralogy	lithosphere
mineral oil	Lydian stone
molten lava	mineral coal
molybdenum	mineral salt
noble metal	mineral vein
ore deposit	molybdenite
orthoclase	native stone
peacock ore	peristalith
pitchstone	petrography
promethium	pissasphalt

MINERALS

pitchblende
potter's clay
quarrystone
quicksilver
rock crystal
sarsen stone
schistosity
stone circle
vermiculite
vesuvianite
volcanic ash
alkali metals
anthraconite
argillaceous
arsenopyrite
black diamond
chalcopyrite
coal measures
duraluminium
electroplate
fuller's earth
metal fatigue
mineral pitch
native metals
oriental opal
praesodymium
protactinium

red sandstone
residual clay
star sapphire
wollastonite
carboniferous
chrome plating
cinnamon stone
copper pyrites
metalliferous
metallurgical
millstone grit
mineralogocal
petrification
Portland stone
quartz crystal
smokeless fuel
copper bottomed
electroplating
metallographer
mineral deposit
mineral kingdom
open cast mining
plaster of Paris
Portland cement
quartz porphyry
stainless steel
Old Red Sandstone

Money

as	bob	mag	pie	sol	yen
bit	écu	mil	sen	sou	anna

bean	fiver	nickel
buck	franc	peseta
cash	grand	rouble
cent	groat	scudos
chip	krona	sequin
coin	krone	shekel
dime	louis	solidi
doit	mohur	specie
kyat	noble	stater
lira	obang	stiver
mark	paolo	tenner
merk	pence	tester
mill	penny	teston
mint	piece	thaler
mite	pound	cordoba
obol	rupee	crusado
peso	sceat	denarii
plum	semis	drachma
pony	soldo	exergue
quid	sucre	guilder
rand	toman	ha'penny
real	verso	milreis
reis	aureus	moidore
rial	bawbee	nummary
ryal	copeck	obverse
thou	copper	pfennig
angel	denier	piastre
asper	dollar	red|cent
belga	drachm	reverse
colon	escudo	sawbuck
conto	florin	sceatta
crown	guinea	sextans
daric	gulden	smacker
dinar	kopeck	solidus
ducat	lepton	ten|spot
eagle	monkey	testoon

two|bits
base|coin
cruzeiro
denarius
didrachm
doubloon
farthing
gold|coin
groschen
louis|d'or
napoleon
new|pence
new|penny
picayune
planchet
quadrans
semissis
semuncia
shilling
short|bit
sixpence
ten|cents
tuppence
twopence
zecchino
dupondius
fourpence
fourpenny
gold|crown
gold|penny
gold|piece
half|crown
half|eagle

half|noble
halfpenny
pistareen
rose|noble
schilling
sovereign
tremissis
yellow|boy
zwanziger
reichsmark
sestertius
threepence
double|eagle
silver|penny
sixpenny|bit
base|shilling
imperial|coin
piece|of|eight
quarter|noble
silver|dollar
brass|farthing
half|sovereign
pieces|of|eight
ten|dollar|bill
almighty|dollar
coin|of|the|realm
debased|coinage
decimal|coinage
half|a|sovereign
half|pennyworth
fifty|pence|piece
handful|of|silver

Mountains

K2
Alps
Jura
Altai
Andes
Eiger
Ghats
Hekla
Urals
Ararat
Exmoor
Kunlun
Pamirs
Pindus
Vosges
Brocken
Helicon
Mendips
Nan Ling
Nan Shan
Rockies
Skiddaw
Snowdon
Sudeten
Caucasus
Cevennes
Cheviots
Chirripo
Cotopaxi

Dartmoor
Demavend
Hymettus
Ida, Mount
Jungfrau
Krakatoa
Nevis, Ben
Pennines
Pyrenees
Tien Shan
Vesuvius
Aconcagua
Allegheny
Apennines
Catskills
Chilterns
Cook, Mount
Cotswolds
Dolomites
Erzebirge
Etna, Mount
Grampians
Helvellyn
Himalayas
Hindu Kush
Huascaran
Meru, Mount
Mont Blanc
Mont Cenis

Monte Rosa
Nanda Devi
Pikes Peak
Puy de Dome
Ras Dashan
Ruwenzori
Stromboli
Zugspitze
Arakam Yoma
Cader Idris
Cairngorms
Chimborazo
Coast Range
Dent du Midi
Elgon, Mount
Kenya, Mount
Khyber Pass
Sinai, Mount
St Gotthard
Adirondacks
Brenner Pass
Brooks Range
Carmel, Mount
Drakensberg
Elbert, Mount
Elbrus, Mount
Erebus, Mount
Hermon, Mount
Katmai, Mount

MOUNTAINS

Kazbek, Mount
Kilimanjaro
Koryak Range
Lammermuirs
Mendip Hills
Nanga Parbat
Scafell Pike
Sierra Madre
Simplon Pass
Appalachians
Cheviot Hills
Gran Paradiso
Illampu, Mount
Kanchenjunga
Monte Cassino
Olympus, Mount
Palomar, Mount
Peak District
Popocatépetl
Rainier, Mount
Roraima, Mount
Ruapehu, Mount
Schiehallion
Sierra Nevada
Triglav, Mount
Whitney, Mount
Blue Mountains
Brecon Beacons

Cameroun, Mount
Chiltern Hills
Cotswold Hills
Grossglockner
Harz Mountains
Kinabalu, Mount
Massif Central
McKinley, Mount
Mitchell, Mount
Mount of Olives
move mountains
Riesengebirge
Sierra Maestra
Stanovoi Range
Sulaiman Range
Table Mountain
Black Mountains
Cleveland Hills
Galty Mountains
Karakoram Range
Kosciusko, Mount
Ozark Mountains
Parnassus, Mount
Snowy Mountains
White Mountains
Mourne Mountains
Taurus Mountains
Zagros Mountains

Muses

Clio	Urania	Melpomene
Erato	Euterpe	Polyhymnia
Thalia	Calliope	Terpsichore

Music

A	me	hay	sax	blow	harp
B	op	hey	ska	brio	hi,fi
C	pp	hit	soh	clef	horn
D	re	hum	sol	coda	hymn
E	sf	jig	tie	dash	jack
f	te	key	uke	disc	jazz
F	ut	kit	wax	disk	jive
G	act	lah	alap	diva	jota
p	air	lay	alto	drum	juba
DC	bar	lip	arco	duet	keen
do	bop	lur	aria	dump	lead
DS	bow	nut	ayre	fife	lied
EP	cat	ode	band	fine	lilt
fa	cue	ped	bard	flat	lira
ff	doh	pes	base	flue	lure
fp	dot	pop	bass	form	lute
gu	duo	rag	beat	fret	lyra
la	fah	ray	bell	glee	lyre
LP	gue	run	bind	gong	mass

MUSIC

mode	tune	corno	luter	proms
mood	turn	crook	lyric	psalm
mute	vamp	croon	major	pulse
neck	viol	dance	march	quint
node	wait	desto	melic	range
noel	wind	dirge	metre	rebec
note	wood	disco	mezzo	reeds
oboe	work	ditty	minim	regal
open	ad|lib	dolce	minor	resin
opus	album	drone	modal	rondo
part	A|side	drums	motet	rosin
peal	assai	elegy	motif	round
pick	atone	Erato	musak	rumba
port	banjo	etude	music	runic
Prom	basso	fancy	naker	scale
raga	baton	farce	nebel	scena
rank	bebop	fifer	neume	score
reed	bells	fifth	ninth	segno
reel	belly	final	nonet	segue
rest	blues	flute	notes	shake
rock	bones	forte	octet	sharp
roll	brass	fugue	odeon	shawm
root	brawl	galop	opera	siren
rote	breve	gamba	organ	sixth
scat	B|side	gamut	paean	slide
sing	bugle	gigue	pause	snare
slur	canon	grace	pavan	sol|fa
solo	canto	grave	pedal	sordo
song	carol	ictus	piano	sound
stop	cello	idyll	piece	space
time	chant	jazzy	piper	staff
tone	chime	jodel	pitch	stave
toot	choir	kyrie	pleno	Strad
trio	chord	large	pluck	strum
tuba	close	largo	point	study
tuck	comma	lento	polka	suite

swell	accent	damper	legato	rounds
swing	accord	decani	Lieder	rubato
tabla	adagio	diesis	lutist	scorer
table	almain	direct	lyrist	second
tabor	almand	do|re|mi	manual	sempre
tacet	answer	double	maxixe	septet
tambo	anthem	drones	medley	sestet
tango	Apollo	dulcet	melody	sextet
tempo	arioso	ecbole	minuet	shanty
tenor	a|tempo	eighth	monody	shofar
theme	atonal	encore	motion	singer
third	aubade	euphon	motive	snatch
throb	ballad	fading	musico	sonata
thrum	ballet	fiddle	needle	spinet
tonic	bolero	figure	neumes	stanza
touch	bowing	finale	nobile	strain
triad	bridge	firing	nowell	string
trill	bugler	fourth	oboist	subito
troll	burden	fugato	octave	syrinx
trope	cadent	giusto	off|key	tabret
tuned	can|can	graces	ottava	tampon
tutti	cantor	grazia	pavane	tam|tam
up|bow	cantus	great|C	period	tattoo
valse	catchy	guitar	phrase	temper
valve	catgut	hammer	pipe|up	tenor|C
verse	chanty	harper	piston	tenuto
vibes	chimes	hepcat	player	tercet
viola	choral	horner	presto	terzet
voice	chorus	hymnal	quaver	timbal
volta	cither	hymner	racket	timbre
volte	citole	in|tune	rattle	tom|tom
waits	cornet	jingle	rebeck	tooter
waltz	corona	keener	record	top|ten
winds	cue|ing	kettle	reggae	treble
woods	cymbal	lament	repeat	tromba
yodel	da|capo	leader	rhythm	troppo

tucket	bazooka	codetta	furlana
tune|up	bellows	compass	fuzzbox
tuning	bombard	compose	gavotte
tymbal	bourdon	con|brio	giocoso
tympan	bourrée	concert	gradual
unison	brasses	concord	G|string
up|beat	bravura	conduct	halling
vielle	buccina	con|moto	harmony
violin	cadence	consort	harpist
vivace	cadency	cornett	hautboy
voices	cadenza	cornist	hit|song
waxing	calando	coupler	hit|tune
zambra	calypso	Cremona	hornist
zither	cantata	crooner	hot|jazz
zufolo	canzona	curtall	humming
agitato	canzone	cymbals	hymnist
allegro	caprice	descant	hymnody
althorn	carioca	discord	intrada
andante	celesta	double|C	introit
animato	cellist	doubles	ivories
arietta	cembalo	down|bow	juke|box
arrange	chanson	drummer	keening
art|song	chanter	episode	key|note
attacca	chantry	euphony	Landler
attuned	chikara	Euterpe	lullaby
bagpipe	chiming	fagotto	maestro
ballade	chorale	fanfare	mandola
bandman	chorine	fermata	mandora
bandore	chorist	fiddle|G	marcato
bar|beat	cithara	fiddler	marimba
bar|line	cithern	flutina	mazurka
baryton	cittern	fluting	measure
bassist	clapper	flutist	mediant
bassoon	clarion	forlana	melisma
battery	classic	fox|trot	melodia
battuta	clavier	furioso	melodic

7/8 LETTERS

middle|C	refrain	taboret	a|piacere
mixture	reprise	tambura	archlute
mordent	requiem	tangent	arpeggio
morendo	respond	the|Nine	arranger
musette	ribible	theorbo	Ave|Maria
musical	ripieno	timbrel	bagpiper
natural	romance	timpani	bagpipes
ocarina	rondeau	tirasse	bandsman
octette	rondino	toccata	banjoist
offbeat	rosalia	top|note	baritone
one,step	roulade	tracker	barytone
organum	sackbut	treble|C	base|clef
Orpheus	salicet	tremolo	base|note
pandora	sambuca	triplet	base|viol
pandore	samisen	tritone	bass|drum
pandura	Sanctus	trumpet	bass|horn
Panpipe	saxhorn	tuneful	bass|oboe
partial	saxtuba	two,step	beat|time
passage	scherzo	ukelele	berceuse
pas|seul	scoring	ukulele	boat|song
pesante	septuor	upright	bouffons
piacere	serpent	vespers	Calliope
pianist	service	vibrato	canticle
pianola	seventh	vihuela	canticum
pibroch	singing	violist	cantoris
piccolo	skiffle	violone	canzonet
piffero	soloist	warbler	carillon
pomposo	song|hit	war|song	cavatina
pop|song	soprano	wassail	chaconne
potlids	sordino	whistle	chanting
prelude	stopped	ziganka	choirboy
Psalter	stretto	Agnus|Dei	choirman
quartet	strings	alto|clef	choragus
quintet	subject	alto|horn	choregus
ragtime	syncope	alto|viol	clappers
recital	taborer	antiphon	clarinet

col|legno	fantasie	leggiero	Panpipes
composer	flautist	libretto	parallel
con|amore	flip|side	ligature	parlando
concerto	flourish	love|song	parlante
continuo	flue|pipe	low|pitch	part|song
coronach	flue|work	lutanist	pastoral
courante	folderol	madrigal	phantasy
cromorna	folk|rock	maestoso	phrasing
cromorne	folk|song	maggiore	pianette
crooning	galliard	major|key	pianiste
crotchet	gemshorn	mazourka	Pierides
cylinder	glee|club	mean,tone	pipe|tune
dal|segno	habanera	measured	plangent
diapason	half|rest	melodeon	plectron
diapente	hand|bell	melodica	plectrum
diatonic	harmonic	melodics	pop|group
doh,ray,me	harp|lute	melodist	pop|music
doloroso	hornpipe	minor|key	post|horn
dominant	humstrum	minstrel	postlude
downbeat	hymeneal	moderato	psalmody
doxology	hymn|tune	monotone	psaltery
drumbeat	in|accord	movement	raga,rock
drumhead	in|chorus	musicale	ragtimer
drumskin	interval	music|box	recorder
duettino	in|unison	musician	reed|pipe
duettist	jazz|band	nocturne	reed|stop
dulciana	jazzed|up	notation	register
dulcimer	jew's|harp	open|note	response
emphasis	jongleur	operatic	reveille
ensemble	Jubilate	operetta	rhapsody
entr'acte	keyboard	oratorio	rigadoon
faburden	key|bugle	organist	ritenuto
falderal	last|post	ornament	saraband
falsetto	lay|clerk	ostinato	scordato
fandango	lay|vicar	overtone	semitone
fantasia	left|hand	overture	semplice

septette	tone|down	antiphony
sequence	tone|poem	arabesque
serenade	tone|poet	archilute
serenata	tonguing	aria|buffa
sextette	tonic|key	baby|grand
sextolet	triangle	bagatelle
side|drum	trombone	balalaika
sing|song	trouvere	ballerina
sliphorn	tunester	band|major
sol|faist	tympanon	bandstand
solo|stop	una|corda	banjolele
sonatina	vamp|horn	barcarole
songbird	Victrola	blow|a|horn
song|book	virginal	blues|song
songplay	virtuosa	bombardon
songster	virtuosi	bow|fiddle
sour|note	virtuoso	brass|band
spianato	vocalion	bugle|call
spinette	vocalism	bugle|horn
squiffer	vocalist	cacophony
staccato	Vorspiel	cantabile
strike|up	warbling	cantilena
strummer	wind|band	capriccio
strummer	woodwind	carolling
swan|song	yodeller	castanets
swell|box	zambomba	celestina
symphony	zarzuela	chalumeau
tamboura	a|cappella	chantress
tenor|cor	accompany	charivari
tenoroon	accordion	choralist
terzetto	acoustics	chorister
the|Muses	adagietto	chromatic
threnody	ad|libitum	citharist
tonalist	alla|breve	clarionet
tonality	allemande	classical
tone|deaf	andantino	claviharp

MUSIC

concentus
conductor
consonate
contralto
cornopean
crescendo
croon|song
cymbalist
dance|band
dance|form
dead|march
death|song
diaphonia
dithyramb
double|bar
drone|bass
drum|corps
drum|major
drumstick
dulcitone
duple|time
echo|organ
ecossaise
entrechat
epicedium
epinicion
euphonium
execution
extempore
farandole
figurante
fine|toned
fingering
flageolet
flute|a|bec
folk|dance

folk|music
fugue|form
full|close
full|organ
full|score
glissando
grace|note
grandioso
Gregorian
guitarist
half|close
hand|bells
hand|organ
harmonica
harmonics
harmonist
harmonium
harmonize
head|voice
hexachord
high|pitch
hit|parade
homophony
hymnology
imitation
impromptu
improvise
inflexion
interlude
invention
inversion
jazz|stick
jitterbug
kent|bugle
krummhorn
langspiel

larghetto
leger|line
Leitmotiv
lyric|bass
lyrichord
major|mode
malaguena
mandoline
mediation
melodious
melodrama
melomania
metronome
mezza|voce
minor|mode
modulator
monochord
monophony
music|hall
music|roll
music|room
music|wire
mute|pedal
obbligato
octachord
offertory
open|notes
open|score
orchestra
organ|stop
orpharion
out|of|tune
overtones
part|music
pas|de|deux
passepied

pasticcio	right|hand	tabor|pipe
pastorale	rondo|form	tail|piece
pedal|note	roundelay	tambourin
performer	saxcornet	tempo|mark
piacevole	saxophone	tenor|clef
piangendo	scherzoso	tenor|drum
piano|keys	scrape|gut	tenor|horn
pianolist	semibreve	tenor|tuba
piano|wire	semitonic	tenor|viol
pipe|organ	seraphine	tessitura
pitch|pipe	serenader	theme|song
pizzicato	sforzando	theorbist
plainsong	shantyman	time|value
play|by|ear	siciliana	timpanist
polonaise	signature	top|twenty
polychord	singspiel	torch|song
polyphony	sink|a|pace	transpose
pop|record	slow|march	tremulant
potpourri	smerzando	triangles
precentor	soap|opera	trumpeter
principal	soft|pedal	tuning|bar
programme	solfeggio	tympanist
prolation	solo|organ	tymp|stick
promenade	song|sheet	undertone
quadrille	sonometer	variation
quartette	sostenuto	viola|alto
quintette	sotto|voce	violin|bow
quodlibet	sound|hole	violinist
recording	sound|post	virginals
reed|organ	spiritoso	virtuosic
remote|key	spiritual	vocalizer
rendering	stockhorn	voice|part
rendition	succentor	Volkslied
resonance	swing|band	voluntary
rhythmics	symphonic	vox|humana
ricercare	tablature	waltz|time

whole|note	bull|fiddle	double|time
whole|rest	cancionero	drummer|boy
whole|step	cancrizans	dulcetness
whole,tone	canto|fermo	Eisteddfod
wind|chest	canzonetta	enharmonic
wind|music	chest|voice	euphonious
wind|trunk	chime,bells	exposition
woodwinds	chitarrone	expression
wrestpins	choir|organ	five,finger
wrong|note	chorus|girl	Flugelhorn
xylophone	cinquepace	folk|singer
zitherist	clavichord	fortepiano
accidental	coloratura	fortissimo
adaptation	comic|opera	French|harp
added|sixth	common|time	French|horn
affettuoso	concertina	golden|disc
allargando	concertino	grace|notes
allegretto	concertist	gramophone
alteration	concordant	grand|opera
antiphoner	conducting	grand|piano
attunement	consonance	great|organ
background	con|sordini	great|stave
ballad|horn	contrabass	Greek|modes
band|leader	cor|anglais	grind|organ
band|master	cornettist	ground|bass
band,waggon	Coryphaeus	harmonicon
barcarolle	cradlesong	harmonizer
basset|horn	dance|music	homophonic
basset|oboe	diminuendo	hornplayer
bassoonist	diminution	horse|opera
bell,ringer	disc|jockey	humoresque
Benedictus	dissonance	hurdygurdy
binary|form	doodlesack	incidental
bottom|note	dotted|note	instrument
brass|winds	double|bass	intermezzo
bridal|hymn	double|flat	intonation

jam|session	musical|ear	quick|march
kettledrum	music|lover	recitalist
leger|lines	music|maker	recitative
light|music	musicology	recitativo
light|opera	music|paper	related|key
long|player	music|stand	repertoire
lyre|guitar	oboe|d'amore	repetition
lyric|drama	opera|buffa	resolution
lyric|tenor	opera|score	responsory
mainstream	ophicleide	rhapsodist
major|chord	orchestral	ritardando
major|scale	organ|point	ritornelle
major|sixth	patter|song	ritornello
major|third	pedal|board	round|dance
major|triad	pedal|organ	sacred|Nine
manuscript	pedal|point	salicional
marimbaist	pentachord	saltarello
melody|part	pentatonic	saxotromba
mezzo|forte	percussion	scherzando
mezzo|piano	perdendosi	scordatura
minor|canon	phonograph	Scotch|snap
minor|chord	pianissimo	seguidilla
minor|scale	pianoforte	semichorus
minor|sixth	pianologue	semiquaver
minor|third	piano|score	set|to|music
minor|triad	piano|stool	shaped|note
minstrelsy	piccoloist	sheet|music
mixed|times	plagal|mode	short|score
modal|scale	Polyhymnia	silver|disc
modern|jazz	polyphonic	simple|time
modulation	ponticello	sonata|form
mouth|music	pop|concert	song|leader
mouth|organ	popular|air	songstress
mouthpiece	portamento	song|writer
musical|bow	prima|donna	sound|board
musical|box	proportion	sousaphone

speaker|key
squeeze|box
Stradivari
strathspey
street|band
stringendo
submediant
supertonic
suspension
swell|organ
swell|pedal
symphonion
symphonist
syncopated
syncopator
tambourine
tarantella
tetrachord
tin|whistle
tone|poetry
tonic|chord
tonic|major
tonic|minor
tonic|sol,fa
transcribe
transition
treble|clef
treble|viol
tremolando
triple|time
trombonist
troubadour
tuning|fork
tuning|pipe
tuning|wire
tweedledee

tweedledum
twelve|note
union|pipes
variations
vibraphone
villanella
vocal|music
vocal|score
accelerando
accompanist
Aeolian|harp
alla|tedesca
arrangement
ballad|maker
ballad|opera
barrel|organ
bass|passage
beat|a|tattoo
beat|the|drum
bell|ringing
blues|singer
broken|chord
calliophone
campanology
canned|music
capriccioso
cat's|concert
chansonette
chanterelle
choirmaster
clarinetist
clarion|call
clavicymbal
common|chord
compact|disc
composition

concertante
concert|band
concert|hall
consecutive
contrapunto
contredanse
counterbase
damper|pedal
decrescendo
descant|viol
discography
discotheque
divided|stop
dominant|key
Dorian|modes
dotted|minim
double|chant
double|fugue
double|sharp
double|touch
dulcet|tones
ear|for|music
English|horn
equal|voices
eurhythmics
extemporize
faux|bourdon
fiddlestick
fife|and|drum
figured|bass
finger|board
fipple|flute
first|fiddle
first|violin
French|pitch
French|sixth

fundamental
funeral|song
German|flute
German|sixth
golden|toned
graphophone
great|octave
half|cadence
harmonizing
harpsichord
hunting|horn
inscription
in|the|groove
keyed|guitar
leading|note
long|playing
Lydian|modes
madrigalist
major|second
mandolinist
mellifluent
mellifluous
mellisonant
Minnesinger
minor|second
mixed|voices
morris|dance
musica|ficta
musical|copy
musical|joke
musical|note
music|lesson
music|loving
music|school
nickelodeon
normal|pitch

opera|ballet
opera|bouffe
orchestrate
orchestrion
organophone
organ|player
over|blowing
Pandean|pipe
partial|tone
part|playing
part|singing
part|writing
passacaglia
passing|bell
passing|note
percussives
performance
piano|player
piano|violin
pitch|accent
plagal|modes
player|piano
polyphonism
popular|tune
preparation
prestissimo
progression
psalm|singer
quarter|note
quarter|rest
ragtime|band
rallentando
relative|key
Requiem|mass
retardation
rock|and|roll

sacred|music
saxophonist
scat|singing
Schottische
Scotch|catch
short|octave
silver|toned
singing|sand
small|octave
solmization
soprano|clef
sound|in|tune
square|piano
Stabat|Mater
stopped|pipe
street|organ
street|piano
string|music
string|plate
subdominant
sweet|voiced
synchronism
syncopation
temperament
tempo|giusto
ternary|form
Terpsichore
time|pattern
Tin|Pan|Alley
tonic|accent
torch|singer
transposing
tunefulness
tuning|slide
vicar|choral
viola|d'amore

287

viol da gamba	concert pitch	light harmony
violin piano	Concertstuck	lyric cantata
violoncello	conservatory	major seventh
vivacissimo	contrapuntal	marching song
voix celeste	counterpoint	martial music
wedding song	counter tenor	mean semitone
willow pipes	country dance	medieval mode
acciaccatura	cushion dance	mellifluence
accompanyist	divertimento	melodic minor
accordionist	dominant note	mezzo soprano
acoustic bass	dotted quaver	military band
agogic accent	drinking song	minor seventh
anticipation	extended play	minstrel song
appassionata	extravaganza	mixed cadence
appoggiatura	false cadence	monochordist
augmentation	fiddlesticks	musical scale
balladmonger	fiddlestring	musical score
ballad singer	florid phrase	musicianship
banjo ukelele	funeral march	musicologist
bass baritone	glockenspiel	mutation stop
bass clarinet	gravicembalo	opening notes
bass trombone	harmonichord	opera comique
beat a retreat	harmonic tone	orchestra pit
boogie woogie	hidden fifths	orchestrator
brass section	hurdygurdist	organ grinder
chamber music	hymnographer	parlour grand
chamber organ	improvisator	passion music
changing note	instrumental	penny whistle
chest of viols	introduction	perfect fifth
chorus singer	inverted turn	perfect pitch
clavicembalo	Italian sixth	philharmonic
comedy ballet	ivory thumper	Phrygian mode
compound time	ivory tickler	piobaireachd
concert grand	jazz musician	pipe and tabor
concertinist	key signature	polytonality
concert music	less semitone	popular music

reciting note
record player
registration
repercussion
rhythmic mode
sarrusophone
sesquialtera
sing in chorus
skiffle group
slow movement
speaking stop
steam whistle
Stradivarius
street singer
stress accent
symphonic ode
tape recorder
theatre organ
thorough bass
tintinnabula
tone measurer
tone painting
top of the pops
tromba marina
trumpet major
upper partial
upright piano
viola da gamba
vocalization
wedding march
wind musician
Zigeunerlied
accompaniment
American organ
capellmeister
cello concerto

choir practice
choral society
choreographer
concrete music
conductorship
conservatoire
contrabassoon
contrafagotto
contrapuntist
cornet a piston
corps de ballet
electric organ
Gregorian mode
harmonic scale
kapellmeister
kettledrummer
meistersinger
melodiousness
music mistress
musicological
orchestration
piano concerto
recorded music
rhythm section
signature tune
singing master
staff notation
string quartet
string quintet
symphonic poem
time signature
transposition
twelve tone row
violoncellist
ballet mistress
chromatic scale

MUSIC

classical|music
concerto|grosso
contrary|motion
demisemiquaver
double|stopping
electric|guitar
male|voice|choir
musical|prodigy
music|publisher
negro|spiritual
open|air|concert
piano|accordion
plantation|song
reed|instrument
smoking|concert
violin|concerto

wind|instrument
Bachelor|of|Music
background|music
Christy|minstrel
concert|overture
concert|platform
electronic|music
flutter|tonguing
incidental|music
instrumentalist
instrumentation
Moog|synthesiser
perfect|interval
string|orchestra
symphony|concert

Mythology

Anu	Gog	nis	Sol	Adad	Ares
Ate	Hel	nix	Sri	Aeon	Argo
Aya	Hob	Nox	Tem	Afer	Askr
Bel	Ida	Nut	Tiu	Agni	Aten
Bor	imp	Nyx	Tiw	Ajax	Aton
Cos	Ino	obi	Tum	Alea	Auge
dea	Ira	Ops	Tyr	Amen	Baal
Dia	Leo	Ore	Ull	Amor	Bast
Dis	Ler	Oya	Vac	Amun	Bora
elf	Lok	Pan	Van	Anax	Bran
Eos	Lug	Ran	Zan	Anna	Bron
fay	Mab	Seb	Zio	Anta	Buto
god	Mot	Set	Ziu	Apis	Ceto

Ceyx	Hera	Ment	Tiki	Atlas	Dione
Civa	Hero	Mors	Troy	Atman	Diral
Clio	Hler	Muse	tyro	Baldr	Dirce
Cora	Hodr	Nabu	Ullr	Batea	Donar
deil	Hora	Naga	Upis	Belus	Dorus
deus	Hoth	Nana	Urth	Bhaga	Draco
Deva	huma	Nebo	Vach	bogey	dryad
Devi	icon	Neph	Vale	Bragi	Durga
Dewa	idol	Nike	Vali	Brute	dwarf
Dian	Idun	Nona	Vans	Cabal	Dyaus
Dido	Ilus	Norn	Vayu	Cacus	Dylan
Dike	Inar	Nott	Vili	Canis	Dymas
Echo	Iole	Odin	Wate	Capta	Egill
Edda	Iris	ogre	Yama	Caria	Ehlis
Eden	Isis	peor	yeti	Carpo	elves
Enyo	jinn	peri	Ymir	Ceres	Enlil
Erda	jinx	Ptah	Zemi	Cerus	Epona
Eric	joss	Puck	Zeus	Cetus	Erato
Eris	Jove	Rahu	Zion	Chaos	Erlik
Eros	juju	Rama	Aegir	charm	Etara
Erua	Juno	Rhea	aegis	Circe	Eurus
Fate	Kali	Rind	Aegle	Coeus	fable
Faun	Kama	Saga	Aeson	Comus	Fagus
Fons	kami	Sati	afrit	coven	fairy
Frey	Kapi	seer	Algol	Creon	Fauna
Fria	Leda	Seth	Ammon	Creus	Faust
Frig	Leto	Shri	angel	Crius	fetch
Fury	Loke	Siva	Arcas	Cupid	fiend
Gaea	Loki	Soma	Arges	Dagda	Flora
Gaia	Luna	Spes	Argos	Dagon	Freya
Gerd	Lyra	Styx	Argus	Damia	Frigg
Gere	magi	tabu	Ariel	Danae	Gauri
Goll	Maia	Tara	Aries	deify	genie
Hapi	mana	Tare	Arion	deity	ghost
Hebe	Mara	Thea	Artio	Devil	ghoul
hell	Math	Thor	Athor	Diana	giant

Gibil	Kotys	Notus	theos	Aglaia
gnome	Laius	nymph	Thoth	Alecto
Grace	lamia	obeah	Thrym	Alseid
Gyges	Lamos	Orcus	Thule	Amazon
Hadad	Lares	oread	Titan	AmenRa
Hades	larva	Orion	totem	Amenti
Harpy	Lepus	ouphe	Troad	Amores
Hatra	Lethe	Paean	troll	amulet
haunt	Liber	pagan	Tyche	Anubis
Helen	Libra	Pales	Uriel	Anytus
Helle	limbo	Parca	Vanir	Apollo
Herse	Lupus	Paris	Varah	Aquila
Hoder	Lycus	Pitys	Venus	Arthur
Holda	Lydia	pixie	Vesta	Asgard
Horae	Magog	Pluto	Vidar	Assama
Horus	magus	Poeas	Virgo	astral
houri	Marut	Priam	Vithi	Athena
Hyads	Mazda	Remus	Wabun	Athene
Hydra	Medea	Robur	weird	Atreus
Hylas	Metis	Satan	Wodan	Attica
Hymen	Midas	satyr	Woden	Auriga
Iasus	mimic	shade	Wotan	Aurora
ichor	Minos	Sheol	Yasna	Auster
Idmon	Moira	Shiva	zombi	Avalon
Iliad	Momos	Shree	Adonai	avatar
Indra	Momus	Sibyl	Adonis	Azrael
Irene	Morna	Sinon	Aeacus	Babbar
Irmin	Morta	siren	Aeetes	Balder
Istar	naiad	Siris	Aegeus	Baldur
Ister	Nanna	spell	Aegina	Baucis
Janus	Nerio	spook	Aeneas	Belial
Jason	Ninos	Surya	Aeneid	Beulah
jinni	Niobe	sylph	Aeolus	Bootes
Karna	nisse	taboo	Aethra	Boreas
kelpy	nixie	Terra	afreet	Brahma
Komos	Njord	Theia	Agenor	brewer

6 LETTERS

Buddha	Freyia	Isolde	Nereus	Saturn
Cabiri	Freyja	Ithunn	Nergal	Sciron
Cadmus	Frigga	jinnee	Nessus	Scylla
Cancer	Ganesa	jumart	Nestor	seagod
Castor	Garuda	kelpie	Nimrod	Sekume
Chandi	Gawain	kobold	numina	Selene
Charis	Gemini	kraken	Oberon	Semele
Charon	genius	Kronos	obiman	seraph
cherub	Geryon	Laputa	occult	Simios
Chiron	goblin	Libera	Oeneus	Sinbad
Clotho	Gorgon	Lilith	ogress	Sirius
Corona	Graces	Locris	Oileus	skygod
Corvus	Graeae	Lucina	OldNed	Somnus
Crater	Haemon	Lugaid	Ondine	Sparta
Creusa	Hathor	maenad	oracle	Sphynx
Cronus	heaven	Mammon	Ormuzd	spirit
Crotus	Hebrus	manito	Osiris	sprite
Cybele	Hecate	Marduk	Ossian	Stator
Cygnus	Hector	Marmar	Pallas	Stheno
daemon	Hecuba	mascot	panisc	Strymo
Danaus	Hekate	Medusa	panisk	sungod
Daphne	Helios	Megara	Parcae	syrinx
Decuma	Hermes	Memnon	Peleus	Tammuz
dragon	Hobbit	Mentor	Pelias	Taurus
durgan	Hoenir	Merlin	Pelops	Tellus
Egeria	hoodoo	merman	Phocis	Tethys
Eirene	Hyades	Merope	Phoebe	Teucer
Epirus	Hyllus	Mithra	Pisces	Thalia
Erebus	Iasion	Moerae	Placia	Thallo
Erinys	Iasius	Moirai	Pollux	Thebus
Erotes	Icarus	Molech	Pontus	Themis
Etolia	Indara	Moloch	Pothos	Thetis
Europa	Iolcus	Myrrha	Psyche	thrall
Euryte	Iseult	nectar	Pythia	Thunor
Faunus	Ishtar	Neleus	Python	Titans
fetish	Ismene	Nereid	Rhodus	Tithon

MYTHOLOGY

Tityus	Ali|Baba	Camelot	Eurytus
Tonans	Amphion	cantrip	Euterpe
Tophet	Antaeus	Capella	evil|eye
Triton	Antenor	Cecrops	Evil|one
Tydeus	Anteros	centaur	Faustus
Typhon	Antiope	Cepheus	fire|god
undine	Aquilon	Cercyon	Fortuna
Urania	Arallis	charmer	Gabriel
Uranus	Arcadia	Chemosh	Galahad
Utopia	Argolis	chimera	Galatea
Varuna	Ariadne	Chloris	Gehenna
Vesper	Artemis	Cisseus	giantry
Victor	Astarte	Clymene	Glaucus
Vishnu	Athamas	Cocytus	Glitnir
vision	Atropos	Curetes	goat|god
voodoo	Avallon	cyclops	goddess
Vulcan	Avernus	Cynthia	godling
war|god	Axierus	Cyzicus	gremlin
wizard	Azapane	Deasura	griffin
wraith	Bacchus	Deipyle	griffon
Wyvern	bad|luck	Demeter	half|god
Yahweh	bad|peri	demigod	Hanuman
ye|gods	banshee	dervish	Harpies
Zephyr	Bellona	dog|star	Helenus
Zethus	bewitch	Echidna	hellion
zombie	Bifrost	Electra	heroine
Abaddon	Boeotia	Eleusis	Hesione
Achalia	boggart	Elysian	Himeros
Achates	Bona|Dea	Epigoni	Horatii
Acheron	Brontes	Erginus	Hygieia
Actaeon	brownie	Erinyes	Iacchus
Ahriman	bugaboo	erlking	Iapetus
Aladdin	bugbear	Eubulus	Icarius
Alcaeus	Cabeiri	Eunomia	Illyria
Alcmene	Calydon	Eupheme	incubus
Alcyone	Calypso	Euryale	inferno

7/8 LETTERS

Iuturna	OldNick	Savitri	Aidoneus
Jocasta	Olympus	Scorpio	ambrosia
Jupiter	Omphale	seamaid	Ameinias
Krishna	Orestes	Serapis	Anchises
Laertes	Orpheus	Serpens	Antigone
Lakshmi	Orthrus	serpent	Apollyon
Laocoon	Ouranos	Shaitan	Aquarius
Laodice	Pandion	Shamash	Arcturus
Laputan	Pandora	Sigmund	Argestes
Leander	Panthus	Silenus	Argonaut
limniad	Pegasus	sorcery	Arimaspi
Lorelei	Penates	spectre	Asmodeus
Lucifer	Perseus	sylphid	Asterope
Lynceus	Pervati	Taygete	Astraeus
Marsyas	Phaedra	Telamon	Astyanax
Megaera	phantom	Thaumus	Astyoche
Mercury	Philtre	thegods	Atalanta
mermaid	Phineus	Theseus	Atlantis
Michael	Phoebus	Titania	Baalpeor
Midgard	Phoenix	Tristan	bacchant
Miletus	Phorcys	Troilus	badfairy
Minerva	Phryxus	Ulysses	blackart
Mordred	Pleione	unicorn	Briareus
Mycenae	Pluvius	vampire	Cabeirus
Nariman	Procris	warlock	caduceus
Nemesis	Procyon	Wieland	Calliope
Nephele	Proteus	windgod	Callisto
Neptune	Pylades	Zadkiel	Capareus
Nerthus	Pyrrhus	Absyrtus	Castalia
Niflhel	raingod	Achelous	Cephalus
Nirvana	Raphael	Achernar	Cerberus
Nisroch	RigVeda	Achilles	Charites
nymphet	Romulus	Acrisius	cherubim
Oceanid	Sagitta	Adrastus	chimaera
Oceanus	Sammael	Aegyptus	Chrysaor
Oedipus	sandman	Aganippe	chthonic

Cimmerii	false|god	Marathon
Clymenus	Favonius	Marnaran
Cockayne	folklore	Melampus
colossus	Ganymede	Meleager
Corythus	giantess	Menelaus
Cretheus	Glasberg	Mephisto
Curiatii	good|luck	Merodach
Cyclopes	gramarye	Messenia
Cynosura	grimoire	Minotaur
Daedalus	Harmonia	morganes
Danaides	Harpinna	Morpheus
Dardanus	hell|fire	Myrtilus
Deiphyle	Hellotis	Nauplius
demiurge	Heracles	Nephthys
demonism	Hercules	Niflheim
Despoina	Hesperis	Odysseus
devaloka	Hiawatha	Oenomaus
devil|god	Himantes	Old|Harry
Diomedes	Horatius	Old|Horny
Dionysus	Hyperion	Olympian
Dioscuri	Iphicles	paganism
dream|god	Juventas	Pan|pipes
earth|god	Kalevala	Pantheon
El|Dorado	Lachesis	Paradise
elf|child	Laconica	Pasiphae
Epicaste	Lancelot	Penelope
Eridanus	Laomedon	Pentheus
Erinnyes	Laputian	Percival
Eriphyle	Leiriope	Pergamus
Erytheia	libation	Periboea
Eteocles	Lilliput	Persides
Eurayale	limoniad	Peter|Pan
Eurydice	Lycurgus	Phaethon
exorcise	Lyonesse	Philemon
exorcism	magician	Philotis
fabulous	Mahadeva	Pierides

Pittheus	zoolater	Cassandra
Pleiades	zoolatry	Centaurus
Podarces	Acarnania	Cephissus
Polyxena	Aegisthus	Charybdis
Portunus	Agamemnon	chthonian
Poseidon	Agapemone	Cimmerian
Quirinus	Aigialeus	Cleopatra
revenant	Aldebaran	cloudland
Sabazius	Alexander	Cockaigne
Sarpedon	Amphiarus	Concordia
Satanism	Andromeda	cupbearer
sea|nymph	Anticleia	Cupidines
Sharrapu	Aphrodite	Davy|Jones
Sisyphus	archangel	Deianeira
Sleipnir	archfiend	Delphinia
sorcerer	Argus|eyed	Delphinus
Steropes	Aristaeus	Dendrites
succubus	Asclepiad	Deucalion
talisman	Asclepios	devil|lore
Tantalus	Asclepius	diablerie
Tartarus	Ashtaroth	diabolism
Teraphim	Assaracus	Discordia
Thanatos	Astydamia	dreamland
the|Deuce	Atalantis	Electryon
the|Muses	Atargatis	enchanter
the|Seven	Atlantica	Eumenides
Thyestes	Attic|salt	Euphorbus
Tithonus	Autolycus	Excalibur
Tristram	Axiocersa	fairyfolk
Tristran	bacchante	fairyland
Valhalla	Beelzebub	fairy|ring
Valkyrie	bewitcher	Friar|Tuck
werefolk	Black|mass	Gilgamesh
werewolf	brimstone	golden|age
Ygdrasil	Britannia	golden|egg
Zephyrus	cacodemon	good|fairy

Great|Bear
Guenevere
Guinevere
hamadryad
Heimdallr
Hippocoon
Hippolyte
Hobgoblin
Holy|Grail
Houyhnymn
Hyppolita
Ilmarinen
Immortals
Jagannath
Kumarpish
labyrinth
Launcelot
love|charm
lucky|bean
Lycomedes
Lyonnesse
maelstrom
magic|wand
magic|word
Marspiter
Meilanion
Melpomene
Mnemosyne
Myrmidons
Narcissus
occultism
Palamedes
Palladium
Pandareus
Parnassus
Parthenon

Phantasus
Philomelo
pied|piper
Polydorus
purgatory
pyrolater
pyrolatry
Robin|Hood
Ruritania
Sangarius
Sarasvati
Shangri¡la
sorceress
Sthenelus
Strategis
Teiresias
Telegonus
the|Furies
Tisiphone
totem|pole
tree|nymph
Trojan|War
Tyndareus
Ursa|major
Ursa|minor
Valkyries
Valkyriur
winged|cap
wood|nymph
Yggdrasil
Zernebock
Zeus|Pater
Alexandros
Amphiaraus
Amphitrite
Amphitryon

Andromache
apotheosis
apparition
Arion's|lyre
Armageddon
Axiocersus
bewitchery
black|magic
broomstick
Callirrhoe
Canis|major
Cassiopeia
cast|a|spell
changeling
Chrysippus
cloven|foot
Cockatrice
Coriolanus
cornucopia
Cretan|Bull
Demogorgon
demonology
Electryone
Epimetheus
Erechtheus
Euphrosyne
Euroclydon
Eurystheus
evil|genius
evil|spirit
fairy|queen
Gargantuan
ghost|dance
Greek|Fates
hagiolatry
Happy|Isles

heathen god	Nebelkappe	sun worship
heliolater	necromancy	Telemachus
heliolatry	Nemean lion	the Dickens
Hellespont	ocean nymph	the Tempter
Hephaestus	Oedipus Rex	Thruthvang
Hesperides	old soldier	Triangulum
Hippocrene	open sesame	underworld
hippogriff	Orion's belt	Vardhamana
hippogryph	Pantagruel	water nymph
Hippolytus	Peripheles	water witch
hippomanes	Persephone	white magic
Hippomenes	Pheidippes	wishing cap
Hitopadesa	Phlegethon	witchcraft
hocus pocus	Phosphoros	Wonderland
Hyacinthus	phylactery	Yggdrasill
idolatrous	pipes of Pan	abracadabra
idolomancy	Polydectes	Aesculapius
invocation	Polydeuces	amphisbaena
ivory tower	Polyhymnia	Aonian fount
Juggernaut	Polymestor	Aonian mount
Juno Lucina	Polyneices	Aristomenes
King Arthur	Polyphemus	bedevilment
leprechaun	Procrustes	Bellerophon
Little Bear	Prometheus	Britomartis
Little John	Proserpina	Brobdingnag
lucky charm	rabbit foot	Capricornus
lucky piece	River of woe	charmed life
magic spell	round table	demigoddess
Maid Marion	salamander	demonolatry
Melicertes	Samothrace	enchantment
Memnonides	Santa Claus	fetch candle
Menestheus	Saturnalia	fire worship
Midas touch	Schamander	flower nymph
minor deity	sixth sense	Gog and Magog
mumbo jumbo	soothsayer	Golden Bough
myrmidones	St Nicholas	golden goose

Gorgon's head
Happy Valley
Helen of Troy
hippocampus
Hypermestra
Juno Curitis
Kabibonokka
kingdom come
Locrian Ajax
lotus eaters
lycanthrope
magic carpet
magic circle
meadow nymph
mecromancer
medicine man
Megapenthes
moon goddess
Morgan le Fay
mother earth
Mudjekeavis
Neoptolemus
nether world
Nymphagetes
Orion's hound
Orion's sword
Pallantides
Pandemonium
Pandora's box
pastoral god
patron saint
Persephassa
Philippides
Philoctetes
poltergeist
Polymnestor

Prester John
Rosicrucian
Sagittarius
Scamandrius
second sight
Shawandasee
spellbinder
Stygian oath
sylvan deity
Symplegades
Terpsichore
the black art
three Graces
thunderbolt
Triptolemos
Trojan horse
tutelary god
ultima Thule
under a spell
ware animals
water spirit
water sprite
wishing well
witch doctor
wooden horse
Achilles heel
Aesop's fables
Aladdin's lamp
Amphion's lyre
Arcadian hind
Athena Pallas
Augean stable
avenging fury
Bower of Bliss
Bull Poseidon
Chrysomallus

Clytemnestra
Doppelganger
Dyanean rock
Erichthonius
exsufflation
Garden of Eden
golden apples
golden fleece
Golden Legend
heavenly host
Hesperethusa
hippocentaur
horn of plenty
household god
Hyperboreans
Isle of Apples
Juno Quiritis
Kriss Kringle
Laestrygones
Lake Tritonis
Land o the Leal
lap of the gods
Lernean Hydra
little people
Marathon bull
Mount Helicon
Mount Olympus
ordeal by fire
Pallas Athene
Parthian shot
Periclymenus
Promised Land
Rhadamanthus
Serpentarius
Stygian creek
Stygian gloom

supernatural	metamorphosis
thaumaturgus	Phoebus|Apollo
Thesmophorus	apple|of|discord
vestal|virgin	Jupiter|Pluvius
Wandering|Jew	mythologically
Weird|Sisters	Never|Never|Land
Will|Scarlett	Walpurgis|Night
wishing|stone	Father|Christmas
witches|coven	Gotterdammerung
Augean|stables	Homeric|laughter
Elysian|fields	sword|of|Damocles

Occupations

AB	dux	bard	feed	peon	adult
BA	fan	beak	firm	poet	agent
CA	guy	bear	girl	pope	baker
DD	job	beau	G\-man	sage	belle
GP	kid	boss	hack	salt	boots
MA	lad	bull	hand	seer	bosun
MC	man	chap	head	serf	boxer
MD	Mrs	char	hero	silk	buyer
MO	nun	chef	hobo	star	caddy
MP	pay	cook	host	task	cadet
Mr	rep	crew	lass	tyro	canon
PA	sir	cure	lead	wage	chief
PM	spy	dean	magi	ward	chips
BSc	tar	demy	maid	whip	chore
CID	vet	dick	miss	work	clerk
deb	aide	diva	monk	abbot	coach
doc	babe	doxy	page	actor	crier
don	baby	dyer	peer	adman	crone

301

crony	luter	sewer	bandit	codist
crook	madam	slave	banker	coheir
decoy	major	smith	barber	consul
demon	maker	sower	bargee	coolie
devil	Maori	staff	barker	cooper
diver	mason	tenor	barman	copier
donor	mayor	thief	batman	copper
doyen	medic	tiler	batter	costar
dummy	miner	tommy	beadle	coster
dutch	minor	trade	bearer	couper
elder	model	tramp	beater	cowboy
envoy	nanny	tuner	beggar	Creole
extra	navvy	tutor	beldam	critic
fakir	nurse	uhlan	Berber	curate
felon	odist	usher	bishop	cutler
fence	owner	valet	boffin	cutter
fifer	padre	vicar	bookie	damsel
friar	party	viner	bowman	dancer
Galen	pilot	wages	broker	deacon
garbo	pinup	wench	bugler	dealer
ghost	piper	witch	bursar	debtor
gipsy	posse	woman	busker	deputy
grass	prior	yokel	butler	divine
guard	proxy	youth	cabbie	docker
guest	pupil	abbess	caddie	doctor
guide	quack	admass	caller	double
hewer	quill	airace	camper	dowser
issue	rabbi	airman	cantor	draper
judge	racer	albino	captor	drawer
juror	rider	alumna	career	driver
laird	rishi	archer	carter	drudge
limey	rival	artist	carver	duenna
local	rover	aupair	casual	editor
locum	saver	aurist	censor	ensign
loser	sawer	author	cleric	escort
lover	scout	backer	client	Eskimo

6 LETTERS

etcher	high|up	mahout	oracle	rookie
expert	hippie	maiden	orator	runner
fabler	hosier	marine	ostler	sailor
factor	hunter	marker	outlaw	sapper
feeder	hussar	master	packer	sartor
fellow	hymner	matron	parson	savage
fitter	iceman	medico	pastor	savant
flunky	inmate	medium	patron	sawyer
flyman	intern	member	pedlar	scorer
forger	jailer	menial	penman	scouse
friend	jester	mentor	pen|pal	scribe
fuller	jet|set	mercer	picket	seadog
gaffer	jobber	mikado	pieman	sealer
gagman	jockey	miller	pirate	seaman
ganger	joiner	minion	pitman	second
gaoler	jumper	mister	plater	seller
garcon	junior	moiler	player	senior
gaucho	junker	monger	Pommie	sentry
German	keener	moppet	porter	server
gigolo	keeper	mortal	potter	sexton
gillie	killer	mummer	prater	shadow
glazer	lackey	munshi	priest	sheila
glover	lancer	musico	punter	shower
golfer	lascar	mystic	purser	shrink
graver	lawyer	nannie	ragman	singer
grocer	leader	native	ranger	sister
grower	lector	Norman	rating	skater
gunman	legate	notary	reader	skivvy
gunner	lender	novice	reaper	skyman
hatter	lessee	nudist	rector	slater
hawker	Levite	nuncio	regius	slavey
healer	limner	oboist	rhymer	slayer
helper	living	odd|job	rigger	sleuth
herald	lodger	office	ringer	smoker
hermit	lutist	oilman	rioter	sniper
hetman	lyrist	optime	robber	soutar

souter	waiter	bandman	citizen
sowter	walk,on	barmaid	cleaner
sparks	warden	baronet	climber
squire	warder	bassist	clippie
status	weaver	Bedouin	coalman
stoker	welder	beldame	cobbler
suitor	whaler	bellboy	cockney
sutler	winner	bellhop	colleen
tailor	wizard	bigname	collier
talent	worker	bigshot	colonel
tanner	wright	bitpart	commere
Tartar	writer	blender	company
taster	yeoman	boarder	compere
tatter	abetter	boatman	comrade
teller	abigail	bookman	convert
tenant	acolyte	bouncer	convict
Teuton	acrobat	breeder	copilot
tiller	actress	brigand	copyist
tinker	actuary	builder	copyman
tinner	admiral	burglar	coroner
toiler	adviser	bushman	corsair
trader	almoner	butcher	Cossack
truant	alumnus	buttons	counsel
turner	amateur	callboy	courier
tycoon	analyst	calling	cowherd
typist	apostle	cambist	cowpoke
tyrant	arbiter	captain	creator
umpire	artisan	captive	crofter
urchin	artiste	carrier	crooner
usurer	assayer	cashier	cropper
valuer	athlete	caulker	curator
vanman	attache	caveman	custode
vendor	auditor	cellist	cyclist
verger	aviator	chemist	danseur
victor	bailiff	chindit	daysman
Viking	ballboy	chorist	debater

denizen	gateman	lockman	patient
dentist	general	lookout	patroon
diviner	ghillie	lorimer	pearler
dominie	glazier	maestro	peasant
doorman	gleaner	magnate	pianist
dragoon	grownup	mailman	picador
drayman	gunmoll	manager	pierrot
dresser	gymnast	mariner	pilgrim
driller	handler	marshal	pioneer
drummer	hangman	masseur	planner
dustman	harpist	matador	planter
elogist	haulier	matelot	plumber
embassy	headboy	meatman	poacher
entrant	headman	midwife	poetess
equerry	heckler	milkman	pollman
escapee	heiress	mobsman	poloist
escaper	heroine	mobster	pontiff
esquire	hipster	modiste	poorman
farceur	histrio	monitor	popidol
farcist	hostess	moulder	popstar
farrier	hymnist	mourner	postboy
fiddler	imagist	mudlark	postman
fighter	invalid	navarch	prefect
fireman	Jacktar	newsboy	prelate
flagman	janitor	newsman	premier
flapper	jemedar	oarsman	presser
flesher	juggler	oculist	primate
florist	junkman	officer	printer
footboy	justice	oldsalt	privado
footman	knacker	omnibus	private
footpad	knitter	oratrix	proctor
foreman	knowhow	orderly	proofer
founder	learner	pageboy	prophet
frogman	lineman	painter	protege
furrier	linkboy	partner	provost
gambler	linkman	passman	prowler

puddler	sharper	trooper	banjoist
punster	shearer	trouper	bankrupt
pursuer	sheriff	tumbler	banksman
railman	shopman	turfman	bargeman
rancher	shopper	veteran	baritone
rat|race	showman	viceroy	beadsman
realtor	skinner	vintner	bedesman
redskin	skipper	visitor	bedmaker
referee	soldier	warrior	beginner
refugee	soloist	webster	benefice
regular	soprano	whipper	bigamist
remover	spartan	wiseman	blackleg
rentier	speaker	witness	blind|man
rescuer	spinner	wolf|cub	boardman
reserve	sponsor	woodman	Bohemian
retinue	spotter	woolman	bondsman
rich|man	stand|by	workman	boniface
routine	starlet	abductor	borrower
rustler	starman	adherent	botanist
saddler	starter	adjutant	bowmaker
sagaman	station	advocate	boxmaker
samurai	steward	aeronaut	boy|scout
sandman	stipend	alderman	brakeman
scalper	student	alienist	brunette
scenist	supremo	allopath	bummaree
scholar	surgeon	ambivert	business
scraper	swagman	anchoret	cabin|boy
sea|cook	tapster	armorist	call|girl
sea|king	teacher	armourer	canoness
sea|lord	tipster	arranger	cardinal
sea|wolf	tourist	assassin	castaway
seminar	trainee	assessor	ceramist
senator	trainer	attacker	chairman
servant	trapper	attorney	chambers
service	trawler	axemaker	champion
settler	tripper	bagmaker	chandler

8 LETTERS

chaperon	dictator	filmstar	Hebraist
chaplain	diet|cook	finalist	helmsman
choirboy	diocesan	finisher	henchman
cicerone	diplomat	fishwife	herdsman
cicisbeo	director	flatfoot	hijacker
civilian	disciple	flautist	hired|gun
claimant	dogsbody	floorman	hired|man
clansman	domestic	forester	hireling
classman	dragoman	forgeman	home|help
clerkess	druggist	freshman	horseman
clothier	duettist	front|man	hotelier
co|author	educator	fugitive	houseboy
comedian	elegiast	fusilier	hula|girl
commando	embalmer	gangsman	huntsman
commoner	emeritus	gangster	identity
compiler	emigrant	gaolbird	idyllist
composer	emissary	gardener	importer
conjurer	employee	garroter	inceptor
convener	engineer	gendarme	informer
corporal	engraver	goatherd	initiate
coryphee	epic|poet	governor	inkmaker
cottager	essayist	gownsman	inventor
courtier	eulogist	graduate	investor
coxswain	examinee	guardian	islander
creditor	executor	guerilla	jailbird
croupier	explorer	gunmaker	jet|pilot
cupmaker	exponent	gunsmith	jeweller
cutpurse	fabulist	ham|actor	jongleur
dairyman	factotum	handmaid	juvenile
danseuse	falconer	handyman	knife|boy
dead|head	fanfaron	hatmaker	labourer
deck|hand	fanmaker	hawkshaw	land|girl
delegate	farm|hand	haymaker	landlady
deserter	ferryman	head|cook	landlord
designer	figurant	head|girl	landsman
detainee	film|idol	headship	lapidary

law|agent	modeller	perfumer	retainer
lawgiver	moralist	perjurer	reveller
law,maker	motorist	picaroon	revenant
laywoman	muleteer	pilferer	reviewer
lecturer	muralist	pillager	rewriter
licensee	murderer	plagiary	rifleman
life,peer	musician	poetling	rivetter
life,work	narrator	poisoner	road,gang
linesman	naturist	polisher	rotarian
linguist	neophyte	pontifex	rugmaker
listener	netmaker	position	saboteur
logician	newcomer	potmaker	salesman
loiterer	news,hawk	practice	salvager
looker,on	nightman	preacher	satirist
lumberer	Norseman	pressman	sawbones
luminary	novelist	prioress	sawsmith
lyricist	objector	prisoner	sciolist
magician	observer	prizeman	scullion
mandarin	occupant	producer	sculptor
mapmaker	official	promoter	seafarer
marauder	onlooker	prompter	seedsman
marksman	op|artist	psychist	selector
masseuse	operator	publican	sentinel
mechanic	opponent	pugilist	sergeant
mediator	optician	purveyor	servitor
melodist	oratress	quarrier	shepherd
mercator	ordinand	radar,man	shipmate
merchant	organist	rag|trade	shopgirl
milkmaid	overlord	ragwoman	showgirl
millgirl	overseer	receiver	side,kick
millhand	pardoner	recorder	sidesman
milliner	parodist	reformer	silk|gown
minister	party|man	reporter	sinecure
ministry	passer,by	research	sketcher
minstrel	patentee	resident	sky,scout
mistress	penmaker	retailer	small|fry

smuggler	torturer	alchemist
solitary	townsman	anatomist
songster	trainman	anchoress
sorcerer	trappist	anchorite
spaceman	tripeman	annotator
spearman	tunester	announcer
speed|cop	unionist	annuitant
sprinter	union|man	antiquary
stageman	vagabond	apologist
star|turn	valuator	applicant
stockman	vanguard	appraiser
storeman	virtuoso	arch|enemy
stowaway	vocalist	architect
stranger	vocation	archivist
stripper	waitress	art|critic
stroller	ward|maid	art|dealer
stunt|man	wardress	artificer
superior	watchman	assistant
superman	waterman	associate
supplier	wayfarer	astronaut
surveyor	wet|nurse	attendant
survivor	wheelman	authoress
swagsman	whiphand	authority
tallyman	whipjack	automaton
taxpayer	whittler	axlesmith
teddy|boy	wig|maker	balladist
teenager	woodsman	ballerina
thatcher	workfolk	bargainer
Thespian	workgirl	barrister
thurifer	workhand	barrow|boy
tin|miner	wrangler	beefeater
tinsmith	wrestler	bee|keeper
Tom|Thumb	yodeller	beermaker
tone|poet	aborigine	beggarman
top|brass	absconder	bellmaker
toreador	aerialist	biologist

OCCUPATIONS

bit|player
boatswain
bodyguard
bodymaker
boilerman
boltsmith
bookmaker
bootblack
bootmaker
brass|hats
brigadier
buccaneer
bunny|girl
bus|driver
bush|pilot
byrewoman
bystander
cab|driver
cabin|crew
cafe|owner
cakemaker
cameraman
candidate
canvasser
cardsharp
caretaker
carpenter
casemaker
celebrity
cellarman
centurion
chain|gang
chartered
charterer
charwoman
chauffeur

choralist
chorus|boy
clergyman
clinician
clogmaker
coadjutor
coal|miner
coenobite
colleague
collector
columnist
combatant
commander
commodore
companion
concierge
concubine
conductor
confessor
confidant
conqueror
conscript
constable
contender
contralto
cornerboy
cosmonaut
cost|clerk
costumier
court|fool
couturier
covergirl
crackshot
cracksman
crayonist
cricketer

cupbearer
custodian
cutthroat
cymbalist
daily|help
day|labour
deaconess
dean|of|men
debutante
decorator
defendant
dependent
designate
desk|clerk
detective
dialogist
dietician
dispenser
dog|walker
dollmaker
dramatist
drum|major
drysalter
ecologist
economist
embezzler
emolument
enamelist
enchanter
engrosser
entourage
errand|boy
espionage
estimator
exchanger
exchequer

exciseman	guest|star	jitterbug
executive	guitarist	jobholder
eye|doctor	gunrunner	key|worker
fieldwork	hand|sewer	kidnapper
figurante	harbinger	lacemaker
film|actor	harbourer	lady's|maid
film|extra	hard|graft	lampmaker
film|maker	harlequin	lampooner
financier	harmonist	land|agent
fire|guard	harpooner	land|force
first|mate	harvester	landowner
fisherman	head|clerk	landreeve
foreigner	herbalist	land|shark
foundling	hillbilly	larcenist
free|lance	hired|hand	launderer
freemason	hired|help	laundress
fruiterer	historian	lawmonger
furnisher	home|maker	lay|figure
garreteer	homeopath	lay|reader
garrotter	Hottentot	lay|sister
gas|fitter	house|dick	legionary
gazetteer	housemaid	lensmaker
gem|cutter	husbandry	librarian
geologist	hypnotist	lifeguard
girl|guide	immigrant	life's|work
gladiator	increment	linotyper
gluemaker	incumbent	liontamer
go|between	innkeeper	lip|reader
goldsmith	inscriber	liveryman
gondolier	in|service	loan|agent
governess	inside|man	lockmaker
grapevine	inspector	locksmith
grenadier	interview	log|roller
guarantor	ironminer	lord|mayor
guardsman	ironsmith	lowlander
guerrilla	jay|walker	lumberman

machinist	outfitter	postulant
major|domo	panellist	postwoman
major|poet	pantomime	poulterer
make|up|man	paparazzo	precentor
male|model	part|owner	precursor
male|nurse	passenger	prelector
man|at|arms	patrolman	presbyter
man|Friday	patroness	president
medallist	paymaster	priestess
mendicant	paysagist	principal
mercenary	pedagogue	privateer
mesmerist	pen|friend	professor
messenger	pen|pusher	profiteer
middleman	pensioner	prud'homme
minor|poet	performer	publicist
model|girl	personage	publisher
monitress	personnel	puppeteer
moonraker	phone|girl	raconteur
mortician	physician	rainmaker
muscle|man	physicist	ransacker
musketeer	picksmith	ranzelman
mythmaker	Pierrette	ratefixer
navigator	pistoleer	ratepayer
neighbour	pitwright	recordist
newsagent	plaintiff	reference
newshound	plasterer	registrar
nursemaid	ploughboy	residency
occultist	ploughman	rhymester
odd|job|man	plunderer	ringsider
office|boy	poetaster	roadmaker
old|master	policeman	rocketeer
old|stager	pop|artist	rocket|man
ombudsman	pop|singer	ropemaker
operative	portrayer	roundsman
osteopath	portreeve	rum|runner
otologist	possessor	rural|dean

sackmaker	spider|man	volunteer
safemaker	spokesman	wassailer
sailmaker	sportsman	waxworker
sales|girl	stagehand	weekender
sales|team	stage|idol	wheelsman
sassenach	star|gazer	winemaker
scarecrow	statesman	woodreeve
scaristan	stationer	workwoman
scavenger	steersman	yachtsman
scenarist	stevedore	youngster
scientist	strike|pay	zitherist
scrapegut	subaltern	zoologist
scribbler	sub,editor	able|seaman
scrivener	suffragan	accomplice
sea,lawyer	swineherd	accountant
secretary	tablemaid	advertiser
seneschal	tailoress	aeronomist
sentryman	tap|dancer	agrologist
seraskier	tax|evader	agronomist
serenader	tentmaker	aide,de,camp
sermonist	test|pilot	air|hostess
servitude	therapist	air|steward
shoemaker	timberman	amanuensis
signaller	toolsmith	ambassador
signalman	town|clerk	Anglo,Saxon
situation	towncrier	anvilsmith
skin|diver	tradesman	apothecary
solicitor	traveller	apprentice
songsmith	tribesman	arbitrator
sonneteer	troubador	archbishop
sophister	trumpeter	archdeacon
sophomore	tympanist	archpriest
sorceress	undergrad	aristocrat
soubrette	usherette	astrologer
space|crew	vigilante	astronomer
speedster	violinist	auctioneer

audit|clerk
au|pair|girl
babe|in|arms
baby|sitter
ballet|girl
ballplayer
bandmaster
bank|robber
baseballer
bassoonist
bear|leader
beautician
bellringer
benefactor
billbroker
billposter
biochemist
biographer
blacksmith
bladesmith
blockmaker
bludgeoner
bluebottle
bluejacket
boatwright
bogtrotter
bombardier
bonesetter
bonus|clerk
bookbinder
book|dealer
bookfolder
bookholder
bookkeeper
bookseller
bookwright

bootlegger
brain|drain
brakemaker
brass|smith
breadmaker
bricklayer
brickmaker
broom|maker
brushmaker
bulb|grower
bumbailiff
bureaucrat
burlesquer
camera|team
campaigner
cartoonist
cat|breeder
cat|burglar
catechumen
cavalryman
ceramicist
chainmaker
chairmaker
chancellor
changeling
chargehand
charity|boy
chauffeuse
chorus|girl
chronicler
cider|maker
cigar|maker
claim|agent
clapper|boy
cloakmaker
clockmaker

clocksmith
clog|dancer
cloisterer
cloistress
clothmaker
clubmaster
coachmaker
coastguard
co|director
collar|work
coloratura
colporteur
comedienne
commandant
commission
competitor
compositor
concertist
consultant
contestant
contractor
controller
copyreader
copywriter
corn|doctor
cornettist
coryphaeus
councillor
counsellor
country|boy
countryman
couturiere
cover|agent
crackbrain
cultivator
customs|man

314

cytologist
day|tripper
demoiselle
dilettante
dirty|nurse
disc|jockey
discounter
discoverer
dishwasher
dispatcher
dog|breeder
donkey|work
doorkeeper
dramatizer
dramaturge
dressmaker
drug|pusher
drummer|boy
dry|cleaner
duty|roster
early|riser
empiricist
employment
equestrian
evangelist
experience
eye|witness
fabricator
faith|curer
farmer's|boy
fellmonger
fictionist
film|editor
firemaster
fire|raiser
fishmonger

flag|bearer
flight|crew
flower|girl
folk|singer
footballer
foot|doctor
forecaster
forerunner
forty|niner
frame|maker
freebooter
fund|raiser
gamekeeper
game|warden
garage|hand
gatekeeper
gatewright
geisha|girl
geneticist
geochemist
geographer
glassmaker
glossarist
goalkeeper
gold|beater
gold|digger
goldworker
grammarian
grand|prior
grindstone
groceryman
gubernator
gunslinger
hall|porter
handmaiden
handshaker

hatchet|man
headhunter
headmaster
head|porter
head|waiter
hedgesmith
henchwoman
highjacker
highlander
high|priest
highwayman
hitchhiker
holy|orders
honorarium
horn|player
horologist
house|agent
husbandman
impresario
incendiary
incumbency
inhabitant
inquisitor
instructor
ironmaster
ironmonger
ironworker
jewel|thief
job|hunting
job|printer
journalist
junk|dealer
kennelmaid
kitchenboy
kitchenman
knifesmith

OCCUPATIONS

land|holder	millwright	peacemaker
land|jobber	mind|curist	pearl|diver
landlubber	mind|healer	pearly|king
land|pirate	mindreader	pedestrian
land|waiter	ministress	pediatrist
lapidarist	missionary	pedicurist
laundryman	model|maker	penologist
law|officer	monopolist	perruquier
lay|brother	moonshiner	petitioner
leading|man	motley|fool	pharmacist
legislator	mouthpiece	piano|tuner
liberty|man	naturalist	piccoloist
librettist	nautch|girl	pickpocket
licentiate	naval|cadet	piermaster
lieutenant	negotiator	plagiarist
lighterman	neutralist	platelayer
lime|burner	newscaster	playbroker
linotypist	news|editor	playwright
livelihood	newsvendor	playwriter
lobsterman	newswriter	poet|artist
lock|keeper	night|float	poet|farmer
loggerhead	night|nurse	poet|priest
loomworker	notability	politician
lumberjack	nurseryman	postmaster
machineman	obituarist	prebendary
magistrate	occupation	priesthood
mail|robber	oil|painter	prima|donna
management	pallbearer	private|eye
manageress	pantomimic	procurator
manicurist	pantry|maid	profession
manservant	papermaker	programmer
medical|man	park|keeper	prolocutor
medicaster	park|ranger	proprietor
message|boy	pastrycook	prospector
midshipman	pathfinder	proveditor
militiaman	pawnbroker	questioner

quizmaster	songstress	timekeeper
railwayman	soundmixer	trafficker
rawrecruit	spacewoman	translator
recitalist	specialist	tripehound
researcher	speculator	tripewoman
retirement	spycatcher	trombonist
revenueman	staffnurse	tweedledee
revivalist	starmonger	tweedledum
rhapsodist	steelmaker	typesetter
ringmaster	stepdancer	typingpool
roadmender	stewardess	underagent
ropedancer	stickupman	understudy
ropewalker	stockrider	undertaker
safeblower	stocktaker	vegetarian
salesclerk	stonemason	versemaker
salesforce	storesmith	versesmith
saleswoman	strategist	veterinary
saltworker	submariner	viceconsul
sanddancer	subscriber	vicemaster
schoolma'am	substitute	victualler
scrutineer	supercargo	vinegrower
sculptress	supervisor	wageearner
seacaptain	supplicant	wageworker
seamstress	swordsmith	wainwright
secondmate	symphonist	watchmaker
seminarian	syncopator	waterguard
sempstress	tallyclerk	wharfinger
serologist	tallywoman	wholesaler
serviceman	taskmaster	winebibber
sessionman	taxidriver	winewaiter
shanghaier	technician	wireworker
shipwright	technocrat	woodcarver
shopfitter	televiewer	woodcutter
shopkeeper	tenderfoot	woodworker
signwriter	thirdparty	woolcarder
sinologist	tilewright	woolcomber

OCCUPATIONS

wool|sorter
wool|winder
workfellow
working|man
workmaster
workpeople
worshipper
abecedarian
academician
accompanist
actor's|agent
antiquarian
appointment
army|officer
astrologist
astronomist
audio|typist
backroom|boy
bag|snatcher
bank|cashier
bank|manager
bargemaster
basketmaker
beauty|queen
bell|founder
beneficiary
billsticker
bingo|caller
bird|fancier
bird|watcher
board|member
body|builder
body|servant
boilermaker
boilersmith
breadwinner

bridgemaker
broadcaster
bronzesmith
bullfighter
bushfighter
businessman
candlemaker
car|salesman
chamberlain
chambermaid
charcoalist
cheerleader
cheesemaker
chiropodist
choirmaster
clairvoyant
clergywoman
coachwright
co,authoress
coffinmaker
cognoscenti
commentator
congressman
conspirator
contributor
conveyancer
co,ordinator
coppersmith
court|jester
crane|driver
crimewriter
crown|lawyer
cub|reporter
cypher|clerk
day|labourer
dean|of|women

delivery|man
demographer
distributor
double|agent
draughtsman
drill|master
drug|peddler
duty|officer
electrician
embroiderer
enlisted|man
entertainer
estate|agent
etymologist
executioner
extortioner
factory|hand
faith|healer
field|worker
fifth|column
fighting|man
filing|clerk
fingersmith
fire|brigade
fire|watcher
flag|captain
flag|officer
flat|dweller
flying|squad
foot|soldier
fruit|picker
funambulist
functionary
galley|slave
games|master
gentlewoman

ghostwriter	laundrymaid	night sister
ginger group	leading lady	night worker
glass blower	leaseholder	novelettist
glass cutter	ledger clerk	numismatist
grave digger	lifeboatman	office party
greengrocer	locum tenens	onion Johnny
gunman's moll	lollipop man	optometrist
haberdasher	Lord Provost	ornamentist
hairdresser	lorry driver	orthopedist
hair stylist	madrigalist	palaestrian
hammersmith	maidservant	pamphleteer
handservant	mandolinist	panelbeater
hardwareman	manipulator	panel doctor
head teacher	masquerader	papal nuncio
hedgepriest	master baker	paperhanger
high sheriff	matinee idol	paragrapher
high society	mechanician	parish clerk
home crofter	medicine man	parlourmaid
horse doctor	memorialist	pathologist
horse trader	merchantman	pearlfisher
housekeeper	metalworker	pearly queen
housemaster	method actor	penny-a-liner
housemother	military man	petrologist
housewright	millionaire	philatelist
ice cream man	mimographer	philologist
illuminator	miniaturist	philosopher
illusionist	money lender	phonologist
illustrator	moonlighter	piece worker
infantryman	mother's help	police cadet
interpreter	mountaineer	policewoman
interviewer	music critic	portraitist
iron founder	naval rating	predecessor
kitchenmaid	needlewoman	prizewinner
lamplighter	neurologist	probationer
landscapist	night hunter	protagonist
land steward	night porter	proof reader

purseholder
questionist
quill driver
radiologist
rag merchant
rank and file
rear admiral
relic monger
research man
resignation
rhetorician
river keeper
roadsweeper
rocket pilot
rugby player
safebreaker
safecracker
sandwichman
saxophonist
school nurse
scorekeeper
scoutmaster
scrap dealer
scythesmith
search party
secret agent
semanticist
semaphorist
semi skilled
senior clerk
sharebroker
sheep farmer
shepherdess
shipbuilder
ship's cooper
ship's tailor

ship's writer
shop steward
silversmith
sister tutor
slaughterer
slave labour
slave trader
smallholder
sociologist
space doctor
spacewriter
speechmaker
stage player
stagewright
stallholder
steeplejack
stenotypist
stereotyper
stipendiary
stockbroker
stockfarmer
stockjobber
stonecutter
storekeeper
storyteller
straight man
stripteaser
subordinate
surrebutter
swordmaster
talent scout
taxidermist
telegrapher
telepathist
telephonist
terpsichore

testimonial
ticket agent
toastmaster
tobacconist
Tommy Atkins
tooth doctor
tooth drawer
town planner
toxophilite
train bearer
train robber
transcriber
travel agent
tree surgeon
truck farmer
typographer
upholsterer
van salesman
versemonger
vice admiral
vine dresser
viola player
war reporter
washerwoman
water doctor
water finder
welfare work
whalefisher
wheelwright
white collar
white hunter
witch doctor
woodchopper
wool stapler
working girl
workmanlike

xylophonist	cerographist	escapologist
youth|leader	check|weigher	exhibitioner
actor|manager	chicken|thief	experimenter
advance|party	chief|cashier	ex|service|man
air|commodore	chief|justice	exterminator
aircraftsman	chief|mourner	family|doctor
air|sea|rescue	chief|of|staff	father|figure
ambulance|man	chimney|sweep	field|marshal
anaesthetist	chirographer	field|officer
armour|bearer	chiropractor	figure|dancer
artilleryman	churchwarden	filibusterer
balladmonger	circuit|rider	film|director
ballad|singer	civil|servant	film|producer
ballet|dancer	civil|service	first|officer
bibliologist	clarinettist	first|reserve
bibliopegist	clerk|of|works	flying|column
board|meeting	coachbuilder	flying|doctor
body|snatcher	collaborator	footplateman
booking|clerk	commissioner	garret|master
bookstitcher	confectioner	general|agent
border|sentry	conquistador	geriatrician
bottlewasher	contemporary	globetrotter
boulevardier	corn|chandler	grandstander
bridgemaster	costermonger	group|captain
brigade|major	customs|clerk	guest|speaker
brinkmanship	deep|sea|diver	gynecologist
cabinet|maker	demonstrator	headmistress
calligrapher	desk|sergeant	headshrinker
camp|follower	doctor's|round	heir|apparent
candlewright	dramaturgist	high|official
caricaturist	ecclesiastic	hockey|player
carpet|bagger	electrotyper	holidaymaker
carpet|fetter	elocutionist	hotel|manager
cartographer	entomologist	housebreaker
casual|labour	entrepreneur	housepainter
cattle|lifter	equestrienne	hydropathist

OCCUPATIONS

immunologist   manual|worker   prison|warder
impersonator   manufacturer   prison|worker
improvisator   mass|producer   quarrymaster
in|conference   master|at|arms   racing|driver
inseparables   mastersinger   radiodontist
instructress   metallurgist   radiographer
intermediary   metropolitan   receptionist
jazz|musician   mezzo|soprano   remuneration
junior|rating   mineralogist   restaurateur
juvenile|lead   money|changer   retaining|fee
king's|counsel   monographist   sales|manager
kitchen|staff   motorcyclist   scene|painter
knifegrinder   musicologist   scene|shifter
knifethrower   naval|officer   schoolmaster
lady|superior   newspaperman   screenwriter
landed|gentry   notary|public   scriptwriter
land|surveyor   nutritionist   scullery|maid
law|stationer   obstetrician   sister|german
lay|out|artist   office|bearer   site|engineer
leader|writer   office|junior   snake|charmer
leathernecks   pastoral|poet   social|worker
legal|adviser   patent|office   soil|mechanic
letter|writer   pediatrician   sole|occupant
lexicologist   penitentiary   special|agent
line|sergeant   petty|officer   speechwriter
literary|hack   photographer   spiritualist
literary|lion   physiologist   sports|master
lithographer   plant|manager   sportscaster
longshoreman   ploughwright   sportswriter
loss|adjuster   plumber's|mate   staff|officer
maid|of|honour   poet|laureate   stage|manager
maitre|d'hotel   post|graduate   statistician
major|general   postmistress   steel|erector
make|up|artist   practitioner   stenographer
man|of|letters   press|officer   stereotypist
man|of|science   principal|boy   stonedresser

stormtrooper
street trader
tax collector
technologist
telegraph boy
telephone man
tennis player
test engineer
theatre nurse
ticket holder
ticket writer
top executive
trained nurse
trichologist
trick cyclist
troutbreeder
undermanager
vaudevillist
vice director
vice governor
warehouseman
water diviner
wind musician
wine merchant
wood engraver
worker priest
working party
workmistress
works manager
alongshoreman
antique dealer
archaeologist
articled clerk
audio engineer
barber surgeon
campanologist

church officer
civil engineer
coastguardman
common law wife
contortionist
contrabandist
cook housemaid
cotton spinner
counter jumper
craftsmanship
cryptographer
dancing master
dental surgeon
district nurse
feature editor
fellow servant
fencing master
fortune teller
guardian angel
gynaecologist
harbour master
health visitor
industrialist
lady in waiting
lift attendant
lighthouseman
livery servant
livery servant
lollipop woman
maid of all work
master builder
master mariner
night watchman
office manager
old clothes man
poultry farmer

OCCUPATIONS

printer's devil
prison visitor
process server
rag and bone man
rent collector
scrap merchant
ship's chandler
shop assistant
shop detective
skeleton staff
skilled worker
still room maid
street sweeper
toastmistress
traffic warden
universal aunt
window cleaner
window dresser
accomplishment
apprenticeship
audiometrician
black marketeer
bus conductress
busman's holiday
casual labourer
charcoal burner
chimney sweeper
clerical worker
coastguardsman
commissionaire
common informer
dramatic critic
elder statesman
gentleman usher
hotel detective
house decorator

house detective
king's messenger
labour exchange
maintenance man
market gardener
marriage broker
matron of honour
mining engineer
munition worker
naval architect
nursing officer
opposite number
prison governor
research worker
Reverend Mother
ship's carpenter
sports reporter
stage carpenter
stamp collector
standard bearer
station manager
store detective
street musician
superintendent
tobacco planter
troubleshooter
turf accountant
valet de chambre
blastfurnaceman
Bow street runner
colliery manager
commission agent
crossing sweeper
customs official
district visitor
Father Christmas

15 LETTERS

funeral director
gentleman farmer
gossip columnist
Jack of all trades
old age pensioner
one parent family
ophthalmologist
planning officer
police constable
police inspector
programme seller
Queen's messenger
research chemist

shorthand typist
shorthand writer
slave trafficker
stamp collection
stretcher bearer
surrogate father
surrogate mother
surrogate parent
ticket collector
tight rope walker
under cover agent
youth club leader

Oceans and Seas

Aegean
Arctic
Baltic
Red Sea
Aral Sea
Dead Sea
Java Sea
Kara Sea
Oresund
Ross Sea
Sulu Sea
Wash, The
Adriatic
Atlantic
Black Sea
Bosporus

Coral Sea
Kattegat
Korea Bay
Minch, The
North Sea
Spithead
Timor Sea
Azov, Sea of
Bantry Bay
Foxe Basin
Hudson Bay
Ionian Sea
Scapa Flow
Skagerrak
Solent, The
Yellow Sea

Zuider Zee
Aden, Gulf of
Andaman Sea
Arabian Sea
Bass Strait
Caspian Sea
Celebes Sea
Cook Strait
Delagoa Bay
Fundy, Bay of
Oman, Gulf of
Palk Strait
Riga, Gulf of
Siam, Gulf of
Aqaba, Gulf of
Beaufort Sea

OCEANS AND SEAS

Bengal, Bay of
Bismarck Sea
Cabot Strait
Dardanelles
Indian Ocean
Korea Strait
Lions, Gulf of
Menai Strait
Persian Gulf
Plenty, Bay of
Saronic Gulf
Solway Firth
Benin, Bight of
Darien, Gulf of
East China Sea
Greenland Sea
Guinea, Gulf of
Mannar, Gulf of
Marmora, Sea of
Mexico, Gulf of

Panama, Gulf of
Tonkin, Gulf of
Torres Strait
Bothnia, Gulf of
Corinth, Gulf of
Finland, Gulf of
Fonseca, Gulf of
Mediterranean
Pentland Firth
South China Sea
Taranto, Gulf of
Tyrrhenian Sea
Van Diemen Gulf
Albemarle Sound
Bristol Channel
English Channel
Macassar Strait
Magellan Strait
Malacca, Strait of
Messina, Strait of

Physical Sciences

AU	coil	lens	unit	cycle	light
amp	core	mass	volt	field	meson
erg	echo	phon	wane	flame	optic
lab	flex	pile	watt	focus	orbit
ray	flux	pion	wave	force	phase
wow	foam	pole	X,ray	gauss	polar
atom	foci	rays	anion	henry	power
beam	fuse	rule	anode	hertz	quark
cell	heat	tone	curie	laser	radar

relay	siphon	density	science
solve	solder	diagram	Sputnik
sound	stress	Doppler	tensile
spark	syphon	dry|cell	tension
steam	theory	elastic	torsion
A|blast	thrust	entropy	vernier
aerial	torque	EURATOM	voltage
albedo	vacuum	fall|out	aerology
ampere	vortex	fatigue	aerostat
atomic	weight	fissile	alpha|ray
baffle	actinon	fission	angstrom
boffin	adaptor	gilbert	anode|ray
bolide	aerator	gimbals	antinode
cation	airlock	gravity	armature
charge	air|pump	heating	atmology
degree	ammeter	impulse	atomizer
dipole	aneroid	inertia	Avogadro
dynamo	angular	isotone	beta|rays
energy	antenna	isotope	betatron
Geiger	aphotic	kiloton	bevatron
H|blast	atomics	megaton	cassette
ignite	atomism	missile	constant
isobar	aureole	monitor	delta|ray
kation	azimuth	neutron	detector
magnet	battery	nuclear	deuteron
megohm	beta|ray	nucleon	dew|point
metric	binocle	nucleus	electron
micron	bipolar	off|peak	enthalpy
mirror	capsule	ohmeter	equation
nuclei	cathode	physics	eutectic
opaque	chamber	positon	excitant
optics	circuit	project	fast|pile
proton	control	quantum	filament
quasar	crystal	radical	formulae
radome	current	reactor	freezing
sensor	decibel	rontgen	friction

PHYSICAL SCIENCES

fuel|cell	pressure	apparatus
gamma|ray	radiator	atom|blast
gas|laser	reaction	atomicity
half₁life	reactive	atomology
harmonic	receiver	barograph
heat|sink	recorder	barometer
hologram	red|shift	baroscope
ignition	research	binocular
impeller	resistor	blast|wave
inductor	rheostat	bolometer
infra₁red	roentgen	Boyle's|law
injector	scanning	canal|rays
ion|drive	scissile	capacitor
ionizing	sine|wave	capillary
iriscope	slow|pile	cold|short
klystron	Space|age	condenser
laser|gun	spectrum	conductor
magic|eye	sub₁atoms	converter
mesotron	thruster	cosmic|ray
molecule	unit|cell	cosmogony
momentum	velocity	cosmology
negative	watt₁hour	cosmotron
negatron	wave|form	countdown
neutrino	X₁ray|tube	cryoscope
nucleate	zoetrope	ctyogenic
ohmmeter	zoom|lens	cyclotron
overload	acoustics	dead|point
paradigm	activated	deflector
particle	activator	deionizer
peak|load	adiabatic	detonator
physical	advection	dineutron
pinacoid	air|pocket	discharge
polarity	altimeter	elastance
positive	amplitude	electrode
positron	annealing	equipoise
power|cut	aperiodic	explosion

field|coil	megascope	stability
flotation	mesic|atom	stop|clock
flow|meter	mesotrons	subatomic
focimeter	microfilm	telephony
frequency	microtron	telescope
galvanize	microwave	threshold
gamma|rays	moderator	time|clock
gyroscope	molecular	tolerance
heat|index	monatomic	triatomic
heliostat	multipole	video|tape
holograph	Newtonian	voltmeter
hydration	phonemics	wattmeter
hydrostat	photocell	wave|guide
hygrostat	physicist	wire|gauge
indicator	pitot|tube	wire|photo
induction	plumb|line	air|cooling
inelastic	pneumatic	amphoteric
inventory	polar|axis	antiproton
isosteric	potential	atmosphere
kilohertz	power|pack	atomic|mass
laser|beam	proton|gun	atomic|pile
Leyden|jar	radiation	atomic|unit
libration	radiology	atom|rocket
light|wave	radio|rays	battery|jar
light|year	recording	biophysics
long|waves	reflector	bleep|bleep
lubricant	reservoir	Bohr|theory
Mach|front	resonance	calorifier
macrodome	scientist	carbonated
magnetism	scintilla	carbon|atom
magnetron	short|wave	catenation
magnifier	side|chain	cathode|ray
manometer	sound|wave	Centigrade
mechanics	spaceship	centrifuge
megacurie	spacesuit	cine|camera
megacycle	spacewalk	cobalt|bomb

329

collimator
combustion
compressor
controller
convection
corrugated
cryogenics
curiescopy
deep|freeze
degaussing
desiccator
Dewar|flask
distortion
elasticity
electronic
elongation
energetics
epithermal
estimation
evaporator
excitation
experiment
Fahrenheit
filter|pump
filter|tube
geophysics
gravimeter
heat|shield
horse|power
hydraulics
hypothesis
hypsometer
inductance
ionosphere
isonuclear
isothermal

laboratory
latent|heat
light|valve
Mach|number
macroprism
magnet|pole
mass|defect
mass|energy
mass|number
megaparsec
megascopic
metacentre
microcurie
micrograph
microphone
microscope
millicurie
multicurie
nanosecond
nucleonics
pentatomic
polycyclic
power|plant
projectile
pronucleus
propellant
propulsion
radiogenic
radiometer
radiometry
radioscope
radioscopy
radio|sonde
reactivity
reluctance
resilience

resistance
resolution
rutherford
scientific
short|waves
space|craft
spallation
stabilizer
step|rocket
supersonic
synchroton
tagged|atom
technology
telegraphy
television
tetratomic
thermistor
thermopile
thermostat
three|phase
time|switch
transistor
transition
triniscope
trochotron
voltameter
volt|ampere
water|gauge
water|level
wave|length
white|light
wind|tunnel
xerography
X,radiation
zwitterion
accelerator

11/12 LETTERS

accumulator
achromatism
actinic|rays
actinometer
anticathode
antineutron
atom|counter
atomic|clock
atomologist
atom|smasher
Auger|effect
baffle|plate
barycentric
bifocal|lens
capillarity
carnot|cycle
cathode|rays
coefficient
conductance
crystalline
cytophysics
diffraction
dynamometer
echo|sounder
Einsteinium
electricity
electrolyte
electronics
engineering
epidiascope
fast|breeder
fibre|optics
fissionable
fluorescent
fluoroscope
fluoroscopy

free|radical
gravitation
gravity|cell
ground|state
heat|barrier
high voltage
iridescence
irradiation
isochronism
kinetic|body
landing|beam
light|shield
lyophilizer
macroscopic
manipulator
opeidoscope
open|circuit
photography
photosphere
polarimeter
polarimetry
polarograph
positive|ray
primary|cell
quantum|jump
radiant heat
radioactive
radio|beacon
radiologist
reactor|pile
regenerator
retro rocket
Rontgen|rays
rule|of|thumb
space|rocket
stroboscope

supercooled
technocracy
temperature
thermionics
thermoduric
thermograph
thermometer
transformer
transmitter
tripod|stand
troposphere
ultrasonics
vacuum|flask
acceleration
acceptor|atom
actinic|glass
aerodynamics
afterburning
Angstrom|unit
antineutrino
antiparticle
astronautics
astrophysics
atomic|energy
atomic|number
atomic|theory
atomic|weight
atom smashing
boiling|point
burning|glass
burning|point
carat|balance
central|force
chain|reactor
cloud|chamber
condensation

critical|mass
crystallites
deceleration
deflagration
displacement
electric|cell
electric|lamp
electron|pair
electronvolt
electroscope
experimental
extranuclear
fluorescence
galvanometer
geomagnetism
high|fidelity
hyperphysics
iatrophysics
infra,red|lamp
interference
law|of|gravity
luminescence
macrophysics
microammeter
microphysics
millerontgen
mirror|nuclei
nuclear|force
nuclear|power
optical|laser
oscilloscope
photofission
photoneutron
polarization
positive|rays
power|reactor

power|station
quantization
radio|compass
reactivation
refrigerator
Roentgen|rays
scintillator
selenium|cell
short|circuit
smash|the|atom
solar|battery
solar|physics
space|station
specific|heat
split|the|atom
stereophonic
stereopticon
stratosphere
thermoscopic
transmission
unified|field
Van|Allen|belt
vaporization
wave|function
X,ray|spectrum
amplification
Appleton|layer
astrophysical
Auger|electron
camera|obscura
chain|reaction
compressed|air
critical|angle
decompression
demonstration
direct|current

discharge tube
Doppler effect
electric field
electric light
electric meter
electromagnet
electrostatic
ferromagnetic
freezing point
Geiger counter
graticulation
heat resistant
high frequency
hydroelectric
kinetic energy
magnetic field
magnetic north
magnetic poles
magnetisation
non conducting
photo electric
quantum theory
radioactivity
radiolocation
semiconductor
spring balance
telephoto lens
thermonuclear
tracer element
under pressure
anacoustic zone
applied science
astrophysicist
audio frequency
bioelectricity
breeder reactor

cathode ray tube
circuit breaker
counter current
disintegration
eigen frequency
electronically
heavier than air
Heaviside layer
magnetic needle
microcomponent
nuclear fission
nuclear physics
nuclear powered
nuclear reactor
phantom circuit
printed circuit
radio telescope
surface tension
thermodynamics
torsion balance
transverse wave
trickle charger
tuner amplifier
centre of gravity
crystallography
electrification
electroanalysis
electrodynamics
electrokinetics
electromagnetic
horseshoe magnet
magneto electric
microtechnology
nuclear reaction
optical illusion
Planck's constant

potential|energy   specific|gravity
specific|gravity   ultra|violet|rays

Plants

bur	ling	blade	panic	borage
fog	lint	bract	plant	bryony
hay	mint	camas	radix	burnet
ivy	moly	canna	ramie	cacoon
mow	moss	caper	rubia	cactus
poa	otto	clary	scrub	camass
rue	peat	clove	sedge	catnip
sod	rape	couch	senna	caulis
tea	reed	cumin	sisal	clover
balm	rhea	cycad	sprig	cockle
bent	rush	dagga	starr	coffee
bixa	rust	dulse	stoma	corkir
burr	sage	erica	sward	cotton
cane	soma	fitch	tansy	crotal
culm	star	frond	thyme	croton
dill	tare	fucus	umbel	cummin
dock	taro	fungi	vetch	darnel
fern	tuft	gemma	wrack	eringo
flax	turf	gloom	yeast	fescue
gale	weed	grass	yucca	fucoid
gall	woad	halfa	acacia	fungus
hemp	abaca	heath	agaric	hedera
herb	abrus	lemna	albino	hyssop
jute	algae	liana	arabis	indigo
kelp	anise	musci	aralia	jungle
lawn	aspic	orpin	balsam	kissme
leaf	basil	osier	bamboo	knawel

lalang	twitch	dogbane	seaweed
lichen	acerose	esparto	seedbox
madder	alecost	foxtail	sorghum
mallee	alfalfa	frogbit	spignel
manioc	alkanet	genista	spurrey
maquis	allheal	ginseng	statice
marram	amanita	guarana	stipule
marrum	aniseed	guayule	tanghin
medick	armilla	hawkbit	tarweed
myrica	auricle	hayseed	tendril
nettle	benthos	heather	thistle
nostoc	bistort	hemlock	timothy
origan	bogbean	henbane	tobacco
orpine	bogmoss	herbage	trefoil
oxalis	bracken	hogweed	truffle
pampas	bugloss	honesty	tussock
pappus	bulrush	labiate	vanilla
phylum	burdock	linseed	verdant
raffia	calamus	lucerne	verdure
ramson	caltrop	lycopod	vervain
redtop	cambium	mayweed	zedoary
sapium	caraway	melilot	zizania
seamat	carline	milfoil	abutilon
sesame	cassava	mudwort	acanthus
simple	catmint	mustard	angelica
sobole	cat'sear	opuntia	asphodel
sorrel	clivers	osmunda	bedstraw
spurge	clotbur	papyrus	bignonia
spurry	cowbane	pinguin	bindweed
squill	cowweed	redroot	blueweed
stolon	creeper	rhizome	boggrass
storax	crinoid	rootage	buckbean
sundew	crottle	saguaro	canaigre
tangle	curcuma	sampire	cardamom
teasel	deutzia	seareed	cat'sfoot
thrift	dittany	seatang	cat'stail

caulicle	knapweed	samphire
centaury	knapwood	sargasso
charlock	knotweed	seaberry
cleavers	lady|fern	sea|blite
clubmoss	licorice	seagrape
clubrush	mandrake	sea|holly
cocculus	marjoram	sea|wrack
conferva	medicago	seedcase
costmary	meristem	seed|leaf
cow|grass	milkweed	shamrock
cow|plant	milkwort	soapwort
cow|wheat	moonwort	spergula
cut|grass	mushroom	spigelia
death|cap	offshoot	spikelet
death|cup	origanum	starwort
dicentra	peat|moss	take|root
dock|leaf	phyllome	tamarisk
dog|grass	pillwort	tarragon
dog|wheat	pinkroot	toad|flax
dropwort	plantage	tree|fern
duckweed	plantain	tree|lily
eel|grass	plant|pot	tree|moss
egg|plant	plantule	tremella
fernshaw	plumbago	tuberose
fireweed	pokeweed	turmeric
flaxseed	pondweed	valerian
gas|plant	puffball	vasculum
glory|pea	purslane	waybread
goatweed	ratsbane	xanthium
greenery	red|algae	acrospire
gulfweed	reed|mace	arrowhead
hedgerow	ribgrass	arrowroot
hepatica	rockweed	arrowroot
hibiscus	root|knot	artemisia
honeydew	ryegrass	astrofell
ice|plant	saltwort	baldmoney

9 LETTERS

bearberry
beech|fern
bent|grass
bird's|foot
bird's|nest
birthwort
bloodroot
bluegrass
bog|myrtle
bog|orchid
bracteole
broomrape
cane|sugar
carrageen
catchweed
centaurea
chain|fern
chickweed
China|root
cockscomb
coral|root
coriander
crab|grass
crazyweed
crosswort
cryptogam
cup|lichen
desert|pea
dittander
dock|cress
duck's|meat
dyer's|weed
earth|star
euphorbia
fairy|ring
fenugreek

flagellum
fly|agaric
galingale
gama|grass
gemmation
germander
glasswort
goosefoot
gramineae
greenweed
ground|ivy
groundsel
hair|grass
halophyte
herbarium
holly|fern
holy|grass
horehound
hornwrack
horsetail
house|leek
idioblast
involucre
Irish|moss
knotgrass
laserwort
leaf|mould
lemon|weed
liquorice
liverwort
luxuriant
lyme|grass
mare's|tail
marijuana
marsh|fern
marshwort

mesophyte
milk|vetch
mistletoe
monk's|hood
musk|plant
navelwort
overgrown
pellitory
pennywort
plant|life
poison|ivy
polygonum
portulaca
quillwort
reed|grass
rocambole
rock|brake
rockcress
rock|plant
royal|fern
sand|grain
sand|grass
scale|moss
screw|pine
seabottle
seagirdle
sea|tangle
silk|grass
sisal|hemp
smartweed
snakeroot
snowplant
spearmint
spikenard
star|grass
stinkweed

337

stonecrop
stonewort
sugar|cane
sun|spurge
sweet|flag
sweetgale
tear|grass
toadstool
toothwort
vernation
water|fern
water|leaf
water|vine
waterweed
wire|grass
worm|grass
aftergrass
arrow|grass
aspidistra
beard|grass
bitterroot
brown|algae
bunch|grass
butterwort
Canada|rice
China|grass
couch|grass
cow|chervil
cow|parsley
cow|parsnip
dead|nettle
dog|parsley
dog's|fennel
dyer's|broom
elecampane
glasshouse

goat's|beard
golden|seal
goosegrass
grama|grass
grasswrack
green|algae
greenhouse
greensward
hemp|nettle
herb|garden
Indian|hemp
indigenous
Jimson|weed
lemon|grass
lycopodium
maidenhair
maidenweed
malaguetta
mandragora
Manila|hemp
manna|grass
motherwort
musk|mallow
new|mown|hay
nipplewort
orangeroot
penny|cress
pennyroyal
peppermint
pepperwort
photometry
planthouse
plume|grass
restharrow
sand|binder
sea|burdock

sea|lettuce
sea|whistle
second|crop
seed|vessel
semination
shield|fern
sisal|grass
slime|mould
spear|grass
spiderwort
springwort
stitchwort
strike|root
sword|grass
thale|cress
transplant
tree|mallow
tumbleweed
vegetation
wall|pepper
waterbloom
wilderness
wild|indigo
willow|weed
Adam's|needle
alpine|plant
bellheather
blue|thistle
bur|marigold
canary|grass
chanterelle
chive|garlic
cotton|grass
cotton|plant
cruciferous
cypress|knee

dame's violet
dog's mercury
dyer's rocket
false acacia
finger grass
French berry
fuller's herb
garden stuff
germination
giant cactus
graft hybrid
green dragon
guinea grass
hart's tongue
horseradish
Iceland moss
kidney vetch
lady's finger
leopardbane
luxuriation
manna lichen
marram grass
myrtle grass
oyster plant
pampas grass
peppergrass
potting shed
pullulation
ribbon grass
Roman nettle
root climber
rubber plant
salad burnet
scurvy grass
sea furbelow
sea lavender

sea milkwort
sea purslane
sesame grass
Spanish moss
swallow wort
switch grass
thistledown
tree creeper
viper's grass
water meadow
water pepper
water violet
wintergreen
witches meat
bladderwrack
buffalo grass
climbing fern
conservatory
esparto grass
feathergrass
fool's parsley
forcing house
green fingers
hassock grass
hound's tongue
Jacob's ladder
lady's fingers
lady's thistle
orchard grass
sheep's fescue
skunk cabbage
snuffbox bean
Spanish cress
Spanish grass
staghorn moss
Timothy grass

PLANTS

tobacco plant	Scotch thistle
umbelliferae	water crowfoot
Venus fly trap	chincherinchee
waterhemlock	circumnutation
watermilfoil	classification
white heather	evergreen plant
zantedeschia	flowering plant
elephant grass	mountain sorrel
golden thistle	Shepherd's purse
horse mushroom	wood nightshade
lady's bedstraw	Virginia creeper
meadow saffron	virgin territory
noli me tangere	woody nightshade

Political Leaders

Fox	Bevan	Caesar	Allende
Blum	Bevin	Carson	Ataturk
Eden	Botha	Castro	Baldwin
Grey	Derby	Cripps	Balfour
Hess	Heath	Curzon	Bolivar
Marx	Laval	Dulles	Canning
Meir	Lenin	Franco	Goering
More	Nehru	Ghandi	Hampden
Nagy	North	Hitler	Hertzog
Peel	Obote	Kaunda	Himmler
Pitt	Peron	Mobutu	Kosygin
Tito	Smuts	Nasser	Luthuli
Tojo	Spaak	Pelham	Mandela
Banda	Attlee	Stalin	Masaryk
Benes	Brandt	Wilson	Menzies
Beria	Bright	Wolsey	Molotov

Nkrumah	Verwoerd
Nyerere	Ben Gurion
Parnell	Bonaparte
Reynaud	Chou en Lai
Russell	Churchill
Salazar	Gaitskell
Trotsky	Garibaldi
Trudeau	Gladstone
Walpole	Gorbachev
Aberdeen	Ho Chi Minh
Adenauer	Kissinger
Andropov	Lafayette
Augustus	Liverpool
Bismarck	Macdonald
Bonar Law	Macmillan
Brezhnev	Melbourne
Bulganin	Mussolini
Burghley	Richelieu
Caligula	Salisbury
Cosgrave	Shelburne
Cromwell	Stevenson
Crossman	Vishinsky
de Gaulle	Alcibiades
de Valera	Che Guevara
Disraeli	Clemenceau
Goebbels	Mao Tse tung
Kenyatta	Metternich
Kruschev	Palmerston
Malenkov	Ribbentrop
McCarthy	Stresemann
Napoleon	Talleyrand
Perceval	Castlereagh
Pericles	Chamberlain
Poincaré	Demosthenes
Rosebery	Douglas Home
Thatcher	Machiavelli

POLITICAL LEADERS

Robespierre	Bandaranaike	Mendes France
Shaftesbury	Julius Caesar	Themistocles

Presidents of the USA

Ford	Pierce	Coolidge
Polk	Reagan	Fillmore
Taft	Taylor	Garfield
Adams	Truman	Harrison
Grant	Wilson	McKinley
Hayes	Harding	Van Buren
Nixon	Jackson	Cleveland
Tyler	Johnson	Jefferson
Arthur	Kennedy	Roosevelt
Carter	Lincoln	Eisenhower
Hoover	Madison	Washington
Monroe	Buchanan	

Relations

ma	mother	divorcee
pa	nephew	grandson
dad	nuncle	helpmeet
kin	orphan	relation
mum	parent	relative
son	senior	son|in|law
aunt	sister	spinster
heir	spouse	triplets
kith	suitor	boy|friend
sire	bestman	firstborn
twin	brother	forebears
mater	cognate	godfather
mummy	consort	godmother
niece	dowager	grand|aunt
pater	fiancée	great|aunt
scion	heiress	kid|sister
sonny	husband	kinswoman
twins	kindred	next|of|kin
uncle	kinsman	offspring
widow	mankind	patriarch
agnate	partner	antecedent
auntie	progeny	babe|in|arms
cousin	sibling	bridegroom
father	stepson	bridesmaid
fiancé	widower	forefather
frater	ancestor	grandchild
godson	bachelor	grand|niece
infant	children	grand|uncle
junior	daughter	grass|widow

RELATIONS

great uncle	blood relation
half sister	Bob's your uncle
kid brother	brotherliness
kith and kin	close relative
maiden aunt	consanguinity
seventh son	daughter in law
son and heir	direct descent
stepfather	distant cousin
stepmother	family reunion
stepsister	first begotten
sweetheart	flesh and blood
blood sister	foster brother
father in law	granddaughter
first cousin	greatgrandson
foster child	identical twin
grandfather	intermarriage
grandmother	marriage lines
grandnephew	materfamilias
grandparent	progenitorial
half brother	fairy godmother
mother in law	foster daughter
sister in law	husband and wife
step brother	identical twins
blood brother	in loco parentis
brother in law	mother and child
cousin german	mother's darling
Darby and Joan	distant relative
foster father	every mother's son
foster mother	greatgrandchild
foster parent	honeymoon couple
foster sister	mother and father
heir apparent	rude forefathers
natural child	surrogate father
near relation	surrogate mother
second cousin	surrogate parent
stepdaughter	wife and children
blood brothers	

Religions

alb	halo	tomb	chela	Hades
ark	harp	tope	choir	Islam
goy	Hell	veil	cotta	Jewry
pew	holy	vows	credo	judge
pie	hymn	wake	creed	knell
pye	icon	zeal	creed	Koran
pyx	idol	abbey	cross	lauds
RIP	joss	abbot	crypt	laver
see	keen	agape	curse	leper
sin	kirk	aisle	demon	Logos
vow	lama	Allah	Devil	magus
alms	mass	almug	dogma	Maker
ambo	monk	Alpha	druid	manna
amen	naos	altar	dulia	manse
apse	nave	ambry	elder	Mazda
bell	oath	amice	ephod	Mecca
bema	pall	angel	exile	Medes
bier	Pope	apron	extol	Media
bull	pray	apsis	faith	mitre
cant	pyre	banns	fanon	motet
cell	raga	beads	feral	mound
cope	rite	Bible	Flood	myrrh
cowl	robe	bigot	friar	Negeb
cure	rood	bless	frock	nones
dean	sect	cairn	glebe	Omega
dome	seer	canon	glory	padre
fast	sext	carol	goyim	paean
font	soul	cella	grace	pagan
guru	text	chant	grail	paten
			grave	

RELIGIONS

piety	cantor	Israel	papacy
pious	casket	Jesuit	parish
prior	censer	Jewish	parson
psalm	chapel	Jordan	pastor
rabbi	cherub	Josiah	plague
relic	chimer	josser	postil
saint	chrism	jubbah	prayer
Satan	church	keener	preach
scarf	clergy	latria	priest
Solon	cleric	lector	primus
spire	coffin	lemuel	priory
staff	corban	litany	pulpit
stall	curacy	litany	Quaker
stole	curate	magian	rector
stoup	deacon	manger	ritual
stupa	Deluge	mantle	rochet
Sumer	devout	mantra	rosary
synod	diadem	manual	rubric
taber	divine	martyr	sacred
tiara	dolmen	matins	satrap
Torah	Easter	maundy	schism
tract	embalm	missal	Scribe
tunic	eunuch	Mormon	sedile
vault	famine	Moslem	Semite
vicar	fannel	mosque	sermon
abbess	Father	mullah	sexton
amulet	flamen	mystic	shaman
anoint	gospel	nimbus	shrine
anthem	hallow	nipter	shroud
armlet	hearse	novena	sinner
barrow	Heaven	novice	sister
beadle	Hebrew	office	stalls
bishop	heresy	ordain	Sunday
Brahma	hermit	orison	suttee
Buddha	homage	pagoda	tablet
burial	homily	palace	talent

Talmud	chaplet	godhead	mourner
temple	chapman	goodman	muezzin
tierce	chapter	gradino	mummify
tippet	charity	heathen	narthex
unholy	charnel	Hebrews	nunnery
vakass	chimere	heretic	obelisk
verger	chorale	holyday	oratory
vestry	collect	holysee	ossuary
vigils	complin	holywar	pallium
vision	convent	Hosanna	papyrus
zealot	convert	hymnary	parable
acolyte	cortege	Ichabod	periapt
Alcoran	Creator	impiety	pietism
almoner	crosier	impious	pilgrim
angelic	crozier	incense	piscina
angelus	crusade	infidel	pontiff
apostle	daysman	introit	prayers
ascents	Dead Sea	Jehovah	prebend
atheist	deanery	jubilee	prelate
Babylon	deodate	Judaism	primate
baptism	devotee	keening	profane
Baptist	diocese	Lambeth	prophet
biretta	diptych	Lebanon	psalter
blessed	diviner	lectern	Puritan
bondage	doubter	lection	pyramid
bondman	Dry Mass	liturgy	pyx veil
brother	Eleazar	Low Mass	rabboni
burying	epitaph	maniple	raiment
buskins	Essenes	mastaba	Ramadan
cabbala	fanatic	memoria	Rameses
calotte	fasting	Messiah	rectory
Cantuar	frontal	Messias	religio
capuche	funeral	minaret	requiem
cassock	gaiters	minster	reredos
chancel	gentile	miracle	retable
chantry	glorify	mission	Sabbath

RELIGIONS

sanctum	beadsman	delubrum	hymn|book
sandals	bedesman	disciple	idolater
Saviour	believer	divinity	idolatry
sceptic	blessing	doctrine	Immanuel
scourge	bless|you	doxology	inner|man
secular	bondmaid	druidess	Jonathan
sedilia	brethren	embolism	lamasery
Semitic	breviary	Emmanuel	lay|vicar
serpent	Buddhist	Epiphany	lich|gate
service	canonics	Epistles	Lord's|day
session	canonize	evensong	Lutheran
Shammah	canticle	exegesis	marabout
sistrum	capuchin	exequial	Mass|book
soutane	cardinal	exequies	mediator
steeple	catholic	exorcism	megalith
stipend	cemetery	faithful	memorial
tonsure	cenotaph	funerary	menology
Trinity	ceremony	funereal	minister
tumulus	chaplain	Gentiles	ministry
tunicle	chasuble	God's|acre	monachal
unction	cherubim	Good|Book	monastic
Vatican	choirboy	governor	monolith
vespers	chrismal	Hail|Mary	monument
Vulgate	cincture	hallowed	mourning
worship	cloister	hecatomb	mozzetta
aetheist	compline	here|lies	neophyte
agnostic	conclave	hic|jacet	Noah's|Ark
Akeldama	corporal	High|Mass	obituary
Almighty	covenant	holiness	oblation
anathema	Creation	holy|city	offering
Anglican	credence	holy|coat	orthodox
antipope	credenda	Holy|Land	Paradise
Apostles	cromlech	holyrood	Parousia
Ave|Maria	crucifix	Holy|Week	Passover
basilica	Crusader	Holy|Writ	penitent
beadroll	dalmatic	Huguenot	Pharisee

pontifex	altar|desk	confessor
praise|be	altar|rail	converted
preacher	Apocrypha	cremation
predella	archangel	cupbearer
prie¡dieu	arch¡druid	deaconess
province	arch¡enemy	decalogue
psaltery	arch¡fiend	dei|gratia
publican	Ascension	desecrate
pyx|cloth	atonement	devotions
religion	baldachin	dignitary
Romanism	barbarian	dog¡collar
rood¡loft	Beatitude	dogmatics
sacellum	Beelzebub	Dominican
sacristy	black|mass	embalming
sanctity	blasphemy	episcopal
scapular	Calvinist	episcopus
seraphic	canonical	Eucharist
seraphim	cantharus	exchanger
Shepherd	canticles	family|pew
skullcap	Carmelite	firmament
Son|of|Man	carpenter	firstborn
surplice	cartulary	firstling
tenebrae	catacombs	fisherman
theology	catechism	footstone
thurible	cathedral	godfather
thurifer	celebrant	godliness
transept	cerecloth	godmother
versicle	cerements	godparent
vestment	Christian	good|works
viaticum	churchman	gospeller
vicarage	claustral	graveside
Wesleyan	clergyman	graveyard
ziggurat	cloisters	hagiarchy
Aaron's|rod	coadjutor	hagiology
adoration	Communion	headstone
Allelujah	concubine	Hereafter

heterodox	mummy|case	sacrarium
Hexateuch	Mussulman	sacrifice
hierarchy	mysticism	sacrilege
hierology	obsequial	sacristan
high|altar	obsequies	sainthood
holocaust	offertory	saintship
holy|cross	officiant	salvation
Holy|Ghost	orthodoxy	Samaritan
Holy|Grail	ossuarium	sanctuary
holy|table	Palestine	scapegoat
holy|water	papal|bull	scapulary
incumbent	Paraclete	schoolman
interment	parchment	Scripture
Israelite	parsonage	sepulchre
Jerusalem	patriarch	sepulture
joss|house	pay|homage	shewbread
joss|stick	Pentecost	Shintoist
Judas|kiss	prayer|mat	shovel|hat
Lamb|of|God	prayer|rug	spiritual
land|of|Nod	precentor	suffragan
last|rites	presbyter	synagogue
laudation	priestess	Synoptics
lay|reader	prime|song	testament
lay|sister	profanity	tombstone
loincloth	proselyte	triforium
Lost|Sheep	proseuche	undersong
mactation	prothesis	unfrocked
Magdalene	psalmbook	Unitarian
martyrdom	reliquary	unworldly
mausoleum	reverence	venerable
mercy|seat	righteous	Zoroaster
Methodist	rood|stair	zucchetta
monastery	rood|tower	zucchetto
Monsignor	rural|dean	absolution
mortcloth	sackcloth	allocution
Mosaic|law	sacrament	allotheist

almsgiving
altar|cloth
altar|front
altar|mound
altarpiece
amen|corner
Anabaptist
antichrist
Apocalypse
archbishop
archdeacon
arch|flamen
arch|priest
Armaggedon
Band|of|Hope
baptistery
bar|mitzvah
battle|hymn
Beatitudes
benedicite
benefactor
Bible|class
birthright
blind|faith
canonicals
Carthusian
catafalque
catechumen
chartulary
choirstall
Church|Army
church|bell
churchgoer
churchyard
Cistercian
clearstory

clerestory
cloistered
collection
Colossians
confession
consecrate
conversion
dedication
diaconicon
divination
doctrinism
Douay|Bible
encyclical
entombment
episcopacy
episcopant
Evangelist
Evil|Spirit
exaltation
false|piety
fellowship
Franciscan
funeral|ode
funeral|urn
godfearing
golden|calf
goody|goody
gravestone
hagiolatry
hagioscope
Hallelujah
Heptateuch
hierolatry
hieromancy
hierophant
high|church

high|places
high|priest
Holy|Family
Holy|Father
Holy|Orders
Holy|Spirit
Holy|Willie
House|of|God
hyperdulia
iconoclast
idolatrous
immolation
incumbency
inhumation
in|memoriam
irreligion
Jacob's|Well
Lady|chapel
Last|Supper
lay|brother
lectionary
lie|in|state
lip|service
Lord's|house
Lord's|table
magnificat
mantellone
Mark|of|Cain
missionary
Mohammedan
Mount|Sinai
Mount|Tabor
necropolis
Needle's|eye
pallbearer
papal|brief

RELIGIONS

Papal|Court	soothsayer	Christendom
paraphrase	superaltar	christening
Pentateuch	synthronus	church|court
Pharisaism	tabernacle	church|mouse
Philistine	tartuffery	City|of|David
phylactery	temperance	commandment
pilgrimage	temptation	communicant
pontifical	theologian	conventicle
poor|sinner	theologist	Convocation
praetorium	unbeliever	crematorium
prayer|bead	undertaker	crucifixion
prayer|book	veneration	Curia|Romana
prebendary	watch|night	decanal|side
Presbytery	widow's|mite	Divine|right
priesthood	wilderness	Epistle|side
procurator	worshipper	eschatology
prophetess	Wycliffite	family|bible
Protestant	agnosticism	first|fruits
Providence	altar|carpet	funeral|pile
regenerate	altar|facing	funeral|pyre
Revelation	apologetics	Geneva|bands
Roman|Curia	arch|heretic	Geneva|cloak
rood|screen	arch|prelate	good|tidings
Sabbath|day	aspergillum	graven|image
sacerdotal	Augustinium	Greek|Church
sacredness	Benedictine	hagiographa
sacrosanct	benediction	hagiologist
sanctimony	bishop's|ring	hierography
Scepticism	bitter|herbs	incarnation
Schismatic	blasphemous	irreligious
scholastic	body|and|soul	Kingdom|Come
Scriptures	Book|of|Books	kirk|session
secularism	burning|bush	last|offices
Septuagint	Catholicism	lawn|sleeves
sepulchral	chapel|royal	Lord|of|Hosts
shibboleth	choir|stalls	Lord's|prayer

Lord's supper	burial ground
missal stand	canonization
monasterial	cardinal's hat
Nicene Creed	chancel table
nullifidian	chapel of ease
original sin	chapter house
parish clerk	charnel house
paternoster	Charterhouse
patron saint	Chosen People
pillar saint	Christianity
pontificals	church living
pontificate	churchmaster
prayer wheel	church nation
Prodigal Son	church parade
protomartyr	churchwarden
pure in heart	City of Refuge
reading desk	collectarium
Reformation	Commandments
religiosity	Common Prayer
remembrance	confessional
requiem mass	confirmation
rest in peace	congregation
river Jordan	consecration
Sacred Heart	Coptic church
saintliness	Damascus road
Sanctus bell	Day of the Lord
sarcophagus	denomination
soteriology	ecclesiastic
take the veil	enshrinement
theological	fiery serpent
triple crown	frankincense
Vatican City	Garden of Eden
vine of Sodom	Good Shepherd
Virgin's Well	hagiographer
Wise Virgins	herald angels
Annunciation	Holy Alliance

Holy|of|Holies
Holy|Thursday
hot|gospeller
Jacob's|ladder
jot|and|tittle
Judgment|Hall
Judgment|Seat
Last|Judgment
major|prophet
marriage|vows
minor|prophet
money|changer
New|Testament
Old|Testament
prayer|carpet
Promised|Land
resting|place
Resurrection
Rose|of|Sharon
sacred|ground
sacrilegious
Sea|of|Galilee
Second|Coming
Sunday|school
thanksgiving
theologician
Three|Wise|Men
Tower|of|Babel
ultramontane
wear|the|cloth
winding|sheet
Abraham's|bosom
aggiornamento
Ancient|of|days
Anglo-Catholic
anthroposophy

Apostles|creed
archbishopric
archidiaconal
beatification
bidding|prayer
bottomless|pit
church|officer
church|service
communion|card
co-religionist
day|of|judgment
divine|justice
divine|service
ecumenicalism
eschatologist
excommunicate
high|churchman
holy|innocents
household|gods
household|gods
incense|burner
infant|baptism
Lambeth|degree
light|of|nature
moral|theology
morning|prayer
nonconformist
nonconformity
pantheistical
pantheologist
pectoral|cross
prayer|meeting
reincarnation
Salvation|Army
Zarathustrism
Anglican|church

apostolic|vicar
archiepiscopal
beatific|vision
cardinal|virtue
church|militant
communion|bread
communion|table
Dean|and|chapter
denominational
devil's|advocate
ecclesiastical
eschatological
evangelicalism
extreme|unction
fisherman's|ring
forbidden|fruit
high|priesthood
intercommunion
Latter|day|saint
mark|of|the|Beast
morning|service
mother|superior
Orthodox|Church
pastoral|letter
recording|angel
reformed|church
Revised|Version
sabbatarianism
sabbath|breaker
sign|of|the|cross
Society|of|Jesus

Tridentine|Mass
Zoroastrianism
anthropomorphic
anticlericalism
archiepiscopacy
archiepiscopate
articles|of|faith
chapter|and|verse
Christadelphian
Church|of|England
confessionalist
devil|worshipper
divine|messenger
episcopalianism
excommunication
General|Assembly
harvest|festival
Holy|Roman|Empire
Jehovah's|witness
laying|on|of|hands
Moral|Rearmament
new|English|Bible
odour|of|sanctity
Plymouth|brother
Presbyterianism
religious|belief
seven|deadly|sins
synoptic|gospels
ten|commandments
transfiguration

Rivers

Ob	Lena	Congo	Rhone	Ganges
Po	Maas	Douro	Saône	Hudson
Si	Main	Drava	Seine	Humber
Bug	Milk	Dvina	Siang	Iguaçú
Dee	Nile	Forth	Snake	Ijssel
Don	Oder	Foyle	Snowy	Irtysh
Ems	Ohio	Green	Somme	Japura
Esk	Oise	Havel	Spree	Jhelum
Exe	Ouse	Indus	Swale	Jordan
Han	Oxus	Ishim	Tagus	Kolyma
Lys	Para	James	Tiber	Leitha
Oka	Prut	Jumna	Torne	Liffey
Red	Saar	Jurua	Trent	Medway
Tay	Spey	Kasai	Tweed	Mekong
Usk	Suir	Lagan	Vitim	Mersey
Wye	Swan	Liard	Volga	Moldau
Aire	Taff	Loire	Volta	Murray
Arno	Tana	Marne	Weser	Neckar
Avon	Tees	Meuse	Xingú	Neisse
Ebro	Tyne	Negro	Yukon	Orange
Eden	Ural	Niger	Abdiel	Ottawa
Elan	Vaal	Osage	Amazon	Parana
Elbe	Wear	Peace	Angara	Ribble
Gila	Yalu	Pearl	Atbara	Sabine
Göta	Adige	Pecos	Chenab	Salado
Juba	Aisne	Piave	Danube	Sambre
Kama	Argun	Plate	Donets	Severn
Kura	Boyne	Purus	Fraser	St|John
Lech	Clyde	Rhine	Gambia	Struma

Sutlej	Waitaki
Thames	Yangtze
Tigris	Yenisei
Vilyui	Zambezi
Wabash	AmuDarya
Wharfe	Arkansas
Alabama	Cheyenne
Berbice	Chindwin
Bighorn	Colorado
Darling	Columbia
Derwent	Delaware
Dnieper	Dniester
Dubawnt	Dordogne
Garonne	Eastmain
Helmand	Flinders
Hooghly	Godavari
HwangHo	Hamilton
Krishna	Illinois
Lachlan	Missouri
Limpopo	Paraguay
Madeira	Parnaiba
Maritsa	Putumayo
Moselle	Savannah
Orinoco	Suwannee
Pechora	Wanganui
Potomac	Athabaska
Roanoke	Churchill
Salween	Euphrates
Scheldt	Irrawaddy
Senegal	Mackenzie
Shannon	Macquarie
SiKiang	Magdalena
Tsangpo	Murchison
Uruguay	Porcupine
Vistula	RioGrande
Waikato	Tennessee

RIVERS

Wisconsin	Brahmaputra	Murrumbidgee
Republican	Mississippi	Saskatchewan
Sacramento	Yellowstone	
Sr|Lawrence	Guadalquivir	

Shakespearean Characters

Ely	Jamy	Bigot	Feste	Philo
Nym	John	Blunt	Flute	Pinch
Say	Juno	Boult	Froth	Poins
Adam	Kent	Boyet	Ghost	Priam
Ajax	Lear	Bushy	Goffe	Regan
Anne	Luce	Butts	Gower	Robin
Bawd	Lucy	Caius	Green	Romeo
Bona	Moth	Casca	Helen	Rugby
Cade	Page	Celia	Henry	Sands
Cato	Peto	Ceres	Hymen	Snare
Davy	Puck	Cinna	Julia	Snout
Dick	Ross	Cleon	Lafeu	Speed
Dion	Snug	Corin	Lewis	Timon
Dull	Vaux	Court	Lovel	Titus
Eros	Wart	Cupid	Lucio	Tubal
Fang	York	Curan	March	Varro
Fool	Aaron	Curio	Maria	Viola
Ford	Alice	Denny	Melun	Adrian
Grey	Angus	Derby	Menas	Aegeon
Hero	Anjou	Diana	Mopsa	Aeneas
Hume	Ariel	Edgar	Osric	Albany
Iago	Bagot	Egeus	Paris	Alonso
Iden	Bates	Elbow	Percy	Amiens
Iras	Belch	Essex	Peter	Angelo
Iris	Bevis	Evans	Phebe	Antony

6/7 LETTERS

Armado	Gremio	Quince	Bedford
Arthur	Grumio	Rivers	Berowne
Audrey	Gurney	Rumour	Bertram
Banquo	Hamlet	Scales	Bourbon
Basset	Hecate	Scarus	Brandon
Bianca	Hector	Scroop	Calchas
Blanch	Helena	Seyton	Caliban
Blount	Hermia	Shadow	Camillo
Boleyn	Horner	Silius	Capulet
Bottom	Imogen	Silvia	Cassius
Brutus	Isabel	Simple	Catesby
Bullen	Jaques	Siward	Cerimon
Cadwal	Juliet	Strato	Charles
Caesar	Launce	Surrey	Chatham
Caphis	Le|Beau	Talbot	Claudio
Cassio	Lennox	Tamora	Conrade
Chiron	Lovell	Taurus	Costard
Cicero	Lucius	Thaisa	Cranmer
Cimber	Marina	Thomas	de|Burgh
Clitus	Morgan	Thurio	Dionyza
Cloten	Morton	Tranio	Douglas
Cobweb	Mouldy	Tybalt	Dumaine
Curtis	Mutius	Ursula	Eleanor
Dennis	Nestor	Verges	Escalus
Dorcas	Oberon	Vernon	Escanes
Dorset	Oliver	Wolsey	Flavius
Dromio	Olivia	Abraham	Fleance
Duncan	Orsino	Aemilia	Francis
Edmund	Oswald	Afriana	Gallius
Edward	Oxford	Agrippa	Goneril
Elinor	Pandar	Alarbus	Gonzalo
Emilia	Pedant	Alencon	Gregory
Exeter	Philip	Antenor	Helenus
Fabian	Pistol	Antonio	Herbert
Feeble	Pompey	Arragon	Holland
Fenton	Portia	Aumerle	Horatio

359

SHAKESPEAREAN CHARACTERS

Hotspur	Orleans	William	Eglamour
Iachimo	Othello	Abhorson	Falstaff
Jessica	Paulina	Achilles	Florence
Laertes	Perdita	Aemilius	Florizel
Lavache	Phrynia	Aufidius	Fluellen
Lavinia	Pisanio	Auvergne	Gadshill
Leonato	Proteus	Baptista	Gargrave
Leonine	Provost	Bardolph	Gertrude
Leontes	Publius	Bassanio	Grandpre
Lepidus	Quintus	Beatrice	Gratiano
Lorenzo	Richard	Beaufort	Griffith
Lucetta	Rutland	Belarius	Harcourt
Luciana	Salanio	Benedick	Hastings
Lymoges	Sampson	Benvolio	Hermione
Macbeth	Shallow	Berkeley	Isabella
Macduff	Shylock	Bernardo	Jack|Cade
Malcolm	Silence	Borachio	Jourdain
Marcade	Silvius	Bullcalf	Laurence
Marcius	Simpcox	Burgundy	Leonardo
Mardian	Slender	Campeius	Leonatus
Mariana	Solinus	Canidius	Ligarius
Martext	Stanley	Capucius	Lodovico
Martius	Suffolk	Carlisle	Lucentio
Messala	Theseus	Charmian	Lucilius
Michael	Thyreus	Clarence	Lucullus
Miranda	Titania	Claudius	Lysander
Montano	Travers	Clifford	Maecenas
Montjoy	Tressel	Cominius	Malvolio
Morocco	Troilus	Cordelia	Margaret
Mowbray	Tyrrell	Cornwall	Marullus
Nerissa	Ulysses	Cressida	Menelaus
Nicanor	Urswick	Cromwell	Menteith
Norfolk	Valeria	Dercetas	Mercutio
Octavia	Varrius	Diomedes	Montague
Ophelia	Vaughan	Dogberry	Mortimer
Orlando	Warwick	Don|Pedro	Overdone

Pandarus	Woodvile	Erpingham
Pandulph	Agamemnon	Ferdinand
Panthino	Aguecheek	Fitzwater
Parolles	Alexander	Flaminius
Patience	Antigonus	Francisca
Pembroke	Antiochus	Francisco
Pericles	Apemantus	Frederick
Philario	Archibald	Glansdale
Philemon	Arvigarus	Glendower
Philotus	Autolycus	Guiderius
Pindarus	Balthasar	Guildford
Polonius	Balthazar	Helicanus
Polydore	Bassianus	Hippolyta
Prospero	Biondello	Hortensio
Rambures	Boatswain	Katharina
Ratcliff	Bourchier	Katharine
Reignier	Brabantio	Lancaster
Reynaldo	Caithness	Lychorida
Richmond	Calpurnia	Macmorris
Roderigo	Cambridge	Mamillius
Rosalind	Cassandra	Marcellus
Rosaline	Chatillon	Nathaniel
Salarino	Cleomenes	Patroclus
Seleucus	Cleopatra	Petruchio
Somerset	Coleville	Polixenes
Stafford	Constance	Posthumus
Stephano	Cornelius	Rotherham
Thaliard	Cymbeline	Rousillon
Timandra	Dardanius	Salisbury
Titinius	Deiphobus	Sebastian
Trinculo	Demetrius	Servilius
Violenta	Desdemona	Simonides
Virgilia	Dolabella	Southwell
Volumnia	Donalbain	Thersites
Whitmore	Elizabeth	Trebonius
Williams	Enobarbus	Valentine

SHAKESPEAREAN CHARACTERS

Ventidius	Abergavenny
Vincentio	Artemidorus
Voltimand	Bolingbroke
Volumnius	Brackenbury
Worcester	Caius|Lucius
Young|Cato	John|of|Gaunt
Alcibiades	Lady|Capulet
Andromache	Mayor|of|York
Andronicus	Mustardseed
Anne|Boleyn	Philostrate
Antipholus	Plantagenet
Apothecary	Rosencrantz
Barnardine	Young|Siward
Brakenbury	Decius|Brutus
Buckingham	Guildenstern
Coriolanus	Julius|Caesar
Duke|of|York	Junius|Brutus
Euphronius	Marcus|Brutus
Fortinbras	Peaseblossom
Gloucester	Popilius|Lena
Holofernes	Sir|Toby|Belch
Hortensius	Titus|Lartius
Jaquenetta	Westmoreland
Longaville	Doll|Tearsheet
Lysimachus	Faulconbridge
Margarelon	Joan|la|Pucelle
Mark|Antony	Young|Clifford
Menecrates	Christopher|Sly
Montgomery	Launcelot|Gobbo
Proculeius	Metellus|Cimber
Saturninus	Northumberland
Sempronius	Octavius|Caesar
Somerville	Sextus|Pompeius
Starveling	Tullus|Aufidius
Touchstone	Menenius|Agrippa
Willoughby	Mistress|Quickly

Robin|Goodfellow   Titus|Andronicus
Sicinius|Velutus

Sports, Games and Pastimes

KO	jig	away	deck	hand	lido
PT	kit	bail	dice	hank	lift
TT	lap	bait	dive	heat	lock
ace	lbw	ball	doll	hike	loom
aim	leg	bank	drag	hold	loop
bat	let	base	draw	hole	love
bet	lie	beat	duck	home	ludo
bid	lob	bend	duel	hook	luge
bow	loo	bias	epee	hoop	lure
box	net	bike	fall	hunt	mall
bye	par	bind	fare	hype	meet
cap	peg	blow	file	iron	meld
cat	pin	blue	fish	I|spy	mile
cox	Pit	bout	fist	jack	nock
cue	pot	bowl	foil	jape	Oaks
cup	run	brag	fore	jest	oars
dan	set	buck	form	jive	odds
die	shy	calx	foul	joke	Oval
DIY	ski	card	gaff	judo	over
fan	tag	chip	gala	jump	pace
fun	tie	chop	game	kail	pack
gin	ton	club	gate	kill	pass
gym	top	coup	gear	king	pawn
hit	toy	crew	goal	kite	play
hop	try	dart	golf	lane	polo
jab	win	dash	grid	lark	pool
jeu	ante	deal	grip	leap	port

puck	trot	catch	fives	notch
putt	turf	chase	fling	ombre
quiz	walk	check	frame	ouija
race	whip	chess	going	pairs
raft	wide	chips	grass	parry
reel	wing	chute	green	pilot
reel	wire	climb	guard	pique
ring	wood	clubs	guide	pitch
rink	yo,yo	coach	gully	piton
rook	alley	conge	halma	pivot
ruck	angle	count	heave	point
ruff	arena	coupe	hobby	poker
rule	arrow	court	inner	polka
sail	baffy	craps	jetty	pools
seat	bathe	crawl	joker	prank
seed	baths	cycle	joust	pro,am
shot	baton	dance	kails	punto
side	bingo	darts	kayak	quart
skat	blade	debut	kendo	queen
skid	blind	decoy	kitty	racer
skip	bluff	Derby	knave	rally
skis	board	deuce	links	range
slam	bogey	diver	lists	relay
slip	bound	divot	loose	rouge
snap	bower	dormy	loser	rough
solo	bowls	drive	lotto	round
spin	boxer	dummy	lunge	rover
spot	break	eagle	mambo	rugby
suit	bully	evens	march	rules
sumo	caber	event	match	rumba
swim	caddy	eyass	medal	rummy
tack	cadge	fault	mid,on	sabre
team	canoe	feint	miler	samba
tice	caper	field	monte	scent
toss	cards	fight	morra	score
trap	carom	final	no|bid	screw

scrum	whist	castle	glider	marina
scull	abseil	centre	gobang	mascot
serve	akimbo	cestus	gobble	mashie
shaft	anchor	cha|cha	go|kart	maxixe
shoot	angler	chasse	golfer	merils
sight	anorak	cherry	googly	mid|off
skier	archer	chukka	ground	minuet
skiff	ascent	circus	gutter	misere
slide	at|ease	conker	hammer	morris
slips	attack	corner	hand|in	mud|pie
smash	bailer	course	hazard	murder
spear	banker	cradle	header	nelson
spoon	bidder	crambo	hearts	no|ball
sport	birdie	crease	helmet	opener
stake	bishop	crosse	hiking	paddle
stalk	bisque	cruise	hockey	pelota
steer	blocks	cup|tie	honour	period
strip	bookie	curler	hooker	piquet
sweep	borrow	dealer	hookey	player
swing	boston	dedans	hoop|la	plunge
sword	bowled	diving	hurdle	pocket
tally	bowler	dog|leg	hurley	pommel
tango	bowman	dormie	ice|axe	popgun
tarot	boxing	driver	jesses	puppet
title	bracer	dry|fly	jigsaw	putter
ton|up	bricks	eleven	jockey	puzzle
touch	bridge	equipe	jostle	quarry
track	bulger	euchre	jumper	quarte
trick	bumper	fencer	karate	quinze
trump	bunker	fisher	knight	quoits
twist	caddie	flight	lariat	rabbit
valse	can|can	flying	leader	racing
venue	cannon	gallop	leg|bye	racket
wager	canter	gambit	mallet	raffle
waltz	car|run	gaming	manege	ramble
wedge	casino	glider	marble	rapids

365

rapier	squash	yoicks	bubbles
rave_ιup	stakes	yorker	camp|bed
record	stance	ace|high	camping
remise	sticks	acrobat	captain
replay	stilts	address	capture
result	strike	also_ιran	carioca
rhumba	stroke	amateur	cassino
riddle	stroll	angling	catcher
riding	stumps	archery	century
roll|in	stymie	arm|hold	charade
roquet	sweeps	arm|lock	charter
rowing	swivel	assault	Chicago
rubber	tackle	athlete	chicane
rugger	target	back|row	chimney
runner	tarots	bad|calx	chipper
safari	tennis	balance	chukker
savate	threes	ballast	circuit
scorer	thrust	balloon	classic
sculls	thwart	bar|bell	compass
seance	tickle	bathing	couloir
second	tipcat	batsman	counter
seesaw	tiptoe	beguine	crampon
shimmy	tivoli	bezique	creases
shinny	torero	bicycle	cricket
shinty	touche	bidding	croquet
shorts	toy|gun	big|game	cue|ball
skater	trophy	bivouac	curb|bit
skiing	truant	bladder	curling
slalom	TT|race	blaster	cushion
sledge	umpire	boating	cutlass
soccer	versus	bonfire	cycling
spades	volley	bowling	cyclist
spikes	wicket	box|kite	dancing
spiral	willow	bracing	day|trip
sports	winger	bran|tub	decider
sprint	winner	brassie	declare

defence	goggles	leg|hold	pinball
descent	golf|bag	leg|side	pinfall
diabolo	golfing	let|ball	pin|high
diamond	golf|tie	line|out	pinocle
dicebox	good|fun	long|bow	pitcher
discard	grounds	long|hop	pit|stop
doubles	guy|rope	long|leg	play|off
drawing	gymnast	lottery	poloist
dribble	hacking	marbles	pontoon
driving	hairpin	matador	potshot
end|game	hand|off	maypole	press|up
end|play	harpoon	mazurka	prowess
en|prise	harrier	meccano	pyramid
entrant	hawking	melding	quarter
fairway	holster	midiron	rackets
fan|club	honours	netball	rag|doll
fencing	hunting	net|cord	rebound
fielder	hurdler	niblick	referee
fifteen	hurling	ninepin	regatta
fine|leg	ice|pick	no|trump	reserve
finesse	ice|rink	oarsman	ripcord
fishing	ikebana	offside	riposte
fixture	infield	old|maid	rockers
fly|half	innings	one|step	rosette
foot|bow	jackpot	on|guard	rowlock
formula	j|adoube	overarm	rubicon
forward	javelin	over|par	running
fox|hunt	jogging	paddock	sailing
foxtrot	joy|ride	pallone	sand|pie
free|hit	ju|jitsu	partner	sand|pit
Frisbee	keep|fit	passade	scooter
frogman	kick|off	passado	scratch
funfair	knock|up	pastime	service
gallery	lancers	penalty	seven|up
gavotte	landing	picador	shot|put
gliding	last|lap	picquet	shuffle

SPORTS, GAMES AND PASTIMES

shuttle	Torpids	body|blow	cross|bat
singles	tourney	bonspiel	cruising
singlet	trainer	boundary	cup|final
skating	tumbler	brackets	dark|blue
skid|lid	twosome	bullring	dead|ball
snaffle	two|step	bull's|eye	dead|heat
snooker	vantage	bully|off	deadlock
snorkel	vaulter	cakewalk	dead|shot
society	walking	campfire	delivery
soft|toy	war|club	camp|site	diamonds
sparrer	war|game	canoeing	dominoes
squails	workout	card|game	doubling
stadium	wrestle	carnival	dragster
stamina	ziganka	carousel	draughts
starter	aerobics	car|rally	draw|lots
stirrup	all|fours	castling	dressage
St|Leger	approach	catapult	drop|goal
striker	apres|ski	cat|stick	drop|kick
stumped	aqualung	champion	drop|shot
sub|aqua	aquatics	charades	dumb|bell
sun|bath	armguard	checkers	even|keel
tacking	away|game	chequers	even|odds
tactics	baccarat	chessman	exercise
take|off	backhand	chess|set	face|card
tally|ho	backheel	chin|hold	fair|play
tangram	backspin	chip|shot	falconer
tantivy	bail|ball	climbing	falconry
tenpins	balk|line	coasting	fandango
tent|peg	ball|game	contract	fast|ball
The|Oaks	baseball	cottabus	field|day
The|Oval	baseline	counters	finalist
throw|in	beagling	coursing	firework
tie|game	biathlon	coxswain	fistiana
tilting	biathlon	crap|game	fivepins
toe|hold	blocking	cribbage	flapping
tombola	boat|race	crossbar	flat|race

flippers	half ball	left wing	pall mall
floating	half blue	leg break	pass line
foilsman	half mile	leg guard	pass roll
foothold	half shot	lifeline	patience
foot race	half time	linesman	pike dive
footwork	handball	long game	ping pong
forehand	handicap	long jump	pinochle
forfeits	hat trick	long odds	pin table
foul goal	haymaker	long rush	playmate
foul line	headlock	long shot	playroom
foul play	helmsman	long stop	plunging
foursome	high dive	lost ball	polo ball
foxhound	high jump	love game	polo pony
free kick	holed out	lucky bag	pony trek
fretwork	hole high	lucky dip	pool room
front row	home game	mah jongg	port tack
full back	hornpipe	marathon	pugilism
full draw	horseman	marksman	pugilist
full toss	how's that	marriage	pushball
gambling	hula hoop	monopoly	pyramids
gamester	hula hula	motorist	quintain
gauntlet	huntsman	multi gym	quiz game
gin rummy	hurdling	napoleon	racegoer
goal kick	ice yacht	natation	radio ham
goalpost	Irish jig	ninepins	rambling
golfball	iron shot	nosedive	reaching
golf club	jiu jitsu	no trumps	recovery
golliwog	joystick	off break	red cloak
good cal x	knock out	off drive	redouble
good shot	korfball	Olympiad	ricochet
gridiron	lacrosse	open file	rink polo
guarding	lawn game	opponent	rope ring
gymkhana	leapfrog	outfield	roulette
gym shoes	left back	outsider	rounders
habanera	left half	oval ball	rucksack
halfback	left hook	paddling	runner up

Ruy|Lopez	stations	all,comers
sack|race	stoccado	all|square
sand|iron	stock|car	anchor|man
sand|trap	stop|shot	arabesque
saraband	straddle	arrow|shot
sardines	straight	astrodome
Scrabble	tap|dance	athletics
scramble	team|game	Aunt|Sally
scrum|cap	tent|pole	back|court
sculling	The|Ashes	back|edges
selector	the|field	back|swing
set|point	third|man	badminton
shell|out	thole|pin	bagatelle
shooting	tie|break	bandalore
short|leg	toreador	bandy|ball
side,blow	Totopoly	barn|dance
side|line	tracking	baulk|line
skin|game	trailing	beach|ball
ski|slope	training	best|bower
ski|stick	train|set	biathlete
skittles	tug,of,war	big|dipper
sledging	underarm	billiards
slow|ball	undercut	black|belt
snapshot	under|par	blackjack
snowball	upper|cut	black|pawn
snow|line	vaulting	bladework
softball	venation	boarhound
southpaw	walkover	boar|spear
sparring	wall|game	bobsleigh
speedway	wing|area	body|check
spoon|oar	wood|club	body|punch
sporting	wood|shot	bossa|nova
sprinter	wrestler	bowstring
stalking	yachting	brown|belt
stand|off	acey,deucy	caddie|car
stand|pat	advantage	camel|spin

card|trick	equalizer	grand|prix
cartwheel	exercises	grand|slam
cavalcade	extra|time	gum|shield
cha,cha,cha	face|guard	gymnasium
chair|lift	favourite	handstand
challenge	field|game	hard|court
checkmate	fieldsman	high|jinks
chess|game	first|half	hill|climb
clock|golf	first|seed	hitch|hike
clog|dance	first|slip	hit|wicket
closing|in	fisherman	hopscotch
club|house	fisticuff	horseback
collector	five,a,side	horseplay
combatant	fletching	horse|race
conjuring	flight|bow	ice|hockey
contender	flyweight	ice|skates
cotillion	foot|fault	infielder
court|card	fore|royal	jackknife
crackshot	forty,love	judo|throw
cricketer	free|reach	kennelman
cross|jack	freestyle	king's|rook
crossword	freewheel	lawn|bowls
cycle|race	full|house	left|bower
cycle|tour	galleries	left|inner
dance|step	game|point	leg|before
dartboard	gardening	leg|spread
decathlon	gladiator	light|blue
decoy|duck	goalposts	long|loser
disengage	go,karting	long|tacks
dog|racing	gold|medal	loose|ball
doll's|pram	golf|links	loose|maul
drawn|game	golf|range	loose|rein
dribbling	golf|shoes	love|forty
enclosure	golf|widow	love|match
en|passant	good|loser	low|volley
en|tout|cas	good|sport	match|play

medallist	quadrille	silver|cup
medal|play	quickstep	singleton
mid|mashie	race|track	skin|diver
motocross	racing|car	sky|diving
music|hall	relay|race	small|bore
Newmarket	relay|team	snow|climb
Nuts|in|May	right|back	solitaire
orienteer	right|half	solo|whist
pacemaker	right|hook	spectator
palaestra	right|wing	speedboat
panel|game	ringsider	spin|parry
pantomime	rock|climb	split|shot
paper|doll	roundelay	spoon|bait
parachute	round|game	sports|day
party|game	round|trip	sportsman
paso|doble	rover|hoop	spot|dance
passepied	safety|net	square|leg
Paul|Jones	sand|yacht	stable|boy
pelmanism	sauna|bath	stalemate
pen|friend	schnorkel	starboard
penthouse	score|card	steersman
philately	scrapbook	step|dance
pickaback	screw|dive	stopwatch
pilot|ball	scrimmage	stud|poker
pinch|draw	scrum|half	surfboard
pirouette	scrummage	sweatband
pitch|camp	second|row	swordplay
plaything	semi|final	swordsman
pogo|stick	shaftment	teddy|bear
poker|dice	shamateur	tennis|net
pole|vault	shinguard	terracing
polonaise	short|game	test|match
potholing	short|odds	the|sticks
puissance	shortstop	three|jump
punchball	shrimping	threesome
push|parry	signal|gun	three|turn

tight rein	blood sport	drop cannon
tip and run	booby prize	drop volley
torch race	boxing ring	equitation
touchdown	catch a crab	Eskimo roll
touch goal	cat's cradle	fairground
touchline	centre half	fantoccini
track suit	challenger	fast bowler
trump card	changeover	feathering
trump suit	charleston	fianchetto
turnstile	checkpoint	field event
twenty one	chessboard	field sport
twist dive	Chinese box	first blood
vingt et un	christiana	fishing net
water polo	clay pigeon	fishing rod
whirligig	coconut shy	flat racing
white pawn	competitor	fly fishing
wristlock	contestant	flying mare
yacht club	contractor	flying shot
yacht race	counted out	footballer
yachtsman	cover point	forced move
youth club	cricket bat	foundation
acrobatics	cricket net	fox hunting
aerobatics	crown green	free for all
agility mat	cyclo cross	full nelson
agonistics	daily dozen	gambit pawn
backgammon	decathlete	ghost train
back marker	deck quoits	goal circle
back stroke	deck tennis	goal crease
balneation	discobolus	goalkeeper
banderilla	diving bell	goal tender
basketball	doll's house	golf course
battledore	dolly catch	grandstand
bee keeping	double axle	gymnastics
betting man	double game	half bisque
binoculars	double peel	half nelson
blind poker	draw stumps	half volley

halieutics	kewpie|doll	playground
halved|hole	kite|flying	point|of|aim
handspring	kriegspiel	poker|chips
hard|tackle	lansquenet	polo|ground
Harrow|game	lawn|tennis	potato|race
hazard|side	league|game	prize|fight
headhunter	little|slam	prize|money
health|club	loaded|dice	punch|drunk
health|farm	loose|scrum	push|stroke
heel|and|toe	love|thirty	queen's|pawn
high|diving	maiden|over	queen's|rook
hitch|hiker	marionette	racecourse
hobbyhorse	marker|buoy	racing|cars
hockey|team	mashie|iron	ratcatcher
hog|hunting	match|point	real|tennis
horseshoes	middle|spot	recreation
horsewoman	minor|piece	relaxation
hunting|bow	non|starter	relegation
ice|dancing	object|ball	rifle|range
ice|skating	off|the|hook	right|bower
Indian|club	opening|bat	right|inner
Indian|file	open|season	right|swing
indoor|golf	open|target	ring|o|roses
injury|time	Ouija|board	rod|and|reel
inside|home	outfielder	roundabout
inside|lane	pancration	round|dance
inside|left	pancratium	rowing|boat
inside|lock	paper|chase	royal|flush
in|the|rough	par|contest	rubber|ball
in|training	pari|mutuel	rubber|duck
isometrics	passed|pawn	rugby|union
jackstones	penalty|try	rumpus|room
jackstraws	pentathlon	run|through
Jockey|Club	philatelic	rush|stroke
jump|the|gun	pigeon|loft	sand|castle
karate|chop	planchette	scoreboard

second half	suspension	willow wand
second slip	sweepstake	win by a head
seconds out	switchback	winning gun
second wind	sword dance	Yarborough
seven a side	take a trick	young entry
short tacks	tarantella	accumulator
show jumper	team spirit	baseball bat
sidesaddle	tennis ball	bearbaiting
side stroke	tennis shoe	bellringing
silly mid on	thirty love	Bengal spear
silly point	thrown goal	betting ring
single file	tiger badge	biased bowls
single game	timekeeper	big game hunt
skateboard	time thrust	boating pond
ski jumping	tin soldier	Bombay spear
skin diving	title fight	bow and arrow
ski running	toe scratch	boxing match
sky jumping	tournament	bronze medal
slow bowler	tour skiing	bull baiting
somersault	toy soldier	canoe slalom
speed trial	track event	casual water
spike shoes	trampoline	Channel swim
spin bowler	trial match	chariot race
sportswear	triple jump	cheer leader
spot stroke	triple peel	cinder track
square ring	true to form	class racing
stamp album	tumble turn	close season
stock cards	turkey trot	compact disc
stop thrust	twelfth man	country walk
strathspey	vantage set	county match
strike camp	Vardon grip	coup de grace
stroke play	volleyball	court tennis
submission	water wings	crash helmet
substitute	whippers in	crawl stroke
sun bathing	whist drive	cricket ball
surf riding	wilful foul	cricket pads

croquet|arch	fox|and|geese	modern|waltz
croquet|ball	free|skating	morris|dance
croquet|hoop	fun|and|games	motor|racing
croquet|lawn	gambit|piece	mountaineer
cross|swords	gambling|man	mystery|tour
curling|pond	gaming|house	nailed|boots
curling|rink	gaming|table	neck|and|neck
cycle|racing	garden|party	offside|rule
daisy|cutter	glove|puppet	Olympic|team
deck|of|cards	gone|fishing	out|of|bounds
deep|fine|leg	good|innings	outside|home
direct|party	grand|salute	outside|left
diving|board	groundsheet	pack|of|cards
diving|dress	hairpin|bend	pair|skating
double|check	half|passage	palaestrian
double|fault	halfway|line	pancake|race
downhill|run	heavyweight	pancratiast
driving|iron	hide|and|seek	parlour|game
egg|and|spoon	hitch|hiking	pawn|and|move
envelopment	hockey|match	penalty|area
eurhythmics	hockey|stick	penalty|goal
false|attack	home|and|away	penalty|kick
fencing|mask	horse|racing	penalty|line
Ferris|wheel	horse|riding	photo|finish
field|events	ice|yachting	picture|card
fifteen|love	inside|right	pigeon|flier
figure|eight	jumping|bean	pigeon|house
first|attack	king's|bishop	pigeon|timer
first|eleven	king's|knight	pig|sticking
fishing|line	lap|of|honour	pillow|fight
flick|stroke	league|table	piscatology
flying|start	lightweight	pitch|and|run
football|fan	lock|forward	playing|card
forced|error	loop|the|loop	playing|line
forward|line	love|fifteen	play|the|game
forward|pass	malibu|board	pole|vaulter

prizewinner	snowglasses	training run
prop forward	snowshoeing	transfer fee
public games	soft landing	triple crown
pyramid spot	spade mashie	Turkish bath
quarterback	speculation	waiting game
rabbit punch	spinning top	walking race
race meeting	sportswoman	water hazard
racing craft	spreadeagle	water skiing
racing shell	springboard	water sports
racket court	square dance	Western roll
record break	square tango	wine tasting
riddle me ree	squash court	wing forward
Roman candle	staghunting	winning post
rouge et noir	starting gun	winning time
round of golf	straight bat	win on points
royal tennis	striker ball	wooden horse
rugby league	sudden death	world record
Schottische	swallow dive	youth hostel
seam bowling	sweep rowing	anchor cannon
self defence	table tennis	approach shot
service grip	target arrow	back straight
service hold	tennis court	bantamweight
service line	tennis match	batting order
service side	tent pegging	beachcombing
shinty stick	Terpsichore	Becher's brook
shovelboard	theatregoer	billiard ball
show jumping	the Olympics	billiard hall
shuttlecock	third player	billiard room
sightseeing	three legged	billiard spot
silver medal	tiddlywinks	bingo session
simple parry	time sharing	bird watching
singing game	tobogganing	body building
skating rink	totalisator	bowling alley
skiing field	touring club	bowling green
sleeping bag	toxophilite	boxing gloves
slow foxtrot	track record	break dancing

break the bank	fast and loose	long distance
breast stroke	field glasses	loose forward
bull fighting	figure skater	losing hazard
butterfly net	first defence	maiden stakes
callisthenic	first innings	marathon race
century break	first reserve	medicine ball
championship	first service	melding score
change bowler	flying tackle	merry go round
change of ends	foursome reel	mincing steps
changing room	freewheeling	mixed doubles
checkerboard	French boxing	National Hunt
classic races	fruit machine	nature ramble
climbing rope	game of chance	noble science
cockfighting	game of points	nursery slope
consequences	gamesmanship	obstacle race
country dance	gone to ground	old time dance
cradle cannon	ground stroke	Olympic games
crapshooting	guessing game	Olympic title
cricket boots	handicap race	Olympic torch
cricket pitch	head scissors	opposing side
croquet court	hill climbing	ordinary foul
cross country	home straight	orienteering
curling stone	homing pigeon	orienteering
cut and thrust	horsemanship	outside right
dead ball line	housey housey	paddling pool
deep sea diver	hundred yards	parallel bars
direct cannon	hunting groom	penalty bully
directors box	in the running	penalty throw
disqualified	investigator	physical jerk
do it yourself	jack in the box	pigeon flying
double sculls	kaleidoscope	ping pong ball
doubles match	knucklebones	pitch and putt
double threes	lampadedromy	pitch and toss
dressing room	landing stage	playing cards
earth stopper	level pegging	playing field
Eton wall game	London Bridge	pleasure trip

point,to,point
pole|position
pony|trekking
prize|fighter
professional
Punch|and|Judy
punto|reverso
putting|green
quarter,final
queen's|bishop
queen's|knight
raffle|ticket
receiving|end
record|holder
redoublement
referee's|hold
return|crease
ride|to|hounds
riding|school
rock|climbing
rocking|horse
roller|skates
running|strip
sand|yachting
sand|yachting
scissors|jump
second|attack
second|eleven
second|player
shadow|boxing
sharpshooter
short|pinocle
shove|ha'penny
shrimping|net
shuffleboard
side|chancery

simple|attack
single|combat
single|sculls
singles|match
skating|boots
skipping|rope
slice|service
slippery|pole
soapbox|derby
speed|skating
sporting|life
sport|of|kings
stabbing|blow
stand,off|half
starting|grid
starting|post
steeplechase
sticky|wicket
stilt|walking
straddle|jump
stranglehold
strong|finish
Sunday|driver
sweep|oarsman
swimming|gala
swimming|pool
sword|fencing
table|turning
tennis|player
tennis|racket
tennis|stroke
three|quarter
tiddleywinks
toss|the|caber
train|spotter
trapshooting

treasure|hunt
treble|chance
trick|cyclist
trigger|happy
tunnel|of|love
umpire's|chair
vantage|point
Virginia|reel
weightlifter
welterweight
wicket|keeper
winter|sports
all|in|wrestler
auction|bridge
beauty|contest
big|game|hunter
billiard|table
blanket|finish
blind|man's|buff
bowling|crease
callisthenics
centre|forward
change|ringing
chequered|flag
climbing|frame
coarse|fishing
county|cricket
cribbage|board
cruiser|weight
double|or|quits
equestrianism
featherweight
figure|of|eight
figure|skating
finishing|post
fishing|tackle

follow|through
football|match
football|pools
funny|peculiar
ghetto|blaster
Grand|National
half|time|score
hare|and|hounds
helter|skelter
hide|and|go|seek
Highland|fling
Highland|games
hunting|ground
international
mashie|niblick
mixed|foursome
nightwatchman
nursery|slopes
peace|offering
physical|jerks
popping|crease
prisoner's|base
prizefighting
return|service
rollerskating
rough|shooting
rugby|football
Russian|ballet
second|innings
shooting|range
shooting|stick
sitting|target
skateboarding
sleight|of|hand
Space|Invaders
sportsmanlike

sportsmanship
sports|stadium
square|dancing
squash|rackets
stalking|horse
starting|price
starting|stall
steeplechaser
straight|flush
surface|worker
table|skittles
tenpin|bowling
three|day|event
train|spotting
ventriloquism
ventriloquist
vulnerability
weight|lifting
aerobic|dancing
approach|stroke
bathing|costume
bathing|machine
billiard|marker
catherine|wheel
champion|jockey
channel|swimmer
cock|a|doodle|doo
conjuring|trick
contract|bridge
country|dancing
crown|and|anchor
fancy|dress|ball
follow|my|leader
football|ground
football|league
golf|tournament

greyhound|Derby
grouse|shooting
halloween|party
high|cockalorum
hop,|skip|and|jump
hunt|the|slipper
marathon|runner
master|of|hounds
mountaineering
nine|men's|morris
nineteenth|hole
opening|batsman
pig|in|the|middle
prima|ballerina
putting|the|shot
ride|a|cock|horse
shove|halfpenny
sit|on|the|splice
smoking|concert
solitaire|board
spectator|sport
speedway|racing
squash|racquets
starting|blocks
starting|stalls
steeplechasing
stock|car|racing
supporters|club
three|card|trick
winter|Olympics
wrestling|match
amusement|arcade
appearance|money
Australian|rules
bodyline|bowling
catch|as|catch|can

cross country run
crossword puzzle
duplicate bridge
egg and spoon race
fancy dress dance
firework display
game, set and match
glorious Twelfth
hit below the belt
Indian rope trick
king of the castle
leg before wicket
nursery handicap
odds on favourite
pipped at the post
puss in the corner

rain stopped play
Roger de Coverley
Royal and Ancient
Russian roulette
shooting gallery
sparring partner
sports equipment
stable companion
stamp collecting
stamp collection
swimming costume
three day eventer
three legged race
three ring circus
throw in the towel
women's institute

Theatre

act	foil	solo	enact	stagy
bit	fool	spot	extra	stall
bow	gods	star	farce	stand
box	grid	tail	flies	still
cue	hall	text	floor	stunt
fan	hero	turn	focus	usher
gag	idol	tutu	foots	wings
ham	joke	unit	foyer	absurd
hit	lead	wing	front	acting
mug	line	zany	heavy	action
pit	loft	actor	house	act|out
rag	loge	ad|lib	lines	appear
rep	mask	agent	mimer	backer
run	mime	angel	mimic	ballet
set	mute	arena	odeum	barker
tab	part	aside	on|cue	Big|Top
bill	play	barre	opera	boards
bowl	plot	break	piece	border
busk	prop	buffo	props	buskin
cast	rant	cloth	Punch	chaser
clap	rave	clown	put|on	chorus
dais	ring	comic	queue	circle
diva	role	corps	revue	circus
dock	rush	debut	rodeo	claque
dots	shot	decor	scena	comedy
drop	show	drama	scene	critic
epic	side	drill	score	dancer
flat	skit	dry|up	spout	depict
flop	sock	eclat	stage	direct

THEATRE

effect	review	callboy	manager
encore	ring|up	casting	marquee
Equity	satire	cat|call	matinee
exodus	scenic	cat|walk	mimicry
farcer	script	charade	miracle
feeder	season	chorine	mummery
filler	singer	circuit	musical
finale	sketch	clapper	mystery
floats	speech	close|up	New|Wave
flyman	stager	comedia	No|drama
gagman	stalls	commere	on|stage
guiser	stanza	company	overact
jester	stooge	compere	pageant
Kabuki	talent	costume	perform
lights	teaser	cothurn	Pierrot
limber	Thalia	coxcomb	play|act
lyceum	ticket	curtain	playing
make|up	·tights	dancing	playlet
masque	timing	danseur	pop|idol
method	tragic	deadpan	pop|star
motley	troupe	dress|up	portray
mummer	up|left	drive|in	present
number	walk|on	fan|club	preview
one|act	warm|up	farceur	produce
on|tour	writer	farcist	proverb
patron	acrobat	gallery	re|enact
patter	act|drop	gate|man	rep|show
person	actress	grimace	Roscius
pit|man	all|star	ham|it|up	rostrum
player	artiste	heroine	scenery
podium	balcony	histrio	scenist
prompt	benefit	ingenue	showman
puppet	bit|part	last|act	show|off
relief	booking	leg|show	soapbox
repeat	buffoon	leotard	spieler
re|take	cabaret	long|run	stadium

stagery	coulisse	off|stage
staging	danseuse	operatic
stand|by	dialogue	operetta
stand|in	Dionysus	overture
stardom	director	paradise
starlet	disguise	parterre
support	down|left	pastoral
tableau	dramatic	peep|show
theatre	dumb|show	pit|stall
the|gods	duologue	platform
Thespis	entr'acte	playbook
tragedy	entrance	playgoer
trouper	epilogue	playland
tumbler	epitasis	playwork
up|right	exit|line	practice
upstage	farceuse	premiere
vehicle	farcical	producer
antimask	fauteuil	prologue
applause	festival	prompter
audience	figurant	property
audition	filmgoer	protasis
backdrop	film|unit	rehearse
balletic	first|act	ring|down
big|scene	front|row	scenario
Broadway	funny|man	sceneman
burletta	gridiron	set|piece
business	grimacer	showboat
carnival	ham|actor	side|show
clapping	headline	smash|hit
claqueur	interval	stagedom
clowning	juvenile	stageman
coliseum	libretto	stage|set
comedian	live|show	star|turn
conjuror	location	stasimon
coryphee	magician	straight
costumer	morality	stroller

subtitle
take|a|bow
the|dance
Thespian
the|stage
third|act
tragical
travesty
typecast
usheress
wardrobe
wigmaker
wireless
absurdist
animation
announcer
arabesque
astrodome
backcloth
backstage
ballerina
bandstand
barnstorm
bit|player
box|office
breakaway
burlesque
carpenter
character
chorus|boy
chorus|man
cinematic
clip|joint
Colosseum
Columbine
costumier

cothurnus
criticism
cyclorama
dead|stage
direction
discovery
down|right
downstage
dramatics
dramatist
dramatize
drop|scene
entertain
entrechat
epirrhema
featuring
figurante
floor|show
greenroom
guest|star
ham|acting
harlequin
headliner
heavy|lead
hoardings
horseshoe
incognito
interlude
left|stage
limelight
live|stage
love|scene
low|comedy
major|role
make|up|man
melodrama

Melpomene
menagerie
minor|role
monodrama
monologue
music|hall
night|club
old|stager
orchestra
panel|game
pantaloon
pantomime
parabasis
pas|de|deux
patronage
patroness
performer
personage
Pierrette
pirouette
play|actor
playhouse
portrayal
programme
prompt|box
publicity
punch|line
raw|comedy
rehearsal
repertory
represent
scenarist
scene|plot
second|act
side|scene
slapstick

soliloquy	comedienne	milk|a|scene
soubrette	comic|opera	mimologist
spectacle	continuity	motley|fool
spectator	coryphaeus	mountebank
spotlight	costumiere	music|drama
stage|door	crowd|scene	on|the|stage
stagehand	denouement	opera|buffa
stageland	disc|jockey	opera|house
stage|name	drama|group	pantomimic
stage|play	dramalogue	pass|holder
staginess	dramatizer	performing
superstar	dramaturge	play|acting
take|a|part	dramaturgy	playbroker
tap|dancer	engagement	playreader
theatrics	exhibition	playwright
the|big|top	expository	playwriter
the|boards	fantoccini	presenting
title|role	first|house	prima|donna
tragedian	first|night	production
triologue	footlights	promptbook
usherette	get|the|bird	properties
wisecrack	high|comedy	proscenium
act|curtain	hippodrome	Pulcinella
act|the|goat	histrionic	puppet|show
act|the|part	impresario	put|on|a|show
afterpiece	impression	rave|notice
appearance	intermezzo	repertoire
apron|stage	in|the|round	right|stage
arena|stage	in|the|wings	Scaramouch
auditorium	leadingman	shadow|show
bandwaggon	legitimate	socio|drama
buffoonery	librettist	stage|boxes
chorus|girl	management	stagecraft
chorus|show	marionette	stage|fever
clog|dancer	masquerade	step|dancer
clown|white	microphone	strip|tease

substitute	dramaticism	play|the|fool
tap|dancing	dramaturgic	play|the|part
tear|jerker	dress|circle	practicable
theatre|box	drop|curtain	protagonist
theatreman	electrician	psychodrama
theatrical	entertainer	Punchinello
the|critics	exeunt|omnes	scene|change
the|unities	fire|curtain	scenewright
tragicomic	galanty|show	set|designer
trial|scene	grease|paint	set|the|scene
understudy	Greek|chorus	set|the|stage
utility|man	histrionics	showmanship
variety|act	histrionism	show|stopper
vaudeville	illusionist	Simon|Legree
walk|on|part	impersonate	skirt|dancer
actor's|agent	jackpudding	sound|effect
actor's|lines	kitchen|sink	spectacular
all|star|bill	leading|lady	stage|design
all|star|cast	light|comedy	stage|effect
a|star|is|born	low|comedian	stage|fright
bag|of|tricks	make|believe	stage|player
balletomane	matinee|idol	stage|school
barnstormer	merry|andrew	stagestruck
black|comedy	method|actor	stageworthy
broad|comedy	mimographer	stagewright
cap|and|bells	miracle|play	star|billing
catastrophe	mise|en|scene	star|quality
charity|show	off|Broadway	star|studded
cliff|hanger	on|the|boards	star|vehicle
comedy|drama	pantomimist	straight|man
comic|relief	pas|de|quatre	strip|teaser
commentator	Passion|play	talent|scout
concert|hall	performance	terpsichore
curtain|call	personality	theatregoer
drama|school	personation	theatreland
dramatic|art	play|actress	theatricals

theatrician
Thespian|art
tragedienne
tragic|drama
tragicomedy
upper|circle
ventriloquy
waiting|line
walking|part
walk|through
word|perfect
academy|award
acting|device
actor|manager
advance|agent
amphitheatre
ballet|dancer
balletomania
booking|agent
borderlights
characterize
character|man
choreography
comedy|ballet
concert|party
dramatic|play
dramaturgist
dressing|room
entrepreneur
extravaganza
first|nighter
Grand|Guignol
Greek|theatre
harlequinade
hold|the|stage
impersonator

introduction
juvenile|lead
make|up|artist
masked|comedy
melodramatic
method|acting
minstrel|show
modern|ballet
morality|play
old|stage|hand
opera|glasses
orchestra|pit
Pepper's|ghost
presentation
principal|boy
publicity|man
Punch|and|Judy
scene|painter
sceneshifter
scene|stealer
scenic|effect
screenwriter
season|ticket
show|business
show|must|go|on
song|and|dance
sound|effects
stage|manager
stage|setting
stage|whisper
standing|room
starring|role
steal|the|show
stock|company
stole|the|show
straight|part

take|the|floor
theatrecraft
theatromania
top|of|the|bill
vaudevillian
vaudevillist
curtain|raiser
curtain|speech
dramatic|irony
dramatisation
emergency|exit
entertainment
impersonation
melodramatist
musical|comedy
one|night|stand
pantomime|dame
safety|curtain
theatre|school
theatricalism
walking|on|part
world|premiere
character|actor
dramatic|critic
dress|rehearsal
open|air|theatre

orchestra|stall
pantomime|horse
prima|ballerina
property|master
proscenium|arch
smoking|concert
speech|training
stage|carpenter
stage|direction
supporting|cast
supporting|part
supporting|role
touring|company
variety|theatre
behind|the|scenes
dramatic|society
gala|performance
legitimate|drama
National|Theatre
orchestra|stalls
raise|the|curtain
shadow|pantomime
situation|comedy
slapstick|comedy
strolling|player
tightrope|walker

Time

AD	mo	ago	due	eld	ere
am	pm	aye	e'en	Eos	eve
BC	age	day	e'er	era	May

3/6 LETTERS

oft	soon	never	Aurora
old	span	night	autumn
sec	term	nonce	Bairam
ult	then	often	brumal
yet	tick	passe	coeval
aeon	tide	pause	coming
ages	till	point	crisis
anon	time	prime	curfew
ante	unto	prior	decade
date	week	Purim	dotage
dawn	when	ready	during
dial	Xmas	shake	Easter
dusk	year	sharp	elapse
even	yore	short	ere|now
ever	Yule	since	extant
fall	again	so|far	ferial
fast	annum	space	Friday
fore	April	spell	future
Ides	as|yet	still	gnomon
inst	brief	style	heyday
jiff	clock	sunup	hiemal
July	cycle	tempo	hourly
June	daily	today	Ice|age
late	dekad	trice	in|time
Lent	delay	until	jet|age
moon	diary	watch	Julian
morn	early	while	Lammas
next	epact	years	lapsed
Noel	epoch	young	lately
noon	fasti	youth	latest
once	flash	actual	latish
over	jiffy	advent	lustre
past	later	always	manana
post	March	annual	May|day
prox	matin	at|once	midday
slow	month	August	minute

TIME

modern	yearly	expired	one time
moment	yester	extinct	overdue
Monday	abiding	fast day	pending
morrow	ack emma	flag day	pip emma
new day	ageless	forever	postwar
o'clock	ages ago	for good	present
off day	all over	for life	proximo
of late	almanac	harvest	quarter
old age	already	high day	quondam
one day	ancient	history	Ramadan
on time	anytime	holiday	ripe age
period	archaic	holy day	Sabbath
presto	at night	infancy	secular
pre war	bedtime	instant	shortly
prompt	belated	interim	sine die
pronto	betimes	Iron Age	some day
pro tem	boyhood	January	stretch
rarely	by and by	journal	Sukkoth
recent	calends	jubilee	sundial
season	century	just now	sundown
second	chiliad	kalends	sunrise
seldom	current	Lady day	teenage
sooner	dawning	long ago	tertian
spring	daylong	long run	this day
sudden	day peep	lustrum	time lag
summer	daytime	manhood	time was
Sunday	diurnal	manhour	tonight
sunset	dog days	matinal	too late
timely	earlier	mid week	too soon
to date	elapsed	monthly	Tuesday
update	endless	morning	twinkle
vernal	epochal	newborn	two two's
vesper	equinox	New Year	unready
weekly	estival	nightly	up to now
whilst	evening	noonday	usually
winter	exactly	October	weekday

weekend	February	lifelong
whereon	fleeting	life span
whitsun	foredawn	lifetime
abruptly	forenoon	livelong
a long day	formerly	long time
antedate	frequent	Lord's day
as soon as	gain time	lose time
biannual	gloaming	lunation
biennial	half hour	make time
birthday	half past	mark time
biweekly	Hanukkah	meantime
blue moon	hereunto	mean time
Brumaire	hibernal	medieval
calendar	high time	menology
darkling	hitherto	meridian
date line	Hogmanay	meteoric
daybreak	holy days	midnight
daylight	Holy week	momently
deadline	horology	natal day
December	ill timed	New Style
Derby day	in a flash	next week
directly	in a trice	noontide
dogwatch	infinity	noontime
doomsday	in future	not often
duration	in no time	November
egg timer	in season	nowadays
enduring	interval	obsolete
entr'acte	juncture	occasion
Epiphany	keep time	ofttimes
eternity	kill time	old times
eventide	lang syne	on the dot
evermore	last time	our times
every day	last week	Passover
evil hour	lateness	pass time
fast time	latterly	postdate
feast day	leap year	postpone

TIME

previous
promptly
punctual
recently
right|now
ringtime
Saturday
seasonal
seedtime
semester
solar|day
solstice
some|time
Space|Age
sporadic
Steel|Age
Stone|Age
suddenly
take|time
temporal
this|week
Thursday
timeless
time|worn
tomorrow
too|early
twilight
ultimate
until|now
untimely
up|to|date
weeklong
whenever
year|book
yearlong
years|ago

yoretime
Yuletide
adulthood
afternoon
after|that
after|time
all|at|once
antiquity
Atomic|Age
at|present
bimonthly
Boxing|Day
Bronze|Age
Candlemas
canicular
centenary
childhood
Christmas
chronicle
civil|time
civil|year
clepsydra
continual
crepuscle
days|of|old
dayspring
decennary
decennial
decennium
due|season
earliness
early|bird
ember|days
Empire|Day
ephemeral
ephemeris

epochally
erstwhile
ever|since
every|hour
far|future
first|time
foregoing
forthwith
fortnight
from|now|on
gnomonics
Golden|Age
great|year
Gregorian
Hallowe'en
Hallowmas
happy|days
hereafter
honeymoon
hourglass
immediacy
immediate
in|a|second
in|due|time
instanter
instantly
interlude
in|the|past
Julian|day
Lammas|day
later|date
latter|day
light|year
local|time
longevity
long|lived

394

long|since	preceding	timepiece
long|spell	precisely	times|past
long|while	premature	timetable
lunar|year	presently	to|this|day
many|a|time	quarterly	transient
many|times	quarter|to	triennial
Mardi|Gras	quotidian	twinkling
Martinmas	recurrent	two|shakes
mature|age	regularly	upon|which
matutinal	remote|age	vicennial
meanwhile	right|time	waste|time
mediaeval	Saint's|day	Wednesday
menstrual	salad|days	well|timed
metronome	sandglass	wherefore
midday|sun	semestral	whereunto
middle|age	September	whereupon
midsummer	short|term	wrong|time
midwinter	short|time	yesterday
mistiming	solar|time	afterwards
momentary	solar|year	after|which
monthlong	sometimes	alarm|clock
nevermore	space|time	Allhallows
nightfall	spare|time	all|the|time
nightlong	spend|time	anno|Domini
nighttide	stop|watch	at|all|times
night|time	Swiss|plan	at|that|time
nocturnal	temporary	at|this|time
octennial	temporize	beforehand
oftentime	therewith	before|long
opportune	till|death	beforetime
out|of|date	time|being	behindhand
overnight	time|check	behind|time
Pentecost	time|clock	better|days
perennial	time|flies	break|of|day
permanent	time|limit	bygone|days
postcenal	time|of|day	by|the|clock

centennial	incidental	ripe|old|age
childermas	in|good|time	Sabbath|day
chronogram	invariably	seasonable
chronology	isochronon	semiweekly
close|of|day	Julian|year	septennial
common|time	just|in|time	sextennial
consequent	Lammastide	short|spell
constantly	last|chance	small|hours
continuous	last|minute	soon|enough
cosmic|time	Lententide	springtide
crepuscule	lunar|month	springtime
days|gone|by	Methuselah	subsequent
days|of|yore	Michaelmas	summertide
Eastertide	middle|aged	summertime
Easter|time	Middle|Ages	thereafter
evanescent	midmorning	this|minute
eventually	millennium	time|keeper
Father's|day	moratorium	timeliness
Father|Time	Mother's|day	time|signal
fiscal|year	near|future	time|to|come
fleetingly	nick|of|time	time|to|kill
frequently	now|or|never	transitory
futuristic	occasional	tricennial
generation	of|the|clock	triple|time
Good|Friday	olden|times	ultimately
half|a|jiffy	one|fine|day	very|seldom
half|an|hour	on|occasion	vespertime
half|a|shake	on|the|eve|of	water|clock
hardly|ever	Palm|Sunday	wedding|day
hebdomadal	posthumous	whensoever
Hebrew|year	prehistory	Whitmonday
henceforth	present|day	Whitsunday
here|and|now	previously	wintertide
heretofore	proper|time	wintertime
historical	repeatedly	with|the|sun
immemorial	retrospect	wristwatch

years|on|end
yesteryear
adjournment
adolescence
after|dinner
against|time
ahead|of|time
All|Fools|day
All|Souls|day
anachronism
anniversary
at|intervals
bicentenary
bygone|times
ceaselessly
chronograph
chronometer
chronoscope
coincidence
concurrence
continually
crack|of|dawn
crepuscular
cuckoo|clock
day|after|day
day|and|night
day|in|day|out
dead|of|night
endless|time
ever|and|a|day
ever|and|anon
everlasting
every|moment
fin|de|siècle
flower|of|age
for|evermore

former|times
fortnightly
Gay|Nineties
golden|hours
good|old|days
halcyon|days
half|a|second
hebdomadary
hereinafter
ides|of|March
immediately
in|an|instant
incessantly
in|due|course
inopportune
interregnum
Judgment|day
lapse|of|time
leisure|time
little|while
livelong|day
long|lasting
long|overdue
march|of|time
microsecond
middle|years
millisecond
modern|times
momentarily
morningtide
morning|time
never|ending
New|Year's|day
New|Year's|eve
night|and|day
once|or|twice

on|the|morrow
opportunely
opportunity
out|of|season
Passion|week
penultimate
perennially
perfect|year
perpetually
play|for|time
point|of|time
present|time
prime|of|life
promptitude
punctuality
quadrennial
quarter|past
sands|of|time
semi|monthly
shining|hour
short|notice
some|time|ago
split|second
straightway
synchronism
synchronize
tempus|fugit
thenceforth
the|other|day
this|morning
this|very|day
time|and|tide
time|drags|by
time|machine
time|to|spare
turret|clock

TIME

twelvemonth
ultramodern
waiting|time
Whitsuntide
with|the|lark
Year|of|Grace
all|of|a|sudden
All|Saints|day
a|long|time|ago
ancient|times
Annunciation
antediluvian
antemeridian
ante|meridiem
Armistice|day
Ascension|day
Ash|Wednesday
auld|lang|syne
bide|one's|time
calendar|year
Christmas|day
Christmas|eve
consequently
contemporary
course|of|time
decisive|hour
decline|of|day
donkey's|years
eleventh|hour
Feast|of|Weeks
following|day
fourth|of|July
from|that|time
Greek|calends
Holy|Thursday
in|days|of|yore

Indian|summer
Innocents|day
in|olden|times
intermission
late|in|the|day
long|standing
many|a|long|day
metachronism
nychthemeron
occasionally
old|fashioned
once|in|a|while
on|the|instant
parachronism
periodically
postdiluvian
postmeridian
post|meridiem
postponement
postprandial
Quadrigesima
quinquennial
quinquennium
rare|occasion
red|letter|day
sempiternity
sidereal|time
sidereal|year
simultaneous
stall|for|time
standard|time
still|of|night
stitch|in|time
tercentenary
the|dawn|of|day
then|and|there

the|year|round
time|and|again
time,honoured
timelessness
time|will|tell
turning|point
Twelfth|night
twelve|o'clock
unseasonable
witching|hour
without|delay
again|and|again
All|Hallow's|eve
April|fool's|day
Ascensiontide
at|short|notice
broad|daylight
calendar|month
Christmas,tide
Christmas,time
chronographer
chronological
days|of|the|week
every|few|hours
every|few|years
every|other|day
financial|year
for|the|present
from|the|outset
from|the|word|go
generation|gap
getting|on|a|bit
golden|jubilee
golden|wedding
Greenwich|time
Michaelmas|day

old|as|the|hills
once|upon|a|time
Passion|Sunday
quincentenary
Quinquagesima
retrospective
right|up|to|date
round|the|clock
Shrove|Tuesday
silver|jubilee
silver|wedding
some|of|the|time
some|other|time
sooner|or|later
speaking|clock
St|Crispin's|day
St|Luke's|summer
St|Swithin's|day
summer|holiday
synchronology
the|time|is|ripe
time|after|time
time|marches|on
time|of|arrival
time|out|of|mind
tomorrow|night
Trinity|Sunday
tropical|month
turn|of|the|year
up,to,the|minute
up|with|the|lark
vernal|equinox
week|in,|week|out
year|in,|year|out
advancing|years
before|and|after

behind|schedule
breathing|space
chronometrical
day|in|and|day|out
daylight|saving
declining|years
diamond|jubilee
diamond|wedding
during|the|night
Easter|holidays
for|ever|and|a|day
for|ever|and|ever
for|the|duration
from|time|to|time
fullness|of|time
geological|time
in|ancient|times
in|course|of|time
interval|of|time
in|the|afternoon
in|the|beginning
in|the|meanwhile
Julian|calendar
keep|early|hours
Maundy|Thursday
midsummer|night
month|of|Sundays
Pancake|Tuesday
past|and|present
Remembrance|Day
Rogation|Sunday
sabbatical|year
septuagenarian
Walpurgis|night

witches|Sabbath
against|the|clock
ahead|of|schedule
chronologically
contemporaneity
contemporaneous
continental|time
continuation|day
dominical|letter
equinoctial|year
every|now|and|then
for|a|year|and|a|day
fourth|dimension
how|goes|the|enemy
in|the|nick|of|time
month|after|month
months|and|months
months|of|the|year
Mothering|Sunday
night|after|night
once|in|a|blue|moon
once|in|a|lifetime
put|back|the|clock
put|the|clock|back
quatercentenary
retrospectively
spur|of|the|moment
St|Valentine's|day
Thanksgiving|day
the|morning|after
this|year|of|grace
tomorrow|evening
tomorrow|morning
world|without|end

Tools

awl
axe
bit
cow
die
dig
hod
hoe
jig
saw
adze
file
fork
hose
jack
mole
pick
pump
rake
tool
auger
brace
burin
delve
drill
gouge
jemmy
jimmy
knife

lever
mower
plane
punch
scoop
spade
tongs
wedge
bob|saw
bodkin
chaser
chisel
dibble
digger
eolith
gadget
gimlet
grater
hammer
harrow
jigsaw
mallet
muller
oil|gun
pliers
plough
ramrod
riddle
rip|saw

roller
scythe
shaver
shears
shovel
sickle
spigot
stylus
tedder
trowel
wrench
bandsaw
bradawl
buzz|saw
cadrans
chopper
cleaver
cold|saw
crowbar
forceps
fretsaw
gripper
hacksaw
handsaw
hatchet
hayfork
hayrake
mattock
pickaxe

pincers
riffler
rotator
scalpel
scraper
shuttle
spanner
spatula
sprayer
stapler
toolbox
woodsaw
air|drill
billhook
calipers
cant|hook
chainsaw
clippers
cross|bit
dividers
Dutch|hoe
edge|tool
flash|gun
flat|iron
handtool
penknife
polisher
power|saw
saw|knife

TOOLS

scissors	cold chisel
spray gun	compass saw
tommy bar	cultivator
tweezers	drop hammer
air hammer	edging tool
arc welder	garden fork
belt punch	garden hose
blow torch	goat sallow
can opener	hole cutter
cement gun	keyhole saw
corkscrew	pantograph
die sinker	paper knife
drop drill	peen hammer
eidograph	pipe wrench
excavator	powder mill
fly cutter	twist drill
grease gun	whirl drill
hair drier	brace and bit
hand drill	butcher's saw
handspike	circular saw
implement	dovetail saw
jackknife	drilling rig
lawn mower	electric saw
pitchfork	electron gun
plumb line	garden spade
road drill	glass cutter
rock drill	machine tool
secateurs	pillar drill
steam iron	ploughshare
telescope	pocketknife
tin opener	power shovel
tyre lever	pruning bill
bowie knife	pruning hook
box spanner	ring spanner
claw hammer	rotary drill
coal shovel	safety razor

sanding disc
screwdriver
steam hammer
steam shovel
surgeon's saw
tamping iron
watering can
wheelbarrow
battering ram
carving knife
electric iron
garden roller
garden shears
garden trowel
hedge trimmer

hydraulic ram
marlinespike
masonry drill
palette knife
pruning knife
ratchet drill
sledgehammer
soldering gun
two handed saw
pick and shovel
precision tool
hammer and tongs
pneumatic drill
hammer and sickle

Trade

CA	due	pro	bank	chip	dues
co	dun	put	bear	coin	dump
HP	EEC	rig	body	co-op	dust
rd	fee	sag	bond	corn	duty
bag	IOU	SET	boom	cost	earn
bar	job	sum	buck	crop	EFTA
bid	lot	tag	bulk	curb	fair
bob	Ltd	tax	bull	deal	fees
BOT	net	tin	bury	dear	file
buy	oof	tip	call	debt	fine
cap	owe	VAT	cant	desk	fire
COD	par	wad	cash	dibs	firm
con	pay	agio	cess	dole	fisc
dot	pit	back	char	drug	free

TRADE

fund	pawn	ware	chips	miser
gain	PAYE	work	chore	money
game	peag	agent	clear	ochre
gift	perk	amass	clerk	offer
gild	pool	angel	costs	order
gilt	post	assay	craft	owing
giro	rags	asset	crash	panic
glut	raid	at|par	cycle	paper
gold	rate	audit	debit	piece
good	reap	baron	depot	pitch
haul	rent	batch	Dives	plant
hawk	risk	beans	dough	pound
heap	roll	bears	dowry	price
hire	roup	bid|up	draft	prize
hive	ruin	block	entry	purse
hold	sack	blunt	Ernie	queer
hype	safe	board	exact	quota
idle	sale	bogus	files	quote
IOUs	salt	bones	float	rails
item	save	bonus	forge	rally
lend	scab	boost	funds	rebuy
levy	sell	booth	gilts	remit
line	shop	brand	gnome	repay
list	sink	brass	goods	rhino
loan	slug	broke	gross	rocks
long	sold	bucks	guild	salve
loss	stag	bulls	hoard	scalp
make	swap	bunce	house	scoop
mart	tare	buyer	index	score
meed	task	buy|up	ingot	scrip
milk	tick	by|bid	issue	set|up
mill	till	cadge	lease	share
mint	tout	cargo	lucre	shark
nail	vend	cheap	maker	shift
note	visa	check	means	short
paid	wage	chink	Midas	skill

404

5/6 LETTERS

slash	accept	change	garage	nugget
slump	accrue	charge	gazump	octroi
smash	admass	cheque	godown	odd|job
smith	afford	client	go,slow	odd|lot
snide	agency	coffer	gratis	office
spend	agenda	consol	grease	on|call
spiel	amount	copper	growth	oncost
spots	appeal	corner	guinea	on|tick
stake	arrear	costly	haggle	option
stall	assets	coupon	hammer	outbid
stand	at|cost	cowrie	hard|up	outcry
stint	avails	credit	hawker	outlay
stock	backer	crisis	import	outlet
store	banker	custom	impose	output
strop	barker	dealer	impost	packet
tally	barter	deal|in	in|bulk	parity
taxes	bazaar	debtee	in|cash	patron
terms	bearer	debtor	income	pauper
tithe	boodle	defray	in|debt	pay|day
token	borrow	demand	in,tray	pay|for
trade	bought	dicker	jobber	paying
treat	bounce	drawer	job|lot	pay,off
trend	bounty	dunner	labour	payola
truck	bourse	emptio	leader	pay|out
trust	branch	enrich	ledger	peddle
usury	broker	equity	lender	pedlar
utter	budget	errand	liable	picket
value	bureau	estate	living	pirate
venal	bursar	excise	luxury	pledge
wages	button	expend	mammon	plunge
wares	buying	export	merger	Plutus
welsh	buy|out	figure	minute	pocket
works	cambio	fiscal	moneys	policy
worth	career	fold|up	monger	profit
yield	cartel	freeze	monies	public
abacus	cash|in	future	notice	purvey

racket	spread	arrears	concern
raffle	stable	article	consols
rating	staker	atelier	contact
ration	stocks	auction	convert
realty	strike	auditor	coppers
rebate	sundry	automat	corn|pit
recoup	supply	average	cottons
redeem	surtax	backing	counter
refund	swings	bad|debt	Croesus
reject	tariff	balance	cumshaw
remedy	taxman	ballast	Customs
render	teller	banking	customs
rental	tender	bargain	cut|rate
resale	tenths	berries	damages
resell	ticker	bidding	daybook
resign	ticket	bonanza	dealing
retail	towage	bondage	declare
retire	trader	boycott	default
return	treaty	bullets	deficit
reward	tycoon	bullion	deflate
rialto	unload	bursary	deposit
riches	unpaid	buy|back	deviser
ruined	usurer	cabbage	dockage
salary	valuta	calling	draw|out
save|up	vendor	cambist	due|bill
saving	vendue	capital	dumping
sell|up	wallet	cash|box	economy
settle	wampum	cashier	effects
shares	wealth	ceiling	embargo
shorts	worker	chapman	emption
silver	wright	charity	endorse
simony	abscond	chinker	engross
smithy	account	clinker	entrust
specie	actuary	coinage	expense
spiral	allonge	coining	exploit
sponge	annuity	company	exports

factory	jobless	payroll	rollers
failure	journal	payslip	roomman
fall|due	killing	peddlar	rouleau
finance	land|tax	pending	royalty
flutter	leading	pension	sacking
foot|lot	lending	pet|bank	salable
foreman	lettuce	plunger	salt|tax
forgery	limited	poll|tax	salvage
for|sale	lockout	poorman	savings
fortune	Lombard	portage	seconds
foundry	long|run	preempt	selling
freebie	lottery	premium	sell|out
freight	lump|sum	prepaid	service
full|lot	manager	pricing	shekels
futures	manmade	produce	shopman
gabelle	mintage	profits	shopper
gift|box	mission	promote	skilled
go|broke	moneyed	pro|rata	smelter
good|buy	nest|egg	prosper	solvent
good|sum	net|gain	provide	sponger
go|under	notions	pursuit	squeeze
guerdon	nummary	pyramid	stipend
half|day	oddment	realize	storage
harvest	on|offer	realtor	striker
haulage	on|terms	receipt	subsidy
head|tax	on|trust	refusal	surplus
holding	opening	regrate	swindle
imports	opulent	reissue	takings
inflate	out|tray	release	taxable
in|funds	package	requite	tax|free
intrust	parlour	reserve	terrier
invoice	parvenu	retiral	the|city
ironmen	payable	returns	tidy|sum
jingler	pay|cash	revenue	trade|in
jobbers	payment	richman	trading
jobbing	pay|rise	rigging	traffic

TRADE

tranche	basic|pay	credit|to	gazumper
trustee	bear|pool	currency	gift|shop
utility	bear|raid	customer	gilt|edge
vacancy	beat|down	cut|price	giveaway
vending	below|par	day|shift	gold|mine
venture	blackleg	dealings	gold|rush
voucher	blue|chip	defrayal	good|will
walkout	board|lot	director	gratuity
war|bond	boardman	disburse	grow|rich
warrant	bondager	discount	hallmark
wealthy	boom|town	disposal	hard|cash
welfare	borrower	dividend	hard|sell
well|off	boutique	dry|goods	hardware
welsher	breakage	earnings	hoarding
wildcat	brochure	embezzle	homework
workday	bull|pool	employee	hot|money
above|par	bull|raid	employer	huckster
accredit	business	emporium	importer
affluent	buying|in	entrepot	in|arrear
after|tax	campaign	estimate	increase
agiotage	carriage	evaluate	indebted
agronomy	carriage	exchange	industry
amortize	cashbook	expended	in|pocket
appraise	cash|down	expenses	interest
at|a|price	cash|sale	exporter	in|the|red
auditing	circular	face|ruin	investor
automate	clientry	finances	issuance
badly|off	close|out	fire|sale	issue|par
bad|money	cold|cash	flat|rate	jeweller
ballyhoo	commands	floorman	junkshop
bankbook	commerce	for|a|song	keep|shop
bank|loan	consumer	free|gift	kitemark
bank|note	contango	free|port	knitwork
bank|roll	contract	function	labourer
bankrupt	converts	gasworks	lame|duck
base|coin	creditor	gazetted	largesse

408

large|sum	overhaul	rent|roll
legation	overhead	requital
levanter	overseer	reserves
lifework	overtime	retailer
live|high	par|value	retainer
live|well	passbook	richesse
long|side	pawn|shop	richling
low|price	pay|talks	round|lot
low|water	pin|money	round|sum
make|a|bid	pipeline	rush|hour
make|good	pittance	salaried
manifest	position	saleroom
man|power	post|paid	salesman
mark|down	poundage	salt|down
material	practice	sanction
maturity	premises	scalping
merchant	price|cut	scarcity
mint|drop	price|war	schedule
monetary	proceeds	security
moneybag	producer	self|made
moneybox	property	shipment
monopoly	prospect	shipyard
mortgage	purchase	shopping
net|price	put|price	short|run
net|worth	quit|rent	showcase
no|charge	rack|rent	showroom
notation	rag|trade	sideline
notecase	rainy|day	sinecure
oddments	receipts	small|sum
off|price	reckoner	soft|cell
on|credit	recorder	solatium
on|demand	recovery	solidity
on|strike	refinery	solvency
operator	register	spending
opulence	regrater	spot|cash
ordinary	rent|free	spot|sale

409

square|up
sterling
sundries
supertax
supplies
swapping
takeover
tallyman
taxation
tax|dodge
taxpayer
time|bill
tolbooth
tool|shop
toolwork
top|price
trade|gap
trade|off
treasure
Treasury
turnover
underbid
undercut
usufruct
valorize
valuable
venality
vendible
vocation
wash|sale
watchdog
well|to|do
wharfage
workaday
work|late
workroom

workshop
write|off
absconder
ad|valorem
affiliate
affluence
aggregate
allowance
amount|due
appraisal
arbitrage
arrearage
avocation
back|shift
bad|cheque
bank|clerk
bank|stock
barrow|boy
bartering
bear|panic
blind|pool
board|room
bond|issue
bon|marché
bonus|bond
borrowing
box|office
brand|name
breadline
brokerage
bucketing
bull|panic
buy|in|bulk
by|auction
by|bidding
by|product

cable|code
cable|rate
call|price
cash|grain
catalogue
cellarage
cheapjack
check|rate
clearance
clientage
clientele
co|emption
coin|money
commodity
costerman
cost|price
craftsman
death|duty
debenture
deduction
defaulter
deflation
depositor
dime|store
directors
direct|tax
dirt|cheap
discharge
dishonour
dismissal
dollar|gap
draw|wages
drug|store
easy|money
easy|terms
economics

economies	hard goods	make a sale
economise	hard money	market day
emolument	head buyer	marketing
establish	heavy cost	means test
exchequer	high price	middleman
exciseman	high value	moneybags
excise tax	holy stone	money belt
executive	hot market	mortgagee
expansion	hush money	mortgager
expensive	import tax	neat price
exploiter	in arrears	negotiate
export tax	incentive	net income
extortion	income tax	night safe
face value	in deficit	officiate
fair price	indemnity	off market
fair trade	inflation	on account
fat profit	insolvent	on the nail
fiat money	insurance	operative
financial	in the city	order book
financier	invention	outgoings
firm offer	inventory	out of debt
firm price	job of work	out of work
flash note	joint bank	outworker
flat broke	keep books	overdraft
flotation	knock down	overdrawn
free trade	late shift	overheads
full purse	legal bond	overspend
gilt edged	liability	patronage
going rate	life's work	patronize
gold piece	liquidate	pay dearly
good price	list price	pay in kind
greenback	long purse	paymaster
guarantee	lossmaker	pecuniary
guarantor	low priced	pecunious
half price	luxury tax	penniless
handiwork	mail order	pennywise

petty|cash
piecework
piggy|bank
plutocrat
poorly|off
portfolio
pound|note
pourboire
practical
priceless
price|list
price|ring
price|rise
prime|cost
principal
profiteer
promotion
purchaser
qualified
quittance
quotation
ratepayer
ready|cash
real|wages
recession
reckoning
reduction
redundant
reference
refinance
reflation
registrar
reimburse
repayment
resources
restraint

sacrifice
sale|block
salesgirl
sales|talk
secretary
sell|short
shift|work
shop|floor
short|sale
short|side
sight|bill
single|tax
situation
soft|goods
sole|agent
soundness
speculate
spendings
spot|grain
spot|price
stability
stamp|duty
statement
stock|list
stockpile
stock|rate
strike|pay
strongbox
subsidize
substance
sumptuary
surcharge
sweatshop
sweet|shop
syndicate
synthetic

take|stock
tax|return
technical
the|actual
the|market
the|street
tie₁in|sale
timocracy
tollbooth
trade|fair
trademark
trade|name
trade|sale
tradesman
traffic|in
treadmill
treasurer
undersell
union|card
unit|trust
unsalable
unskilled
up|for|sale
utilities
utterance
valuation
vendition
wage|claim
wage|scale
warehouse
wash|sales
wealth|tax
well₁lined
whitewash
wholesale
work|force

workhouse	capitalism	department
work|study	capitalist	depository
World|Bank	capitalize	depreciate
acceptance	chain|banks	depression
accountant	chain|store	direct|cost
accounting	chancellor	dirty|money
accumulate	chargeable	dividend|on
adjustment	chargehand	dollar|bill
advertiser	cheapening	dummy|share
appreciate	cheap|skate	Dutch|treat
apprentice	cheque|book	easy|market
assessment	chrematist	economizer
assignment	chrysology	efficiency
at|a|bargain	closed|shop	employment
at|a|premium	closing|bid	encumbered
at|the|spear	collateral	end|product
auctioneer	colporteur	enterprise
auction|off	commercial	estate|duty
automation	commission	Eurodollar
average|out	compensate	evaluation
bank|credit	conference	ex|dividend
bankruptcy	consortium	exorbitant
bearer|bond	contraband	exposition
bear|market	cost|centre	false|money
best|seller	coupon|bond	fancy|goods
bill|broker	credit|card	fancy|price
bill|of|sale	credit|slip	fancy|stock
blood|money	curb|broker	filthy|rich
bondholder	curb|market	first|offer
bonus|stock	daily|bread	fiscal|year
bookkeeper	dead|market	fixed|price
bucket|shop	deep|in|debt	fixed|trust
bulk|buying	defalcator	flat|market
buy|and|sell	defrayment	floor|price
buy|futures	del|credere	forced|sale
calculator	demand|bill	free|gratis

free market
free sample
free trader
freightage
full stocks
funded debt
give credit
gold nugget
go on strike
go shopping
government
green pound
grindstone
half stocks
handicraft
hand market
have in hand
head office
heavy purse
high priced
hold office
honorarium
import duty
imposition
in business
income bond
incumbered
incur a debt
industrial
insolvency
instalment
in the black
in the money
investment
job hunting
joint bonds

joint stock
jumble sale
laboratory
lighterage
liquidator
livelihood
living wage
loan market
long market
long seller
loss leader
management
man of means
marked down
marketable
market hall
mass market
meal ticket
member bank
mercantile
merchantry
Midas touch
monetarism
monetarist
moneyed man
money order
monopolist
monopolise
moratorium
negotiable
never never
nightshift
nominal fee
nominal par
nonpayment
note of hand

numismatic
obligation
occupation
off licence
oil of palms
on the block
on the cheap
on the rocks
on the shelf
opening bid
open market
out of funds
overcharge
paper money
pawnbroker
peppercorn
percentage
picket duty
pig in a poke
pilot plant
plutocracy
pocketbook
power plant
pre emption
preference
prepayment
price index
price level
printworks
Prix unique
production
profession
profitable
prospector
prospectus
prosperity

provide|for	short|bonds	trade|price
purchasing	sick|market	trade|route
pure|profit	skilled|man	trade|union
put|and|call	slave|trade	treaty|port
ration|book	slow|market	typewriter
ready|money	smart|money	typing|pool
real|estate	soft|market	underwrite
recompense	sole|agency	unemployed
recoupment	speciality	upset|price
redeemable	speculator	wad|of|notes
redundancy	split|shift	wage|freeze
remittance	spondulies	wage|policy
remunerate	statistics	walk|of|life
repair|shop	steelworks	Wall|Street
reparation	steep|price	waterworks
repository	stock|issue	wealthy|man
repurchase	stockpiles	well|afford
retail|shop	stony|broke	well|heeled
retirement	straitened	wholesaler
rock|bottom	stronghold	window|shop
round|trade	strongroom	working|day
run|up|a|bill	sum|of|money	work|to|rule
salability	swap|horses	written|off
sales|force	take|a|flier	accountancy
saving|bank	taskmaster	account|book
saving|game	tax|evation	acquittance
scrip|issue	technician	advertising
second|hand	technocrat	agriculture
securities	the|needful	antique|shop
serial|bond	thin|margin	appointment
settlement	Third|World	asking|price
settle|with	ticker|tape	association
share|index	tour|of|duty	at|face|value
shoestring	trade|board	auction|ring
shopkeeper	trade|cycle	bank|account
shop|window	trade|guild	bank|balance

bank holiday
bank manager
bank of issue
Barclaycard
bargain sale
bear account
bear the cost
betting shop
big business
billionaire
bill of costs
black market
blank cheque
bonus scheme
book keeping
bottom price
bread winner
brisk market
budget price
bull account
businessman
capital gain
carbon paper
cash account
catallactic
caught short
central bank
certificate
chamberlain
chancellery
chemist shop
chrysocracy
circulation
closing down
come to terms
commodities

common stock
company rule
competition
competitive
comptometer
consumption
cool million
co-operative
co-operative
copperworks
corn in Egypt
corporation
cost benefit
counterfeit
cover charge
cum dividend
custom house
customs duty
danger money
defence bond
delinquence
demand curve
demarcation
deposit slip
devaluation
display case
distributor
dividend off
double entry
down payment
drive a trade
earn a living
economic law
economic man
economy size
embarrassed

endorsement
established
estate agent
expenditure
fabrication
fetch a price
filthy lucre
fixed assets
fixed income
floor broker
floor trader
fluctuation
foot the bill
foreclosure
free harbour
future grain
future price
gingerbread
gross income
hard bargain
high finance
horse market
hypermarket
impecunious
indirect tax
industrials
inexpensive
institution
intercourse
ironmongery
joint return
key industry
king's ransom
lap of luxury
legal tender
liberty bond

life savings
line of goods
liquidation
local branch
local office
long account
long service
loose change
machine made
machine shop
made of money
manufactory
manufacture
market place
market price
mass produce
merchandise
millionaire
minimum wage
mint of money
money broker
money dealer
moneylender
money's worth
money to burn
negotiation
nest factory
net interest
net receipts
nuisance tax
numismatics
on easy terms
on good terms
on the market
open account
open end bond

out of pocket
outstanding
overpayment
package deal
paper credit
partnership
pay cash down
pay on demand
pay spot cash
pay the piper
piece of work
pilot scheme
place of work
pocket money
polytechnic
possessions
postal order
pots of money
poverty line
poverty trap
premium bond
pretty penny
price fixing
price freeze
price spiral
price ticket
property tax
proposition
provided for
purchase tax
put up market
Queer Street
quoted price
raw material
reserve bank
resignation

restriction
retiring age
risk capital
rummage sale
run into debt
safe deposit
sales ledger
sales person
savings bank
self service
sell at a loss
sell forward
sell futures
sharebroker
shareholder
share ledger
shopping bag
short change
short seller
single entry
sinking fund
slot machine
small change
small trader
sole emption
speculation
sponsorship
stagflation
stockbroker
stock dealer
stockholder
stock jobber
stock ledger
stock market
stockpiling
stocktaking

storekeeper
subsistence
supermarket
take home pay
take over bid
Tattersall's
tax assessor
tax gatherer
technocracy
the have nots
tight budget
tight market
time bargain
tired market
to the tune of
trade school
trading post
transaction
travel agent
truck system
undercharge
underwriter
vendibility
wherewithal
working life
workmanlike
workmanship
works outing
world market
active market
ad valorem tax
amalgamation
amortization
amortizement
arithmometer
assembly line

auction stand
balance sheet
bank examiner
bargain offer
bargain price
barter system
be in business
bill of lading
board meeting
Board of Trade
bond to bearer
bottom dollar
bottomry bond
branch office
broker's agent
brokers board
business deal
business life
businesslike
buyer's market
buying public
callable bond
capital gains
capital goods
capital stock
cash and carry
cash register
casual labour
catallactics
circular note
clearing bank
closing price
common market
compensation
consumer good
cook the books

costermonger
cost of living
counting room
credit rating
critical path
currency note
current price
customs union
denomination
depreciation
direct labour
disbursement
discount rate
distribution
dollar crisis
durable goods
Dutch auction
early closing
earned income
econometrics
economy drive
entrepreneur
exchange rate
exhaust price
extend credit
extravagance
fair exchange
fill an office
first refusal
fiscal policy
fixed capital
floating debt
folding money
foreign trade
gate receipts
general store

get rich quick   money matters   redeployment
going concern   mortgage bond   regional bank
gold standard   national bank   remuneration
goods for sale   nearest offer   remunerative
great expense   nine till five   reserve price
haberdashery   nominal price   retaining fee
hard currency   nominal value   retrenchment
high pressure   nouveau riche   rigged market
hire purchase   odd lot dealer   rig the market
hungry market   offered price   rising prices
impulse buyer   offer for sale   rolling stock
in conference   office junior   rubber cheque
indebtedness   open end trust   sale by outcry
interest rate   opening price   sale or return
internal bond   organization   sales gimmick
in the gazette   packing house   sales manager
joint account   pay as you earn   salesmanship
keep accounts   pay in advance   satisfaction
labour of love   pegged market   sell on credit
laissez faire   peg the market   severance pay
leather goods   ply one's trade   share company
line of credit   porte monnaie   shareholding
live in clover   pressure belt   short account
lively market   price ceiling   show business
long interest   price control   slender means
make a bargain   price current   sliding scale
make a fortune   price of money   state lottery
make delivery   price rigging   steady market
make one's pile   productivity   sterling area
manipulation   professional   stock company
manufacturer   profiteering   stock dealing
marginal cost   profit margin   stockholding
mass produced   profit motive   stock in trade
mercantilism   purse strings   stock jobbery
monetization   rags to riches   street market
money changer   rate of growth   strike action

strike|it|rich
strong|market
superannuate
sustain|a|loss
tax|collector
tax|exemption
ten|cent|store
the|long|green
ticker|market
trade|balance
trade|mission
trading|stamp
travel|agency
treasury|bill
treasury|note
trial|balance
trustee|stock
unemployment
variety|store
watered|stock
Welfare|State
without|a|bean
working|class
working|order
advertisement
asset|stripper
bank|messenger
Bank|of|England
bank|overdraft
bank|statement
budget|account
budget|surplus
bulls|and|bears
burial|society
business|hours
cash|dispenser

cash|in|advance
cash|on|the|nail
clearance|sale
clearing|house
commercialism
commercialist
company|report
concessionary
confetti|money
confidence|man
consumer|goods
copartnership
cost|effective
counting|house
credit|account
credit|balance
credit|company
credit|squeeze
crossed|cheque
current|assets
depressed|area
discount|house
discount|store
excess|profits
eye|to|business
falling|prices
filing|cabinet
financial|year
fire|insurance
free|trade|area
fringe|benefit
going|for|a|song
impulse|buying
incorporation
industrialism
in|Queer|Street

life assurance
life insurance
Lombard Street
man of business
millionairess
modernisation
money no object
multinational
multiple store
Parkinson's Law
payment in kind
payment in lieu
penalty clause
petticoat lane
price increase
private income
private sector
profitability
profit and loss
profit sharing
protectionism
protectionist
public company
purchase price
raise the money
rate for the job
rates and taxes
regular income
sellers market
service charge
small business
small investor
spending spree
stock exchange
strike breaker
subcontractor

tax deductible
trade discount
trade unionism
trade unionist
trading estate
value added tax
white elephant
wild cat strike
accident policy
asset stripping
balance of trade
bargain counter
bill discounter
capitalisation
cash on delivery
certain annuity
clearance house
company meeting
concessionaire
consumer demand
corporation tax
cost accountant
cost accounting
cost efficiency
current account
deposit account
direct debiting
discount broker
distressed area
expense account
eye for business
family business
finance company
free enterprise
free of interest
full employment

gnomes of Zurich

holding company

imprest account

inertia selling

letter of credit

lighting up time

limited company

Lloyd's register

market research

mass production

merchant banker

monthly payment

national income

national wealth

ordinary shares

over production

over the counter

penny in the slot

peppercorn rent

Peter principle

private company

production line

pyramid selling

quality control

rate of exchange

rate of interest

second hand shop

shopping centre

simple interest

superannuation

surrender value

tariff reformer

three mile limit

under the hammer

unearned income

vending machine

vested interest

visible exports

window shopping

working capital

American Express

bargain basement

building society

business as usual

business circles

business contact

business manager

business studies

business venture

capital gains tax

carriage forward

cash transaction

closing down sale

commission agent

company director

company promoter

complete annuity

cottage industry

deferred annuity

deferred payment

department store

development area

distress warrant

dividend warrant

do a roaring trade

electricity bill

endowment policy

entrepreneurial

exchange control

family allowance

floating capital

foreign exchange

franking machine
friendly society
golden handshake
income tax demand
income tax rebate
income tax relief
income tax return
insurance broker
insurance policy
investment trust
invisible import
labour intensive
lightning strike
marine insurance
money for old rope
national savings
no claim discount

non profit making
preference stock
public ownership
purchasing power
registration fee
regular customer
reserve currency
rock bottom price
service industry
settle an account
sleeping partner
supply and demand
suspense account
under the counter
unemployment pay
world of commerce

Transport and Communications

Al	cab	guy	leg	rut	UFO
AA	cam	HMS	log	sea	van
go	car	hop	map	ski	via
GT	cat	hoy	MOT	SOS	way
M1	cog	hub	mph	STD	yaw
ABC	cox	jet	oar	sub	ahoy
ace	fan	jib	oil	tar	A one
aft	fin	jog	ply	ton	auto
air	fly	key	ram	top	axle
ark	gad	lag	rev	tow	back
bay	gas	lap	rig	tub	bail
bus	gig	lee	run	tug	bank

TRANSPORT AND COMMUNICATIONS

bark	flow	luff	sail	warp	cleat
beak	ford	Mach	salt	wash	climb
beam	fore	mail	scow	wire	coach
bend	fork	mast	ship	yard	coast
biga	gaff	mini	sink	yawl	coble
bike	gait	moke	skid	zoom	coupe
bitt	gear	mole	skip	abaft	craft
blip	gyro	moor	skis	afoot	crank
boat	hack	navy	sled	afoul	crash
boom	haul	nose	span	alley	crate
boot	head	oars	spar	aloft	cycle
brig	heel	pace	spin	amble	dandy
bunk	helm	park	stay	araba	davit
buoy	hike	pass	stem	avion	ditch
buss	hold	path	step	awash	dodge
cart	hood	pier	tack	balsa	dolly
case	horn	poop	tail	barge	drift
code	hove	port	tank	beach	drive
cork	hulk	post	taxi	below	drome
crew	hull	pram	tide	berth	E,boat
curb	idle	prop	toll	bilge	embus
dash	jack	prow	tour	blimp	facia
deck	jeep	pull	tram	board	fanal
dhow	junk	punt	trap	bosun	ferry
dial	keel	push	trek	brail	flare
dive	kerb	quay	trim	brake	fleet
dock	kite	raft	trip	buggy	flier
dory	knot	rail	trot	byway	float
drag	land	reef	tube	cabby	flota
draw	lane	ride	tyre	cabin	fluke
dray	lift	ring	vang	cable	foist
duck	line	road	veer	canal	forth
fare	list	roam	vent	canoe	glide
fast	lock	roll	wain	cargo	going
flee	loop	rove	wake	choke	guard
flit	lost	saic	walk	chute	guide

haste	pylon	stage	adrift	bumper
hatch	Q|boat	stall	afloat	busman
hawse	racer	stamp	airbus	by|lane
hiker	radar	stamp	airing	by|pass
hobby	radio	start	air|log	bypath
hoist	rally	steam	airman	byroad
horse	range	stern	air|ram	caique
hurry	reach	stray	airway	calash
jaunt	relay	strip	alight	call|up
jetty	rev|up	strut	anchor	camber
jolly	rider	stunt	argosy	canard
jumbo	ropes	sweep	armada	canter
kayak	rotor	Telex	arrive	canvas
kedge	route	thole	artery	careen
ketch	royal	ton|up	ascent	career
lay|by	sally	track	astern	carfax
leech	screw	trail	avenue	carina
lie|to	sedan	train	aweigh	chaise
light	shaft	tramp	back|up	clutch
liner	sheer	tread	banger	coaler
loran	sheet	trike	bargee	cobble
lorry	shell	truck	barque	cockle
march	shift	trunk	barrow	conner
morse	shunt	U|boat	basket	con|rod
motor	sidle	umiak	bateau	convoy
mount	skiff	U|turn	beacon	copter
naval	skirt	valve	berlin	course
nomad	skull	visit	big|end	cruise
on|tow	slips	way|in	bireme	cut|out
orbit	sloop	wharf	boatel	cutter
pedal	smack	wheel	bomber	decked
pilot	smash	xebec	bonnet	de|icer
pitch	spars	yacht	bowser	depart
plane	speed	Z|bend	braces	detour
praam	spill	aboard	bridge	dinghy
prang	sprit	abroad	bucket	divert

TRANSPORT AND COMMUNICATIONS

diving	hurtle	nip|off	saloon
dogger	hustle	nose|up	sampan
driver	idling	octane	sculls
dry|run	impact	on|deck	seaman
dugout	intake	one|way	seaway
earing	in|trim	on|foot	sender
egress	island	onward	set|out
elevon	jalopy	outing	sheets
embark	jet|lag	outset	shoran
engine	jetsam	oxcart	shroud
escape	jet|set	packet	siding
exodus	jib|guy	paddle	signal
fender	jigger	petrol	skates
fiacre	jostle	pharos	skyway
flight	junket	pickup	sledge
flying	kit|bag	pile|up	sleigh
fo|c's|le	klaxon	piston	smoker
funnel	landau	porter	sortie
galiot	lascar	propel	sparks
galley	lateen	pursue	spiral
gallop	launch	radial	splice
garage	leeway	ramble	spring
gas|jet	letter	ram|jet	stocks
gasket	litter	randem	stoker
glider	lock|up	rating	strake
gocart	lorcha	ratlin	street
gunnel	lugger	reefer	stride
hangar	mahout	return	stroll
hansom	marina	rigged	subway
haul|to	marker	rigger	surrey
hawser	mayday	ring|up	swerve
hearse	mirror	rocket	tackle
hooker	mizzen	rudder	tandem
hot|rod	mobile	runner	tanker
hove|to	module	runway	tannoy
hubcap	motion	sailor	tartan

6/7 LETTERS

tender	airfoil	bollard	chopper
ticker	air|jump	bomb|bay	chutist
ticket	air|lane	booking	circuit
tiller	air|legs	booster	clipper
timber	airlift	bow|fast	coaster
tin|can	airline	bowline	cockpit
toddle	air|miss	boxhaul	collide
toggle	airpark	box|kite	collier
torque	airport	boxseat	commute
totter	airship	britzka	compass
towbar	airsick	bulwark	contact
travel	air|taxi	busline	co|pilot
troika	ambages	bus|stop	coracle
trudge	arrival	buzzing	courier
tunnel	autobus	buzz|off	crack|up
turret	autocar	caboose	crewman
unmoor	autovac	call|box	crock|up
valise	aviator	capsize	cruiser
vessel	aviette	capstan	cyclist
volant	baby|jib	capsule	day|trip
voyage	baggage	captain	descent
waggon	bail|out	caravan	detrain
wander	ballast	caravel	dodgems
way|out	balloon	cariole	dogcart
whaler	banking	carpark	draught
wherry	barge|in	carport	drayman
whisky	battery	carrack	dredger
address	bay|line	carrier	drifter
aerobus	beeline	catboat	drive|in
aground	bicycle	cat|head	droshky
aileron	biplane	cat's|eye	dry|dock
air|base	birdman	catwalk	dry|land
airboat	blister	channel	ejector
air|crew	boating	chariot	emplane
airdrop	boatman	charter	engaged
air|flow	bobstay	chassis	en|route

TRANSPORT AND COMMUNICATIONS

entrain	gunboat	killick	monitor
exhaust	gun|deck	killock	mooring
explore	guy,rope	landing	mud|hook
express	gyro,car	lanyard	nacelle
fairing	hackney	L,driver	no|entry
fairway	halyard	learner	oarsman
felucca	hammock	lee|helm	odyssey
fetch|up	handbag	lee|tack	offside
flattop	harbour	leeward	old|salt
flivver	hardtop	leewide	omnibus
flyboat	harness	lift,off	on|board
flyover	haywain	lighter	ongoing
fly|past	head|for	logbook	on|the|go
foretop	head|off	L,plates	opening
formula	headset	luggage	orbital
founder	headway	lugsail	outride
four,oar	heave|to	lymphad	painter
freeway	helibus	Mae|West	parking
frigate	helipad	magneto	parting
frogman	highway	mail|van	passage
futtock	holdall	maintop	pathway
galleon	hot|line	make|for	payload
galleys	hurry|up	make|off	phaeton
gangway	iceboat	man,o,war	pig|boat
gearbox	impetus	mariner	pillion
getaway	impulse	marline	pinnace
get|lost	ingress	Martian	piragua
gliding	Jack|Tar	matelot	pirogue
go,ahead	jaw,rope	meander	polacca
go|below	jet|pipe	migrant	polacre
go|by|air	jib|boom	milk|run	pontoon
go,devil	jibstay	minibus	postage
gondola	journey	minicab	postman
grapnel	joy|ride	minicar	precede
growler	keelson	minisub	proceed
guichet	keep|off	mission	Pullman

pull|out	set|sail	tonneau	volante
push|car	shallop	top|deck	voyager
railway	shipway	topmast	wanigan
ratline	shuttle	topsail	warship
rebound	side,car	topside	waybill
re,entry	skid|pan	torsion	wayfare
retrace	skipper	tourist	wayworn
retreat	skysail	towards	welcome
reverse	sleeper	towboat	winging
ride|out	slipway	towpath	wingtip
rigging	smash,up	towrope	wrecker
ring|off	spanker	tractor	yardarm
ripcord	sputnik	traffic	zooming
road,hog	starter	trailer	aerodyne
road,map	start|up	traipse	aerofoil
road,tax	station	tramcar	aerogram
rolling	steamer	tramway	aeronaut
rope,tow	steward	transit	aerostat
ropeway	stopway	travels	airborne
rowboat	surface	trawler	air|brake
rowlock	sweeper	tripper	air|coach
run|away	swifter	trireme	aircraft
run|into	tackler	trolley	airfield
runners	tail|end	trundle	airframe
sailing	tail|fin	trysail	airliner
satchel	take,off	tugboat	air|route
saunter	tartane	tumbrel	air|scout
scamper	taxicab	tumbril	airscrew
scooter	taxiing	turning	airspace
scupper	taxiway	twin,jet	air|speed
scuttle	telpher	vagrant	airstrip
sea|lane	Telstar	vehicle	airwoman
sea|legs	termini	viaduct	all|at|sea
seasick	test|hop	vis,a,vis	alleyway
seaward	tilbury	visitor	altitude
send,off	to|horse	voiture	approach

area|code	caracole	drag|wire	fore|jack
arterial	carriage	driftway	fore|lift
at|anchor	cast|away	drive|off	foremast
autobahn	catapult	driveway	foresail
autogyro	cat's|eyes	dust|cart	foreship
aviation	causeway	eight|oar	forestay
aviatrix	clarence	elevator	foretack
backfire	clearway	emigrant	foreyard
back|seat	coachbox	emigrate	forkroad
backstay	coachman	entrance	fuel|ship
backwash	coachway	envelope	full|load
bargeman	coasting	equipage	fuselage
barnacle	cockboat	Europort	gad|about
barouche	commuter	evacuate	galleass
beam|ends	Concorde	even|keel	garboard
bearings	converge	exchange	gasoline
becalmed	corridor	excursus	get|ahead
bilander	corvette	fall|back	go|aboard
binnacle	coxswain	farewell	go|ashore
black|box	crabbing	fast|line	go|astray
boat|deck	crescent	ferryman	go|before
boat|hook	crossing	fireboat	go|by|rail
boat|line	crossply	flagging	Godspeed
bodywork	cruising	flagship	gradient
bolt|rope	cul|de|sac	flatboat	grounded
bowsprit	curricle	flat|spin	half|deck
Bradshaw	cylinder	flat|tyre	handcart
brancard	dahabeah	floating	hang|back
broach|to	deck|hand	flotilla	hatchway
brougham	derelict	flywheel	hawse|bag
bulkhead	dipstick	fogbound	head|fast
bulwarks	dismount	footfall	head|into
cabin|boy	ditty|bag	footpath	heel|over
cable|car	downhaul	footslog	heliport
cableway	dragoman	footstep	helmsman
camshaft	dragster	forefoot	highroad

high|seas	level|off	motorist	porthole
homeward	life|belt	motorway	portside
horse|box	lifeboat	muleteer	port|tack
horseman	life|buoy	multi|jet	post|boat
icebound	life|line	navarchy	postcard
ice|yacht	life|raft	nearside	postcode
ignition	lift|wire	nose|cone	progress
in|flight	log|canoe	nosedive	pulsejet
in|motion	longbeat	nose|down	puncture
inner|jib	longeron	nose|into	pushcart
intercom	long|haul	oil|gauge	put|to|sea
ironclad	loose|box	old|crock	quadriga
jackstay	mail|boat	oleo|gear	radiator
jerrican	main|deck	oncoming	railroad
jet|pilot	main|lift	one|horse	receiver
jet|plane	mainline	on|the|run	red|light
jet|power	mainmast	open|road	reef|band
jettison	main|road	operator	reef|knot
journeys	mainstay	ordinary	rickshaw
joy|rider	main|yard	outboard	ring|road
joystick	manifold	outer|jib	road|sign
jumbo|jet	man|of|war	overhaul	roadster
junction	maritime	overland	rockaway
jurymast	masthead	overpass	roof|rack
jury|sail	mine|ship	overseas	ropeband
kamikaze	momentum	overtake	ropework
keel|over	monorail	overturn	rucksack
kickback	moon|base	passer|by	runabout
knapsack	moonsail	passover	run|ahead
land|ahoy	moon|ship	passport	rush|hour
landfall	moonshot	pavement	sailboat
larboard	moonwalk	periplus	sail|free
lateener	moorings	pilotage	sail|loft
launcher	motorbus	platform	schedule
leeboard	motorcar	Plimsoll	schooner
lee|sheet	motoring	poop|deck	scout|car

seafarer	staysail	under|way
seagoing	steerage	unicycle
seaplane	steering	velocity
sea|route	sternway	victoria
set|forth	stock|car	vol̦atile
shanghai	stopover	volplane
sheer̦leg	stowaway	wagon̦lit
sheer|off	straggle	wardroom
ship|ahoy	straying	warplane
shipmate	stunt|man	water|bus
ship|oars	suitcase	waterway
shipping	tackling	wayfarer
short|hop	tag|along	way̦train
shoulder	tail|boom	wear|ship
show|a|leg	tailpipe	wheelies
showboat	tail|skid	wind|cone
side|road	tail|spin	wind|drag
sideslip	taxi|rank	wind|sock
side|step	telegram	windward
sidewalk	teletype	wing|over
silencer	terminal	wireless
skidding	terminus	withdraw
skid|mark	thole̦pin	yachting
slip|road	throttle	Zeppelin
slow|down	toboggan	zero|hour
slow|lane	tollgate	abouțship
snap|roll	tramline	addressee
sociable	traverse	aerodrome
spaceman	tricycle	aeromotor
spar|deck	trimaran	aeroplane
speeding	trim|sail	after|deck
squad|car	trim|ship	air|bridge
staff|car	turbojet	air|pocket
stanhope	turn|away	air|sleeve
start|off	turn|over	airworthy
start|out	turnpike	all|aboard

altimeter
ambulance
amidships
amphibian
anchorage
applecart
astrodome
astronaut
atom|liner
autopilot
autopista
backropes
back|water
bandwagon
bargepole
basic|load
Bath|chair
below|deck
bilge|keel
bilge|pump
black|gang
blockship
blue|peter
boathouse
boatswain
boat|train
bobsleigh
bon|voyage
boulevard
bowl|along
box|waggon
broadside
bubble|car
bulldozer
bus|driver
cab|driver

cablegram
cabriolet
canalboat
cargo|boat
carpet|bag
cartwheel
catamaran
charabanc
chauffeur
chief|mate
clearance
clew|lines
coach|road
coachwork
collision
combat|car
concourse
conductor
cosmonaut
couchette
countdown
crankcase
crash|boat
crash|land
crocodile
crossjack
cross|road
crosstree
crowd|sail
crow's|nest
curbstone
cut|and|run
dashboard
Davy|Jones
day|letter
day|return

deceleron
departure
depot|ship
destroyer
diesel|oil
diligence
dining|car
dip|switch
direction
dirigible
dirt|track
disembark
diversion
dodgem|car
drag|force
drift|wire
drive|away
drop|a|line
duffel|bag
Early|Bird
earphones
empennage
escalator
esplanade
estate|car
excursion
extension
false|keel
family|car
fare|stage
ferryboat
first|mate
first|rate
flying|jib
footropes
forebrace

foreroyal	headphone	lower|boom
foresheet	helidrome	lower|deck
freeboard	hit,and,run	lunar|base
free|wheel	hitch|hike	Mach|meter
freighter	hoist|sail	mail|coach
French|lug	hook|a|ride	mainbrace
front|seat	horseback	mainroyal
fuel|gauge	houseboat	mainsheet
funicular	hump|speed	major|road
gain|speed	hydrofoil	make|haste
gallivant	ice|skates	manoeuvre
gangplank	immigrant	mass|media
gather|way	immigrate	milestone
gear|lever	inch|along	milkfloat
ghost|ship	indicator	milometer
give|a|ring	itinerant	mine|layer
globe,trot	itinerary	miss|stays
go|aground	jaunty|car	mizzentop
gondolier	jaywalker	monoplane
goose|step	jet|bomber	moonraker
grand|tour	jollyboat	morse|code
grapevine	kerb|drill	motorbike
gross|lift	kerbstone	motorboat
groundhog	kick|start	motorcade
guard|ship	lag|behind	mule|train
guard's|van	landaulet	multi,prop
guess|warp	landplane	navigable
guest,rope	land|rover	navigator
gyropilot	launching	newsflash
gyroplane	launch|pad	nosewheel
handbrake	leave|home	ocean|lane
hansom|cab	letter|box	ocean|trip
hatchback	leviathan	on|the|move
haversack	lightship	on|the|wing
hawse|hook	limousine	orientate
hawsepipe	lose|speed	orlop|deck

outrigger	river|boat	sidetrack
overboard	road|block	sight|land
overdrive	road|sense	sightseer
overshoot	roadstead	signal|box
pack|horse	road|works	signalman
palanquin	rocket|car	single|jet
pancaking	rocket|man	skyriding
parachute	rotor|ship	slowcoach
party|line	round|trip	slow|train
passenger	royal|mast	small|boat
patrol|car	royal|road	snowshoes
periscope	royal|sail	sonic|boom
phone|book	rudder|bar	sonic|wall
phone|call	saddlebag	space|crew
pillar|box	sailplane	spacedock
pilot|boat	sally|port	spaceport
point|duty	saloon|car	spaceship
police|car	sand|yacht	space|suit
police|van	satellite	spacewalk
portfolio	saucerman	spare|part
post|haste	sea|anchor	speedboat
postilion	seafaring	speedster
powerboat	sea|gasket	spinnaker
power|dive	seaworthy	sports|car
pressgang	semaphore	spritsail
privateer	set|on|foot	stage|boat
prize|crew	sharp|bend	stanchion
promenade	sheer|hulk	starboard
propeller	shipboard	stateroom
racing|car	ship|of|war	steal|away
radar|nose	ship|plane	steamboat
radio|beam	ship|route	steam|line
radiogram	ship's|crew	steamship
ram|rocket	shipshape	steersman
reach|land	shipwreck	step|aside
reef|point	sidelight	stern|fast

sternpost	tramlines	air|control
stevedore	transport	air|cruiser
stokehold	traveller	air|hostess
storeship	triptyque	air|service
storm|boat	troopship	air|steward
stratojet	trunk|call	air|support
streetcar	trunk|line	Al|at|Lloyd's
stretcher	trunk|road	amber|light
strike|out	turboprop	ambulation
stringers	turbopump	ambulatory
sub,chaser	turn|aside	anchor|deck
submarine	turn|round	antifreeze
surfacing	turret|top	automobile
surfboard	twin,screw	ballooning
switch|off	two,seater	balloonist
tailboard	ufologist	ball|turret
tail,light	underpass	barkentine
tailplane	under|sail	barrel,roll
tail|rotor	upper|deck	batten|down
tail|shaft	vehicular	battleship
take|leave	war|galley	bear|down|on
taximeter	water|line	Bermuda|rig
taxiplane	whaleback	Black|Maria
tea|waggon	whaleboat	blind|alley
telegraph	wheel|base	boneshaker
telemotor	wheel|spin	branch|line
telepathy	white|line	breakwater
telephone	wirephoto	bridge|deck
telephony	yachtsman	bridle|path
telephoto	able|seaman	brigantine
test|pilot	aboard|ship	bubble|hood
third|mate	access|road	bucket|seat
timenoguy	adventurer	bus|service
timetable	aerobatics	bus|station
touch|down	aeronautic	cabin|plane
traipsing	a|head|start	camouflage

cantilever	drift|along	ground|loop
cargo|plane	drift|angle	hackney|cab
cast|anchor	drop|anchor	hawsepiece
catch|a|crab	dusk|rocket	headlights
catch|a|ride	emigration	heatshield
chapel|cart	evacuation	heave|round
clear|house	expedition	heave|short
clew|garnet	expressway	helicopter
coach|horse	fall|behind	High|street
cockleboat	feed|system	hitch|hiker
column|gear	fire|engine	hit|the|deck
command|car	first|class	home|and|dry
congestion	flight|deck	homecoming
connection	flight|path	hovercraft
contraflow	flight|plan	hydroplane
control|rod	flight|time	icebreaker
conveyance	floatplane	inflatable
cosmodrome	fly|by|night	inter|urban
country|bus	flying|boat	invalid|car
covered|way	flying|wing	jaywalking
cow|catcher	footbridge	jet|fatigue
crankshaft	fore|and|aft	jet|fighter
crossroads	forecastle	jigger|mast
dandy|horse	forerunner	Jolly|Roger
dawn|rocket	foresheets	Joyce|stick
day|tripper	forge|ahead	juggernaut
decampment	four|in|hand	jury|rigged
delta|wings	four|master	jury|rudder
dickey|seat	gain|ground	knockabout
disemplane	gather|head	landing|run
dive|bomber	gear|change	landlubber
diving|bell	glass|coach	lateen|sail
double|bend	go|in|the|van	lead|the|way
double|prop	goods|train	lettergram
double|reef	green|light	lie|athwart
downstream	ground|crew	life|jacket

lighthouse	patrol|boat	round,house
locomotion	pedestrian	roustabout
luggage|van	Penny|Black	rowing|boat
main|artery	petrol|pump	safety|belt
make|tracks	petrol|tank	safety|wire
manipulate	picketboat	sail|teaser
manoeuvres	pilgrimage	sally|forth
marker|buoy	pilothouse	seamanship
martingale	pilot|plane	second|mate
middle|deck	pipe|aboard	sedan|chair
midshipman	port|anchor	sens|unique
mizzenmast	port|of|call	servo,pilot
mizzen|sail	post|chaise	set|the|pace
mizzen|stay	Post|Office	sheepshank
monkey|deck	propellant	shipmaster
monkey|rail	propulsion	sidesaddle
motorcoach	public|walk	side|street
motorcycle	quadrireme	single,prop
motor|truck	quadruplex	skyscraper
naval|cadet	radial|tyre	sky|writing
navigation	rear|mirror	slipstream
nose|turret	reduce|sail	sloop|of|war
ocean|going	rendezvous	smoking|car
ocean|liner	repair|ship	solo|flight
on|a|bowline	rescue|boat	spacecraft
on|the|march	rev|counter	spare|wheel
on|the|rocks	ride|and|tie	speed|limit
open|waggon	ride|a|storm	square|away
outer|space	right|of|way	square|sail
overbridge	road|safety	stagecoach
packet|boat	roadworthy	stand|first
packet|line	robot|plane	state|barge
packet|ship	rocket|boat	static|tube
paddle|boat	rocket|ship	step,rocket
parcel|post	rope|bridge	stewardess
pathfinder	roundabout	streamline

submariner	two|wheeler	assault|boat
sun|compass	undershoot	attack|plane
supercargo	under|steam	balloon|sail
supersonic	useful|lift	battleplane
supply|ship	vanity|case	beaten|track
suspension	velocipede	belaying|pin
switchback	veteran|car	bid|farewell
tachometer	V,formation	blind|corner
tanker|ship	vintage|car	blind|flying
target|boat	volitation	break|ground
tea|clipper	volplaning	built,up|area
telegraphy	wanderings	bullock|cart
telepathic	wanderlust	carburetter
television	watercraft	card|compass
telewriter	water|plane	carriageway
telpherage	watertight	carrick|bend
test|flight	way|station	catch|a|train
test|rocket	way|traffic	caterpillar
thumb|a|lift	wheel|chair	cat's|whisker
ticker|tape	wheelhouse	centreboard
tip,up|lorry	whirlybird	close,hauled
toll|bridge	windjammer	club|topsail
topgallant	windscreen	coach|driver
touring|car	wing|mirror	cockleshell
tracklayer	abandon|ship	combat|plane
traffic|jam	accelerator	come|forward
train|ferry	aeronautics	compartment
trajectory	afterburner	contraprops
travelling	after|shroud	convertible
travel|sick	air|controls	country|road
travel|worn	airsickness	cover|ground
triaconter	air|terminal	crash|helmet
triphibian	air,umbrella	crash|waggon
trolley|bus	anchor|fluke	crowd|of|sail
true|course	armoured|car	delivery|van
turret|ship	articulated	destination

distributor
double march
dreadnought
driving test
ejector seat
engaged line
engine gauge
entrainment
escape hatch
escape route
exhaust pipe
fares please
find one's way
fishing boat
fishing dory
fishtailing
fleet of foot
flight strip
flying kites
flying speed
flying visit
forced march
fore topsail
forward deck
galley slave
gather speed
get under way
go alongside
goods waggon
go overboard
Gran Turismo
ground speed
gyrocompass
hawse timber
head for home
highway code

hit the trail
horse litter
hug the shore
ignition key
immigration
interceptor
in the saddle
in the wake of
jaunting car
journeyings
journey's end
kedge anchor
keep station
kite balloon
laminar flow
landing deck
landing skis
lazy painter
leading edge
leave taking
limber board
line engaged
loop the loop
lorry driver
lose one's way
luggage rack
lunar module
magic carpet
main skysail
main topsail
make headway
make sea room
make strides
man from Mars
merchantman
mess steward

minesweeper
mizzen royal
montgolfier
moon landing
moon station
mooring buoy
mooring mast
morse signal
Moses basket
motor launch
motor vessel
mystery tour
naval rating
naval vessel
near the wind
night letter
orientation
ornithopter
out of the way
outside loop
package tour
paddle wheel
parachutist
paratrooper
penteconter
peregrinate
peripatetic
petrol gauge
phone number
pick up speed
pillion seat
pony and trap
portmanteau
private line
push bicycle
put into port

quarter deck	sightseeing	telpher line
quarter jack	sinking ship	testing area
quinquereme	skysail mast	three in hand
racing shell	sleeping bag	three master
radio beacon	sleeping car	ticking over
radio mirror	soft landing	torpedo boat
request stop	solar rocket	trafficator
rescue plane	space centre	transmitter
reservation	space flight	transporter
retroaction	space island	travel agent
retro rocket	space patrol	true heading
reverse turn	space rocket	trysail gaff
road haulage	space travel	tube station
road licence	spanker boom	under canvas
road traffic	spanker gaff	underground
rocket motor	speedometer	vapour train
rocket plane	stagger wire	waggon trail
rocket power	standing lug	waggon wheel
rotorblades	steal a march	waiting room
running knot	steam engine	walking tour
sailing boat	steam launch	weather deck
sailing ship	step rockets	weather side
scuttlebutt	stern anchor	weigh anchor
search plane	stern sheets	wheelbarrow
seasickness	straphanger	wing loading
second class	string along	wrong number
self starter	stunt flying	aircraftsman
send packing	submersible	airfreighter
set in motion	subsonic jet	air sea rescue
Shanks's mare	switchboard	all systems go
Shanks's pony	synchromesh	approach road
sheet anchor	tailless jet	arrester hook
shelter deck	take the lead	arterial road
ship the oars	tandem plane	autorotation
shroud lines	telecontrol	baby carriage
shuttle trip	teleprinter	Bailey bridge

beaching|gear	entrance|lock	landing|strip
beacon|lights	escape|rocket	launching|pad
bearing|plate	fighter|pilot	level|landing
belly|landing	fishing|fleet	light|cruiser
between|decks	fishing|smack	long|distance
blind|landing	flight|tester	longshoreman
cabin|cruiser	flying|circus	lost|and|found
cable|railway	flying|saucer	luggage|label
caulking|iron	flying|tanker	luggage|train
centre|anchor	forestaysail	maiden|flight
change|course	forward|march	maiden|voyage
channel|patch	free|wheeling	main|staysail
chart|a|course	freight|train	make|good|time
citizen's|band	fuel|injector	make|progress
clear|the|land	Gladstone|bag	manned|rocket
coach|and|four	glide|landing	man|overboard
coach|and|pair	globetrotter	merchant|ship
coachbuilder	go|by|the|board	monkey|rigged
companionway	ground|tester	motor|scooter
conning|tower	hackney|coach	night|fighter
control|stick	happy|landing	off|like|a|shot
control|tower	harbour|light	overnight|bag
counter|march	heavy|cruiser	pantechnicon
crash|barrier	hedgehopping	parking|light
crash|landing	hospital|ship	parking|meter
cylinder|head	inclinometer	parking|orbit
desobligeant	in|the|train|of	passing|place
dialling|code	inverted|spin	perambulator
dialling|tone	Jacob's|ladder	petty|officer
dispatch|boat	jet|propelled	pilot|balloon
double|decker	king's|highway	plain|sailing
draught|horse	landing|craft	platform|deck
dual|controls	landing|field	pleasure|boat
East|Indiaman	landing|light	pleasure|trip
ejection|seat	landing|speed	Plimsoll|line
end|of|the|line	landing|stage	Plimsoll|mark

postage|stamp
pressure|suit
puddle|jumper
pursuit|plane
quarterlight
radar|scanner
radar|station
radio|compass
radio|monitor
radio|station
raise|the|dead
return|ticket
ride|at|anchor
ride|bareback
road|junction
rocket|assist
rocket|engine
rocket|glider
roller|skates
rolling|stock
rolling|stone
rough|passage
running|board
running|light
sailing|barge
sailing|canoe
sailing|yacht
season|ticket
shape|a|course
shipping|line
shoot|ballast
single|decker
slacken|speed
sonic|barrier
sound|barrier
space|capsule

space|station
spanker|sheet
sparking|plug
speed|of|sound
square|rigged
square|rigger
stall|landing
steer|clear|of
steering|gear
stream|anchor
streamlining
Sunday|driver
sunshine|roof
survival|suit
take|bearings
take|off|strip
tallyho|coach
tearing|hurry
tender|rocket
the|bitter|end
thoroughfare
three|wheeler
through|train
ticket|office
touch|the|wind
tourist|class
traffic|light
train|service
transmission
travel|agency
trolley|track
tubeless|tyre
upset|the|boat
utility|plane
VIP|transport
walk|the|plank

TRANSPORT AND COMMUNICATIONS

Wandering Jew
weatherboard
weather sheet
windward side
aerial railway
armoured train
begging letter
Belisha beacon
booking office
breakdown gang
bridge of sighs
bush telegraph
carriage drive
Channel tunnel
coach building
command module
communication
conducted tour
conductor rail
container port
container ship
corridor train
distant signal
driving lesson
driving mirror
driving school
electric train
excess luggage
express letter
flying machine
foot passenger
forced landing
globe trotting
ground control
homeward bound
horse and buggy

jet propulsion
landing ground
left hand drive
level crossing
number engaged
paddle steamer
panda crossing
penny farthing
peregrination
peripatetical
petrol station
pontoon bridge
postal address
postal service
poste restante
power steering
press campaign
press cuttings
pressure cabin
printing press
promenade deck
public address
public highway
Queen's highway
radiotelegram
railway engine
railway system
railway tunnel
restaurant car
return journey
road transport
roller coaster
roll on roll off
rule of the road
sailing orders
scenic railway

shock absorber
shooting brake
space platform
speed merchant
station master
steering wheel
stepping stone
strato cruiser
telegraph pole
telegraph wire
telephone book
telephone call
telephone line
through ticket
traffic island
traffic lights
transportable
transport cafe
transport ship
transshipping
trunk dialling
turning circle
turn the corner
unadopted road
undercarriage
zebra crossing
automatic pilot
breakdown truck
catenary system
coaling station
deadman's handle
diesel electric
disembarkation
excursion train
filling station
first class mail

first class post
flight recorder
floating bridge
full steam ahead
inland waterway
luggage carrier
no thoroughfare
observation car
package holiday
passenger train
personal column
person to person
platform ticket
quarantine flag
radiotelegraph
radiotelephone
rear view mirror
registered mail
registered post
reversing light
road traffic act
running repairs
service station
shuttle service
space traveller
steering column
telegraph cable
telephone kiosk
telephotograph
three point turn
three speed gear
through traffic
traction engine
traffic manager
traffic signals
transportation

TRANSPORT AND COMMUNICATIONS

trustee|account
wild|goose|chase
carriage|and|pair
double|white|line
dual|carriageway
excursion|ticket
express|delivery
Grand|Union|canal
hackney|carriage
invalid|carriage
marshalling|yard
message|received
motorway|madness
mountain|railway
moving|staircase
pelican|crossing
picture|postcard
pleasure|steamer
point|of|no|return

prairie|schooner
press|conference
public|transport
radiotelegraphy
railway|carriage
railway|crossing
refreshment|room
road|fund|licence
second|class|mail
second|class|post
special|delivery
stamping|machine
telephone|number
temperance|hotel
ticket|collector
ticket|inspector
vertical|take|off
victualling|ship
windscreen|wiper

Trees

ash	sal	coca	sorb	alder	briar
bay	sap	coco	teak	algum	brier
ben	yew	cone	tree	almug	broom
box	akee	cork	twig	arbor	brush
elm	bark	dhak	upas	aspen	cacao
fig	bass	dita	whin	balsa	carob
fir	bast	ilex	wood	beech	cedar
gum	bole	palm	abele	birch	copse
log	bosk	pine	abies	bough	cubeb
oak	bush	root	acorn	brake	ebony

446

elder	banyan	sallow	foliage
frith	baobab	sapota	foliose
furze	bogoak	sappan	genipap
glade	botree	souari	gumtree
gorse	bransh	spruce	hickory
grove	carapa	sumach	holmoak
hedge	cassia	sylvan	hoptree
henna	catkin	timber	juniper
holly	caudex	walnut	leafage
hurst	cornel	wattle	leaflet
jarul	daphne	willow	lentisk
kokra	deodar	ailanto	logwood
kokum	forest	ambatch	madrona
larch	gingko	arbutus	margosa
lilac	jarool	babussu	oakling
maple	jarrah	bebeeru	palmyra
myrrh	jujube	bluegum	pinetum
palay	jungle	boscage	platane
pipal	kalmia	boxwood	pollard
plane	kittul	bullace	pruning
ramus	laurel	cajuput	rampick
roble	lignum	catalpa	rampike
roots	linden	chamise	redpine
rowan	loquat	chamiso	redwood
sapan	manuka	conifer	sapling
shrub	myrtle	coppice	sapwood
sumac	papaya	coquito	sequoia
thorn	pinery	corkoak	service
tilia	platan	cowtree	spinney
trunk	poplar	cypress	sundari
zamia	privet	dagwood	syringa
abroma	prunus	dogwood	taproot
acajou	queach	duramen	teatree
antiar	rattan	durmast	thicket
arbute	redbud	figleaf	waxtree
arolla	redfir	fircone	wychelm

TREES

Yule|log	kingwood	tamarind
ailantus	laburnum	viburnum
alburnum	lavender	witch,elm
allspice	magnolia	woodland
arboreal	mahogany	wood|pulp
ash,plant	mangrove	adansonia
barberry	manna|ash	albespyne
basswood	mesquite	algarroba
beam|tree	milk|tree	aloes,wood
beefwood	milkwood	alpine|fir
caatinga	oleander	andromeda
calamite	palmetto	arboretum
carnauba	palm|tree	balsam|fir
chestnut	pear|tree	balsa|wood
cinchona	piassava	brier|bush
cinnamon	pinaster	brushwood
clearing	pine|cone	buckthorn
coco|tree	pine|tree	bully|tree
coco,wood	quandong	bussu|palm
cork|tree	rain|tree	butternut
date|palm	rambutan	casuarina
date|tree	red|cedar	chaparral
deadwood	red|maple	chincapin
dendroid	rosemary	cocoa|wood
forestry	rosewood	crowberry
Greek|fir	royal|oak	deciduous
guaiacum	sago|palm	dwarf|tree
hardwood	sapindus	evergreen
hawthorn	shadbush	forsythia
hemp|palm	sloetree	grape|tree
hemp|tree	softwood	greenwood
holly|oak	sweet,bay	ground,ash
hornbeam	sweetsop	heartwood
iron,bark	sycamine	hydrangea
ironwood	sycamore	in|blossom
jack|tree	tamarack	ivory|palm

ivory|tree
Judas|tree
lancewood
lilac|tree
maple|leaf
outer|bark
paulownia
peach|palm
petty|whin
pitch|pine
plane|tree
poison|oak
pyracanth
quebracho
rose|apple
rowan|tree
royal|palm
sagebrush
sapodilla
sassafras
satinwood
Scotch|elm
Scotch|fir
Scots|pine
shade|tree
shrubbery
silver|fir
sloethorn
snowberry
soapberry
star|anise
stone|pine
thorn|tree
tulip|tree
underwood
wax|myrtle

whitebeam
widow|wail
wych|hazel
almond|tree
annual|ring
blackbully
blackthorn
bladder|nut
bottle|tree
brazilwood
bullet|tree
butter|tree
button|bush
buttonwood
calamander
chinquapin
coniferous
coral|berry
cowrie|pine
crown|graft
dead|finish
dendrology
Diana's|tree
Douglas|fir
dragon|tree
Durmast|oak
eucalyptus
fiddlewood
goat's|thorn
greasewood
greenheart
hackmatack
laurustine
manna|larch
nothofagus
olive|grove

orange|wood
palm|branch
paper|birch
pine|needle
plantation
prickly|ash
quercitron
raffia|palm
rain|forest
red|sanders
rose|laurel
sandalwood
silver|bell
silver|tree
spring|wood
sugar|maple
tallow|tree
tree|of|life
tree|tomato
turpentine
underbrush
white|cedar
white|thorn
witch|hazel
yellow|wood
African|teak
amboyna|wood
American|elm
burning|bush
cabbage|palm
cabbage|tree
cajuput|tree
camel's|thorn
coconut|palm
copper|beech
cotoneaster

honey|locust
hound's|berry
Japan|laurel
juniper|tree
laurustinus
lignum|vitae
mammoth|tree
mountain|ash
olive|branch
palm|cabbage
poison|sumac
prickly|pear
purpleheart
pussy|willow
shittah|tree
silver|birch
slippery|elm
spindle|tree
sweet|willow
undergrowth
varnish|tree
white|poplar
wintersweet
xanthoxylum
balsam|of|Peru
balsam|of|Tolu
bougainvilia
calabash|tree
Canada|balsam
checkerberry
chestnut|tree
Christ's|thorn
cucumber|tree
decorticated
dragon's|blood
frankincense

massaranduba
monkey|puzzle
Norway|spruce
Philadelphus
piassava|palm
plantain|tree
poison|laurel
quaking|aspen
ramification
rhododendron
sea|buckthorn
snowdrop|tree
Spanish|broom
spurge|laurel
tree|of|heaven
umbrella|tree
virgin|forest
wellingtonia
afforestation
almond|blossom
amygdalaceous
arboriculture
bird's|eye|maple
Christmas|tree
cranberry|tree
deforestation
dendrological
horse|chestnut
savanna|forest
weeping|willow
arboricultural
cedar|of|Lebanon
flowering|shrub
Lombardy|poplar
maidenhair|tree
mistletoe|bough

arboriculturist   Spanish|chestnut
Dutch|elm|disease   tree|of|knowledge

Vegetables

cos	cress	murphy	pumpkin
pea	cubeb	pea|pod	salsify
pod	kraut	pepper	seakale
rue	onion	potato	seed|pod
sot	patch	radish	shallot
bean	pease	runner	skirret
beet	roots	savory	soybean
cole	salad	sprout	spinach
dill	savoy	tomato	sprouts
herb	swede	turnip	succory
kale	thyme	bay|leaf	weed|out
leek	tuber	blewits	beetroot
mace	borage	cabbage	borecole
mint	carrot	caraway	brassica
okra	celery	cardoon	broccoli
peas	chilli	chervil	camomile
root	cow|pea	chicory	capsicum
sage	endive	collard	celeriac
sium	fennel	gherkin	chick|pea
slaw	floret	haricot	coleslaw
spud	garden	lettuce	cole,wort
basil	garlic	olitory	crucifer
caper	ginger	oregano	cucumber
chard	greens	parsley	dillseed
chive	growth	parsnip	egg,apple
cibol	legume	potherb	egg,fruit
clove	marrow	produce	egg,plant

VEGETABLES

escarole	love apple
greenery	navy beans
green pea	new potato
kohlrabi	pinto bean
Lima bean	red pepper
mad apple	snap beans
main crop	soya beans
marjoram	sugar beet
peasecod	sword bean
plantain	tree onion
potherbs	vegetable
root crop	alexanders
rosemary	broad beans
rutabaga	butter bean
scallion	coffee bean
soy beans	cos lettuce
split pea	cotton tree
tuberose	cotton wood
turmeric	cruciferae
zucchini	French bean
artichoke	garden peas
asparagus	green beans
aubergine	jardiniere
beet sugar	kidney bean
carob bean	potato peel
chick peas	red cabbage
cold frame	runner bean
cole garth	salad plant
colocynth	sauerkraut
coriander	Scotch kale
crucifera	sea cabbage
dried peas	string bean
garden pea	vanilla pod
green bean	water cress
green peas	Welsh onion
Lima beans	wolf's peach

butter|beans	lamb's|lettuce
cauliflower	mangel,wurzel
celery|stick	market|garden
French|beans	marrowfat|pea
green|pepper	marrow,squash
horseradish	Spanish|onion
runner|beans	spring|greens
scarlet|bean	St|John's|bread
sea,colewort	water|parsnip
spring|onion	kitchen|garden
string|beans	mangold,wurzel
sweet|potato	root|vegetable
winter|cress	cabbage|lettuce
asparagus|tip	green|vegetable
cabbage|patch	Brussels|sprouts
chilli|pepper	globe|artichokes
corn|on|the|cob	vegetable|garden
Covent|Garden	vegetable|marrow
haricot|beans	

Virtues

hope	charity	fortitude
love	justice	temperance
faith	prudence	

Visual Arts

ART	glue	batik	model	study
cut	head	block	motif	style
dye	kiln	brush	mould	throw
gum	lake	burin	mural	tinct
hue	lens	cameo	op|art	tinge
lac	limn	carve	paint	trace
oil	line	chalk	photo	turps
pen	mark	chase	piece	virtu
pot	mask	china	pin|up	wheel
sit	nude	craft	plate	artist
urn	oils	crock	point	azo|dye
arty	oven	curio	prime	bedaub
boss	pose	delft	print	bisque
bust	roll	drawn	prism	bite|in
calk	seal	dryer	pupil	blazon
cast	shot	easel	rough	blow|up
clay	show	fired	scape	bronze
copy	snap	frame	scene	calque
daub	soup	genre	sculp	camera
dope	tile	glass	shade	canvas
draw	tint	glaze	shape	carved
etch	tone	gloss	slide	carver
film	tool	glyph	smear	chased
fire	turn	grave	Spode	chaser
flat	turn	hatch	spool	chisel
flux	vase	image	stain	chroma
form	view	inlay	stamp	colour
gild	wash	Japan	still	crayon
gilt	work	lines	stone	crible

cubism	pastel	coating	off|tone
cubist	pencil	collage	outline
dauber	plaque	colours	painter
déjà|vu	pop|art	copyist	palette
depict	poster	Dadaism	pattern
design	potter	dash|off	picture
doodle	primer	develop	pigment
drawer	relief	diorama	plaster
dyeing	rococo	draught	portray
eat|out	school	drawing	pottery
effigy	screen	ebauche	preview
enamel	sculpt	ecorche	primary
engild	shadow	enchase	profile
etcher	sketch	engrave	realism
figure	statue	enlarge	relievo
filter	studio	etching	scenist
firing	symbol	faience	scratch
fresco	talent	fast|dye	shading
glazed	tripod	Fauvism	shutter
graven	viewer	furnace	spatula
graver	acid|dye	gallery	stencil
incise	acushla	gilding	stipple
limner	aniline	glyphic	tableau
madder	art|deco	glyptic	tachism
magilp	art|form	gouache	tempera
mallet	art|work	graphic	tessera
marble	atelier	graving	the|arts
master	baroque	gravure	thinner
medium	biscuit	high|art	tinting
megilp	camaieu	imagism	tintype
mobile	cartoon	incised	tooling
mock|up	carving	lacquer	touch|up
mosaic	ceramic	linocut	tracery
museum	chasing	montage	tracing
opaque	classic	moulded	varnish
parget	close|by	moulder	woodcut

VISUAL ARTS

abstract	eclectic	majolica
acid|kiln	eggshell	mandorla
aesthete	emblazon	modelled
airscape	emulsion	modeller
anaglyph	enchased	monument
aquatint	engraved	movement
art|autre	engraver	negative
art|class	enlarger	original
artcraft	exposure	paint|box
artefact	exterior	paintbox
artifact	fair|copy	painting
artiness	figurine	panorama
artistic	fine|arts	pargeter
artistry	fire|clay	pastiche
art|paper	fixative	pastille
autotype	freehand	pastoral
autotypy	frescoes	photomap
Barbizon	fretwork	picturer
basic|dye	futurism	plein|air
burinist	glyptics	portrait
calotype	graffiti	positive
ceramics	graffito	potsherd
charcoal	graphics	printing
chromism	Greek|urn	repousse
ciselure	grouping	sculptor
clayware	half|tint	seapiece
colorama	half|tone	seascape
creation	hatching	sketcher
curlicue	in|relief	skiagram
dark|room	inscribe	skyscape
demitint	intaglio	slapdash
depicter	interior	snapshot
designer	intimism	spectrum
dry|paint	lapidary	staining
dry|plate	likeness	statuary
dyestuff	limekiln	stop|bath

symbolic	cityscape	lithotint
tachisme	clean line	lithotype
tapestry	cloisonné	low relief
tessella	collodion	manual art
the brush	collotype	medallion
tinction	colorific	mezzotint
tincture	colourful	microcopy
turn a pot	colouring	microfilm
vignette	colourist	miniature
virtuoso	crayonist	modelling
zoom lens	cyanotype	modern art
aesthetic	cyclorama	modernism
anastasis	decorator	objet d'art
anastatic	delftware	off colour
aquarelle	designing	oil paints
art critic	developer	old master
art lesson	distemper	oleograph
art minded	enameller	paintress
art school	encaustic	paper clip
bas relief	enchasing	pargeting
beaux arts	engraving	parge work
blackware	ferrotype	pasticcio
blueprint	flash bulb	pen and ink
box camera	flash tube	photocopy
bric a brac	glassware	photogram
brick kiln	goldsmith	photostat
brushwork	Gothicism	pictorial
cameo ware	grisaille	porcelain
cameraman	grotesque	portrayal
cartridge	headpiece	portrayer
cerograph	heliotype	prefigure
champleve	heliotypy	prismatic
china clay	inscriber	projector
chinaware	kalamkari	reflector
chiseller	landscape	represent
chromatic	lay figure	rice paper

rotograph	xylograph	crosshatch
rough|copy	zinc|plate	crouch|ware
scrimshaw	acid|colour	Crown|Derby
sculpture	aesthetics	dead¡colour
secondary	anaglyphic	decoration
sgraffito	aniline|dye	delineator
sketching	art|gallery	draughting
sketch|pad	art|nouveau	drawing|pin
skiagraph	arty¡crafty	emblazonry
statuette	automatism	embossment
still¡life	avant|garde	enamel|kiln
stippling	background	enamelling
stoneware	beaten|work	enamellist
symbolism	Berlin|ware	enamelware
symbology	bibliofilm	exhibition
tablature	block|print	figuration
tailpiece	cameo|glass	figurehead
talbotype	caricature	flashlight
technique	carmagnole	foreground
telephoto	cartoonist	full|colour
tenebrist	cement|kiln	functional
throw|a|pot	ceramicist	futuristic
townscape	cerography	glazed|ware
treatment	china|stone	grand|stone
triquetra	chiselling	graphic|art
undercoat	chromatics	Grecian|urn
vitascope	chromatism	half|relief
vorticism	chromogram	handicraft
wax|figure	chromotype	heliograph
whiteware	cinecamera	high|colour
whitewash	classicism	high|relief
wirephoto	cloudscape	illuminate
wood|block	coloration	illustrate
woodcraft	colour|film	impression
woodprint	colourless	jasper|ware
work|of|art	comic|strip	kinetic|art

lightmeter	proportion	zincograph
linography	pure colour	zylography
linseed oil	queen's ware	abstract art
lithograph	Raphaelite	abstraction
luminarist	repoussage	achromatism
lustreware	rich colour	alto relievo
masterwork	riverscape	anaglyptics
metalcraft	Rockingham	brush stroke
micrograph	scenograph	cavo relievo
microprint	sculptress	ceramic ware
monochrome	sculptural	cerographer
monumental	sculptured	ceroplastic
mordant dye	sculpturer	charcoalist
natural dye	Sèvres ware	chef d'oeuvre
naturalism	shadowgram	chiaroscuro
neoclassic	show of work	Chinese clay
oil colours	silhouette	cloisonnage
oil painter	sketchbook	coat of paint
ornamental	sling paint	colorimeter
paintbrush	statuesque	colouration
pastellist	steel plate	colour blind
pedal wheel	stereotype	colour cycle
photoflash	stonecraft	colour gamut
photoflood	stovehouse	colour print
photogenic	surrealism	composition
photograph	surrealist	connoisseur
photometer	terra cotta	copperplate
photomural	tessallate	delineation
photoprint	turpentine	dichromatic
phylactery	view finder	discoloured
picaresque	warm colour	draughtsman
pigmentary	water glass	earthenware
plasticine	waterscape	eclecticism
polychrome	wax etching	electrotype
port crayon	wax process	engravement
power wheel	wood carver	enlargement

etching|ball
flash|camera
French|chalk
gild|the|lily
glass|blower
glyphograph
graphic|arts
heliochrome
ichnography
illuminator
illustrator
in|low|relief
insculpture
landscapist
life|drawing
Limoges|ware
linographer
lithography
living|image
local|colour
madder|bloom
masterpiece
Meissen|ware
miniaturist
museum|piece
object|of|art
objet|trouvé
oil|painting
ornamentist
papier|mâché
perspective
photography
photorelief
picturesque
pinacotheca
plein|airist

pointillism
pointillist
portraiture
potter's|clay
press|camera
primitivism
proportions
psychedelic
range|finder
romanticism
rotogravure
rough|sketch
Satsuma|ware
scenewright
scenography
sculpturing
shadowgraph
silversmith
snap|shooter
snapshotter
solid|colour
still|camera
tile|painter
tissue|paper
water|colour
wood|carving
xylographer
zincography
aestheticism
architecture
artist's|model
artist's|proof
basso|relievo
brass|rubbing
bright|colour
camera|lucida

candid|camera
caricaturist
cave|painting
ceramography
ceroplastics
chaleography
chiaro|oscuro
Chinese|paper
chromaticity
colour|circle
colour|filter
cottage|china
design|centre
drawing|board
drawing|paper
Dresden|china
Elgin|marbles
etching|point
fashion|plate
genre|painter
glyphography
heliogravure
hollow|relief
illumination
illustration
in|high|relief
kaleidoscope
lantern|slide
lignographer
line|engraver
lithographer
lithographic
lithogravure
magic|lantern
metallograph
mezzo|relievo

old|Worcester
opaque|colour
paint|the|lily
palette|knife
panchromatic
photoengrave
photoetching
photographer
photographic
photogravure
photomontage
picture|frame
pointelliste
pointillisme
portrait|bust
poster|colour
potter's|earth
potter's|wheel
reflex|camera
reproduction
riot|of|colour
rough|draught
rough|outline
scene|painter
sculptograph
self|portrait
shadow|figure
sneak|preview
spectrograph
stained|glass
stereo|camera
street|artist
technicolour
time|exposure
tracing|paper
tripod|camera

wall|painting
water|colours
wax|engraving
wax|modelling
Wedgwood|ware
well|composed
white|pottery
zincographer
action|painter
art|exhibition
black|and|white
calligraphist
cross|hatching
daguerreotype
expressionism
expressionist
Flemish|school
glass|printing
impressionism
impressionist
pre|Raphaelite
primary|colour
willow|pattern
action|painting
art|for|art's|sake
foreshortening
pavement|artist
picture|gallery
vanishing|point
abstract|painter
charcoal|drawing
draughtsmanship
picture|restorer
portrait|gallery
portrait|painter

Warfare

AB	van	dart	impi	rout	arrow
GI	vet	Dᵈday	jack	rush	at|bay
GI	war	dike	jamb	shot	at|war
MP	ally	dirk	jeep	slug	baton
RA	ammo	dove	Jock	spit	beset
RE	Ares	duck	keep	spur	blade
RN	arms	duel	kill	stab	blank
arm	army	dump	kris	stab	blast
axe	Aˌwar	duty	levy	tank	blitz
bow	AWOL	epee	load	tuck	Boche
cap	ball	exon	lock	unit	bolas
cut	band	feud	mail	WAAF	brave
dud	barb	file	Mars	WACS	broch
foe	bard	fire	mere	wage	Buffs
gat	bill	fish	mine	wall	burst
gun	bird	flak	MIRV	ward	cadre
Hun	bola	foil	moat	WAVE	chute
NCO	bolt	fort	mole	wing	clash
POW	bomb	fray	navy	WRNS	corps
RAF	bone	guns	Odin	yomp	cover
ram	bout	hate	peel	zone	ditch
rat	Bren	hawk	peon	Zulu	draft
rod	butt	helm	pike	AAˌgun	drive
row	camp	hero	post	Aˌbomb	enemy
sap	club	hilt	rack	aegis	feint
spy	cock	hold	rank	arena	fence
sub	coif	host	rath	armed	field
TNT	Colt	Hˌwar	riot	armet	fight
Tyr	cosh	ICBM	rock	array	flail

flank	rebel	tommy	battle	enlist
fleet	recce	tommy	beaver	ensign
foray	redan	train	bellum	escarp
fosse	repel	troop	big|gun	escort
front	rifle	truce	billet	Exocet
fusee	rowel	U|boat	bomber	fewter
fusil	sally	uhlan	breech	flight
grape	salvo	visor	bugler	foeman
guard	scarp	WAACS	bullet	forage
harry	scene	WAAFS	bunker	forces
H|bomb	scout	waddy	camail	gabion
H|hour	sepoy	Woden	cannon	galoot
jerid	serve	wound	casque	glacis
Jerry	shaft	WRACS	castle	glaive
jihad	shako	Wrens	casual	gorget
jingo	shell	abatis	charge	greave
knife	shoot	ack|ack	cohort	gunner
kukri	siege	action	column	gun|shy
lager	skean	air|arm	combat	Gurkha
lance	sling	air|gun	convoy	gusset
leave	snake	alpeen	cordon	hagbut
Luger	sowar	Amazon	corium	hammer
melee	spahi	ambush	creese	hanger
mound	spear	animus	cudgel	hanjar
onset	spike	Anzacs	cuisse	harass
orgue	spray	archer	curfew	heaume
parry	spurs	Archie	curtal	helmet
pavis	squad	argosy	dagger	hot|war
plate	staff	armada	defeat	hussar
poilu	steel	armour	defend	impact
posse	stick	askari	detail	impale
power	stone	assail	donjon	in|arms
Provo	storm	attack	dry|run	inroad
rally	sword	barbel	duello	jereed
range	targe	barrel	dugout	jingal
ranks	tasse	batman	dumdum	laager

labrys	rapier	tom,tom	bayonet
lancer	rappel	trench	bazooka
legion	ray|gun	troops	beat|off
lorica	razzia	tulwar	Bellona
mailed	rebuff	turret	big|guns
maquis	reduit	vallum	big|shot
marine	report	valour	blowgun
Mauser	revolt	Vandal	Boer|War
merlon	rioter	victor	bombard
minnie	rocket	volley	bombing
morion	rookie	war|cry	booster
mortar	salade	war|dog	bravado
musket	sallet	war|god	Bren|gun
muster	salute	weapon	bricole
muzzle	sangar	womera	brigade
oilcan	sapper	yeoman	buckler
outfit	sconce	Zouave	bulldog
panzer	scutum	abattis	bulwark
parade	sentry	advance	caisson
parole	set|gun	air|raid	caitiff
patrol	shield	amnesty	calibre
pavise	slogan	archery	caliver
pellet	sniper	armoury	caltrop
pepper	sortie	arsenal	cap,a,pie
petard	sparth	assault	carbine
picket	spying	assegai	carcass
pierce	strafe	atom|gun	carrier
pistol	strike	atom|war	cashier
pogrom	swivel	baldric	cavalry
pompom	talion	barrack	chamade
powder	target	barrage	chamber
pow,pow	tenail	barrier	charger
quiver	thrust	bar|shot	chicken
rafale	to|arms	basinet	citadel
Rajput	tocsin	bastion	cold|war
ramrod	Toledo	battery	command

7 LETTERS

company	gas bomb	javelin	petrary
conchie	gas mask	jollies	phalanx
conquer	germ war	jump jet	pikeman
cordite	gisarme	knifing	pillbox
corslet	go to war	kremlin	platoon
cossack	grapnel	lambast	poleaxe
coupure	grenade	lamboys	poniard
courage	gunboat	longbow	private
courser	gundeck	Long Tom	quarrel
crusade	gunfire	lookout	rampage
cudgels	gunlock	lunette	rampart
cuirass	gunnage	lyddite	ravelin
curtain	gunnery	machete	recruit
curtana	gunning	make war	red army
cutlass	gun park	maniple	redcoat
dastard	gunplay	mantlet	redoubt
defence	gun port	marines	regular
disband	gunroom	martial	repulse
distaff	gunshot	matross	retreat
dragoon	hackbut	megaton	riposte
draught	halberd	militia	Sabaoth
dry fire	handjar	missile	sabaton
dudgeon	harness	mission	salient
dueller	hatchet	morrion	samurai
dungeon	hauberk	neutral	sandbag
echelon	heroism	offence	Seabees
enomoty	Hessian	on guard	section
fall out	heyduck	open war	self bow
fend off	hold off	outpost	service
fighter	holster	outwork	shoot at
firearm	holy war	paladin	shooter
fortify	hostage	panoply	shotgun
fortlet	invader	parados	soldier
foxhole	jackman	parapet	Spartan
gallant	jambeau	patriot	sparthe
gallery	jankers	pedrero	spinner

WARFARE

sten|gun	aceldama	bomb|site	drumhead
supremo	activate	brattice	duellist
tactics	air|force	brickbat	dynamite
teargas	air|rifle	broadaxe	embattle
tenable	air|to|air	Browning	enfilade
testudo	all|clear	buckshot	enlistee
theatre	alliance	buttress	entrench
the|fray	ammo|dump	buzzbomb	envelope
torpedo	anabasis	campaign	errantry
traitor	anti|mine	cannonry	escalade
trigger	arbalest	casemate	exercise
trooper	armament	catapult	falchion
tumbril	armature	cavalier	falconet
uniform	armoured	chaffron	fasthold
veteran	arms|race	chamfron	fastness
victory	arquebus	champion	fencible
wage|war	art|of|war	chasseur	field|gun
war|club	atom|bomb	chivalry	fighting
ward|off	attacker	civil|war	file|fire
war|drum	aventail	claymore	fireball
warfare	ballista	cold|feet	fire|bomb
war|game	banderol	commando	firelock
warhead	barbette	conflict	fire|upon
warlike	barbican	corselet	flotilla
warlord	barracks	crossbow	fortress
warpath	bartisan	cry|havoc	fugleman
warring	baselard	culverin	furlough
warrior	battalia	cylinder	fusilier
warship	battling	defender	gambeson
war|song	bear|arms	demilune	garrison
weapons	besieger	deserter	gauntlet
wind|gun	betrayer	destrier	Great|War
woomera	blockade	division	guerilla
wounded	blowpipe	doughboy	gunflint
yatagan	bludgeon	drum|call	gunmetal
yomping	bomb|rack	drumfire	gunpoint

gunsmith	marksman	reveille
gunstick	martello	revolver
gunstock	massacre	ricochet
hang|fire	Maxim|gun	rifleman
heavy|gun	melinite	risalder
hedgehog	militant	runagate
herisson	military	safehold
hill|fort	mobilize	scabbard
hireling	muniment	scimitar
hornwork	munition	sentinel
howitzer	mushroom	shrapnel
infantry	musketry	side|arms
informer	nerve|gas	siege|cap
invading	open|fire	skean|dhu
invasion	ordnance	skirmish
invasive	orillion	soldiery
ironclad	outguard	solleret
janizary	overkill	space|gun
jazerant	pacifist	spadroon
jingoism	palisade	spearman
jump|area	palstaff	spontoon
killadar	palstave	squadron
knuckles	partisan	stabbing
lancegay	password	stalwart
land|army	pauldron	Star|Wars
land|mine	petronel	stave|off
langrage	pikehead	stiletto
last|post	poltroon	stockade
launcher	puncheon	strafing
Leon|mine	quisling	strategy
Lewis|gun	quo|vadis	struggle
loophole	recreant	surprise
magazine	regiment	surround
mailclad	renegade	take|arms
man|of|war	repulsor	tenaille
mantelet	reserves	the|front

467

the|sword	army|corps	brown|bill
time|bomb	army|issue	camouflet
tomahawk	army|lists	cannonade
Tommy|gun	arrowhead	cannoneer
total|war	artillery	caparison
transfix	assailant	carronade
trenches	atomic|gun	carry|arms
turnback	atomic|war	cartouche
turncoat	attacking	cartridge
turntail	attrition	casemated
up|in|arms	automatic	castellan
uprising	auto|rifle	cease|fire
vambrace	backplate	chain|mail
vamplate	ballistic	chain|shot
vanguard	banderole	challenge
vanquish	bandolier	chamfrain
vendetta	bastinado	chassepot
war|cloud	battalion	cold|steel
warcraft	battleaxe	combatant
war|dance	battlecry	combative
warfarer	beachhead	conquerer
war|horse	beefeater	conscript
war|hound	beleaguer	crackshot
war|paint	bellicism	cross|fire
war|whoop	bellicose	defensive
Waterloo	Big|Bertha	derringer
wayfarer	blackjack	desert|rat
weaponry	bloodshed	deterrent
world|war	bomb|happy	detonator
yeomanry	bombs|away	discharge
zero|hour	bombshell	doodlebug
accoutred	bombsight	double|sap
aggressor	booby|trap	drop|a|bomb
air|to|ship	boomerang	earthwork
ambuscade	broadside	embattled
arch|enemy	Brown|Bess	encompass

enemy|camp	heavy|fire	munitions
enemy|fire	heroic|act	musketeer
escopette	Home|Guard	musketoon
espionage	hostility	needle|gun
explosive	hydrobomb	nose|guard
face|guard	incursion	nosepiece
fence|wall	incursive	offensive
field|army	in|defence	onslaught
fieldwork	ironbound	open|order
fire|a|shot	irregular	operation
firepower	irruption	other|side
fireworks	janissary	overthrow
first|line	jesserant	panoplied
flintlock	katabasis	parachute
flying|sap	keep|guard	peel|house
fortalice	keep|vigil	peel|tower
fortified	lance|jack	pikestaff
fourth|arm	langridge	prick|spur
free|lance	last|ditch	projector
front|line	legionary	protector
fulgurite	levy|war|on	pugnacity
fusillade	lie|in|wait	pyroxylin
gas|attack	lionheart	ram|rocket
gelignite	logistics	rearguard
gladiator	long|range	rebel|call
grapeshot	Luftwaffe	rebellion
grenadier	make|war|on	rerebrace
guardsman	man|at|arms	ressaldar
guerrilla	manoeuvre	rifle|ball
gun|battle	march|past	rocket|gun
guncotton	matchlock	rocket|man
gunpowder	mercenary	roundhead
gun|turret	militancy	round|shot
habergeon	minefield	rowel|spur
harquebus	minuteman	Royal|Navy
headpiece	monomachy	sally|port

saltpetre
sea|battle
seat|of|war
sentry|box
shellfire
signalman
single|sap
ski|troops
skyrocket
sky|troops
slaughter
slingshot
slung|shot
small|arms
small|bore
small|shot
smoke|bomb
soldierly
soldier|on
sonic|mine
son|of|a|gun
spearhead
spring|gun
stand|fire
stink|bomb
strategic
subaltern
submarine
super|bomb
surprisal
surrender
swivel|gun
sword|play
take|sides
tank|corps
target|day

task|force
tit|for|tat
torpedoed
torpedoer
trainband
trench|gun
troopship
truncheon
under|arms
under|fire
vigilante
volunteer
warmonger
War|Office
war|rocket
watchword
white|flag
woomerang
zumbooruk
activation
active|army
active|duty
active|list
adventurer
aerial|bomb
aerial|mine
aggression
aggressive
Air|Command
air|service
ambushment
ammunition
antagonism
Armageddon
armed|force
armed|guard

armed|truce
armigerous
armipotent
arm's|length
atomic|bomb
atomic|pile
atom|rocket
ballistics
barbed|wire
battle|flag
battle|hymn
battle|line
battlement
battleship
blitzkrieg
blockhouse
bold|stroke
bombardier
bowie|knife
box|barrage
breastwork
bridgehead
brigandine
broadsword
bugle|corps
call|to|arms
camel|corps
camouflage
campaigner
cannon|ball
cannon|shot
cantonment
carabineer
carry|on|war
cavalryman
coastguard

coat of mail
combat area
combat team
commandant
contingent
cross staff
cuirassier
declare war
defendable
defensible
demobilize
detachment
direct fire
dragonnade
dragoonade
drawbridge
drummer boy
embankment
encampment
engarrison
eprouvette
escalation
expedition
faint heart
fieldpiece
field train
fiery cross
fire trench
firing area
flying bomb
flying tank
Foot Guards
foot rifles
Gatling gun
ground fire
ground mine

ground zero
halberdier
heavy armed
impalement
incendiary
investment
jingoistic
knighthood
knobkerrie
kriegspiel
lambrequin
lay siege to
Life Guards
light armed
line of fire
loaded cane
long knives
lookout man
machine gun
martiality
militarism
militarize
militiaman
missile man
mob tactics
mount guard
mural crown
musket shot
mustard gas
napalm bomb
no man's land
nuclear war
obsidional
occupation
old soldier
on the march

operations
other ranks
over the top
oyster mine
paratroops
percussion
petrol bomb
picket duty
point blank
portcullis
private war
projectile
raking fire
rally round
raw recruit
Resistance
revolution
rifle range
rocket bomb
rocket fire
rules of war
run through
second line
sentry duty
serviceman
shellshock
shillelagh
short range
siegecraft
siege train
six shooter
slit trench
smallsword
smooth bore
spill blood
stand guard

state|of|war
strategist
stronghold
submachine
sure|as|a|gun
sword|fight
swordstick
sworn|enemy
take|to|arms
tenderfoot
ten|pounder
test|rocket
touch|paper
trajectile
trajectory
under|siege
vanquisher
volunteers
war|goddess
Winchester
air|to|ground
anti|missile
anti|tank|gun
area|bombing
armed|combat
armed|forces
armoured|car
auxiliaries
barnstormer
battle|array
battledress
battlefield
battle|order
battle|plane
battle|royal
beach|master

bersaglieri
besiegement
blockbuster
bloody|shirt
blunderbuss
bombardment
bomber|pilot
bomb|release
bow|and|arrow
breastplate
British|Army
British|Navy
buck|private
bulletproof
buoyant|mine
bushwhacker
cameraderie
castellated
castle|guard
caterpillar
change|sides
combat|train
contentious
countermine
crack|troops
declaration
demibastion
depth|charge
dive|bombing
emplacement
enemy|action
engine|of|war
enlisted|man
envelopment
fighting|man
fire|a|volley

fire|tactics
firing|party
firing|squad
firing|table
first|strike
fission|bomb
flare|rocket
flying|corps
footed|arrow
footslogger
foot|soldier
forced|march
force|of|arms
friend|or|foe
full|harness
full|of|fight
gang|warfare
generalship
germ|warfare
giant|powder
ground|to|air
guerrillero
guncarriage
hair|trigger
hand|grenade
heavy|armour
heavy|bomber
high|dudgeon
hill|station
Horse|Guards
horse|pistol
hostilities
infantryman
Irish|Guards
iron|rations
land|warfare

light|bomber	safe,conduct	up|and|at|them
lionhearted	safety|catch	warlikeness
Lochaber|axe	Scots|Guards	war|of|nerves
loggerheads	service|call	warriorlike
look|daggers	ship,to,shore	war|to|end|war
magazine|gun	shock|troops	water|cannon
Maginot|line	shooting|war	wooden|horse
Marine|Corps	shoot|to|kill	wooden|walls
might|of|arms	shuttle|raid	acoustic|mine
military|man	Signal|Corps	anti,aircraft
mine|thrower	smell|powder	appeal|to|arms
moral|defeat	smoke|rocket	armour,plated
mountain|gun	smoke|screen	army|reserves
naval|bomber	sneak|attack	artilleryman
naval|forces	soldatesque	atomic|cannon
nitre|powder	soldierlike	awkward|squad
nitrocotton	soldiership	banzai|charge
nuclear|bomb	spent|bullet	battering|ram
open|warfare	stand|at|ease	battleground
pattern|bomb	stand|of|arms	beat|a|retreat
peace|treaty	step|rockets	belligerence
picket|guard	stormtroops	breakthrough
plate|armour	stray|bullet	breechloader
platoon|fire	subdivision	buccaneering
postern|gate	Swiss|Guards	bushfighting
powder|grain	sword|in|hand	cannon|fodder
Provisional	take|by|storm	cannon's|mouth
put|to|flight	thin|red|line	civil|defence
rallying|cry	Tommy|Atkins	council|of|war
rank|and|file	torpedo|boat	counter|march
rebel|action	trench|knife	court|martial
reconnoitre	trigger|talk	cut,and,thrust
recruitment	true|colours	daggers|drawn
regular|army	trusty|sword	deadly|weapon
retro,rocket	under|attack	demi,culverin
rolling|fire	Underground	dumdum|bullet

Dutch|courage	Medical|Corps
electron|bomb	medium|bomber
encirclement	military|zone
engines|of|war	mine|detector
entrenchment	mobilization
escaramouche	moral|courage
false|colours	moral|support
field|of|blood	moral|victory
flame,thrower	muzzle,loader
floating|mine	naval|militia
flying|column	naval|reserve
forward|march	naval|warfare
fowling|piece	on|the|warpath
gladiatorial	Parthian|shot
go|over|the|top	Pearl|Harbour
grand|tactics	picked|troops
ground|forces	pioneer|corps
guerrilla|war	plunging|fire
guided|weapon	powder|charge
heavy|dragoon	pyrotechnics
home|reserves	quarterstaff
homing|rocket	reactivation
horse|and|foot	religious|war
horse|marines	rifled|cannon
hydrogen|bomb	rifle|grenade
lady|from|hell	rocket|attack
launching|pad	second|strike
leathernecks	sharpshooter
Light|Brigade	shock|tactics
light|dragoon	shoulder|a|gun
line|of|action	shoulder|arms
line|of|battle	siege|warfare
machicolated	signal|rocket
magnetic|mine	single|combat
march|against	standing|army
marching|song	stormtrooper

stouthearted
sudden attack
supply troops
sword bayonet
tactical unit
take the field
theatre of war
tooth and nail
trench mortar
trigger happy
under the flag
vertical fire
virus warfare
warmongering
white feather
who goes there
yellow streak
active service
Andrew Ferrara
armaments race
armed conflict
arms and the man
army exercises
articles of war
assault course
baptism of fire
battle cruiser
battle honours
battle scarred
bayonet charge
beleaguerment
bomber command
breechloading
British Legion
cartridge belt
cavalry charge

cheval de frise
Churchill tank
cobelligerent
combat fatigue
comrade in arms
counter attack
desert warfare
disengagement
dispatch rider
drill sergeant
evasive action
Exocet missile
field hospital
field of battle
fighter patrol
first world war
Flammenwerfer
flying colours
flying officer
force de frappe
foreign legion
fortification
generalissimo
guard of honour
guided missile
gunnery school
high explosive
lance corporal
light infantry
line of defence
listening post
machine gunner
Messerschmitt
Military Cross
Military Medal
mine detection

mini submarine
muzzle loading
non resistance
nuclear weapon
order of battle
order of the day
passage of arms
Peninsular War
pitched battle
prisoner of war
put to the sword
quarter gunner
quartermaster
reinforcement
royal air force
running battle
sabre rattling
scorched earth
senior service
sergeant major
Siegfried line
staff sergeant
striking force
sublieutenant
submachine gun
trench warfare
two edged sword
unarmed combat
Victoria Cross
war department
war to the death
wing commander
yeoman service
action stations
airborne forces
airborne troops

aircraftswoman
Air Vice Marshal
ammunition dump
army cadet force
army manoeuvres
barrage balloon
battle stations
blank cartridge
blockade runner
captain general
cavalry officer
chevaux de frise
cloak and dagger
coastal battery
coastal command
colonel in chief
colour sergeant
comrades in arms
conquering hero
demobilisation
field ambulance
field artillery
fifth columnist
fighter command
fight to a finish
flag lieutenant
freedom fighter
guerrilla chief
guerrilla force
heavy artillery
horse artillery
incendiary bomb
liaison officer
light artillery
marching orders
militarisation

military|police
military|tattoo
muzzle|velocity
non,operational
nuclear|warfare
nuclear|warhead
operations|room
orderly|officer
ordinary|seaman
pincer|movement
powder|magazine
Pyrrhic|victory
reconnaissance
regimental|band
Royal|Artillery
Royal|Engineers
Royal|Fusiliers
Royal|Tank|Corps
squadron,leader
street|fighting
supreme|command
unknown|soldier
unknown|warrior
urban|guerrilla
warrant|officer
Wars|of|the|Roses
winter|quarters
adjutant|general
air|chief|marshal
aircraft|carrier
Anderson|shelter
armed|to|the|teeth
armoured|cruiser

Brigade|of|Guards
chemical|warfare
displaced|person
first|lieutenant
gentleman,at,arms
Grenadier|Guards
light|machine|gun
military|mission
military|service
Molotov|cocktail
Morrison|shelter
Mulberry|harbour
national|defence
national|service
naval|engagement
naval|operations
non,commissioned
observation|post
officer|of|the|day
on|active|service
orderly|corporal
orderly|sergeant
parachute|troops
rearguard|action
recruiting|drive
regimental|march
second,in,command
spoils|of|victory
sword,and,buckler
telescopic|sight
territorial|army
up|guards|and|at|em

Weight

- lb
- oz
- cwt
- ton
- dram
- gram
- kilo
- mass
- carat
- gerah
- grain
- libra
- livre
- minim
- pound
- scale
- stone
- tonne
- uncia
- denier
- dirhem
- drachm
- gramme
- netton
- shekel
- longton
- quintal
- scuple
- tonneau
- assay ton
- decagram
- decigram
- gram atom
- gross ton
- kilogram
- short ton
- centigram
- hectogram
- metric ton
- milligram
- myriagram
- ounce troy
- troy ounce
- carat grain
- troy weight
- avoirdupois
- centigramme
- gram molecule
- hundredweight
- imperial weight

Wonders of the World

- Colossus, The
- Pyramids, The
- Palace of Cyrus
- Temple of Diana
- Hanging Gardens
- Tomb of Mausolus
- Statue of Zeus, The

Works of Literature and Music

Job	Lolita	Giselle	Carnival
Kim	Martha	Ivanhoe	Catriona
She	Mignon	Lord Jim	Cenci, The
Aida	Nuages	Lycidas	Coppelia
Emma	Oberon	Macbeth	Cranford
Lulu	Otello	Manfred	Endymion
Maud	Rienzi	Marmion	Everyman
Brand	Rob Roy	Ma Vlast	Falstaff
Comus	Rokeby	Mazeppa	Gloriana
Faust	Salome	Messiah	Hay Fever
Fetes	Semele	Nabucco	Hiawatha
Kipps	Sylvia	Othello	Hudibras
La Mer	Trilby	Rebecca	Hyperion
Manon	Utopia	Ring, The	Idiot, The
Medea	Walden	Shirley	Idomeneo
Norma	Adonais	Sirenes	Iliad, The
Scoop	Aladdin	Ulysses	In the Wet
Tosca	Amadeus	Volpone	Iolanthe
Alcina	Babbitt	Werther	Jane Eyre
Amelia	Beowulf	Wozzeck	King Lear
Becket	Camilla	Adam Bede	La Boheme
Ben Hur	Candida	Adam Zero	L'Allegro
Carmen	Candide	Alcestis	Lavengro
En Saga	Don Juan	Anabasis	Les Noces
Ghosts	Dracula	Antigone	Lucky Jim
Hassan	Electra	Arabella	Moby Dick
Helena	Erewhon	Bells, The	Parsifal
Iberia	Euphues	Born Free	Patience
Jenufa	Fidelio	Carnaval	Peer Gynt

Pericles
Rasselas
Sea Drift
Swan Lake
Tom Jones
Turandot
Villette
Waves, The
Aeneid, The
Agamemnon
Beau Geste
Billy Budd
Brigg Fair
Capriccio
Cavalcade
Checkmate
Choephori
Coningsby
Cox and Box
Critic, The
Cymbeline
Dandy Dick
Don Carlos
Dr Zhivago
Dubliners
East Lynne
Egoist, The
Eumenides
Euryanthe
Hard Times
Hobbit, The
I, Claudius
I Puritani
Kidnapped
Kubla Khan
Les Biches

Lohengrin
Mein Kampf
Men at Arms
Mikado, The
No Highway
On Liberty
Papillons
Prince, The
Pygmalion
Rigoletto
Rivals, The
Ruddigore
Saint Joan
Siegfried
Tom Sawyer
Venusberg
Vice Versa
Warden, The
All for Love
Animal Farm
Appalachia
Bleak House
Borough, The
Cannery Row
Casabianca
Cinderella
Citadel, The
Coriolanus
Das Kapital
Die Walkure
Don Quixote
Dunciad, The
Dynasts, The
Howards End
Il Seraglio
Inferno, The

In Memoriam
Intermezzo
I Pagliacci
Jamaica Inn
John Gilpin
Kenilworth
Kingdom, The
La Gioconda
La Traviata
Les Troyens
Lorna Doone
Lysistrata
My Fair Lady
My Son, My Son
Nelson Mass
Odyssey, The
Oedipus Rex
Only Way, The
On the Beach
Our Village
Pantagruel
Persuasion
Petroushka
Planets, The
Prelude, The
Prince Igor
Relapse, The
Rural Rides
Seagull, The
Seasons, The
Semiramide
Tannhauser
Tempest, The
Tono Bungay
Trojans, The
Uncle Remus

Uncle Vanya	Love for Love	Alchemist, The
Vanity Fair	Luisa Miller	Anna Karenina
Vile Bodies	Mary Poppins	Antiquary, The
War Requiem	Middlemarch	Apple Cart, The
Water Music	Minute Waltz	Archduke Trio
Westward Ho!	Mrs Dalloway	Areopagitica
American, The	Mr Standfast	Ash Wednesday
Apostles, The	Newcomes, The	Barnaby Rudge
As You Like It	Now We Are Six	Blithe Spirit
Big Sleep, The	Noye's Fludde	Brighton Rock
Black Beauty	Ode to Autumn	Buddenbrooks
Blue Bird, The	Oliver Twist	Caretaker, The
Boule de Suif	Peter Grimes	Charley's Aunt
Cakes and Ale	Peter Simple	Childe Harold
Creation, The	Pippa Passes	Cosi fan Tutte
Cruel Sea, The	Princess Ida	Danse Macabre
Doll's House, A	Princess, The	Decameron, The
Don Giovanni	Puss in Boots	Dogs of War, The
Don Pasquale	Redgauntlet	Dombey and Son
Firebird, The	Rosmersholm	Epithalamion
Georgics, The	Salut d'Amour	Eugene Onegin
Greenmantle	Sea Symphony	Excursion, The
Harp Quartet	Silas Marner	Four Quartets
Hedda Gabler	Sorcerer, The	Frankenstein
High Windows	South Riding	Golden Ass, The
HMS Pinafore	Stalky and Co	Grand Duke, The
Hymn of Jesus	Stenka Razin	Guy Mannering
I Like it Here	Tale of a Tub, A	Handley Cross
Il Penseroso	Talisman, The	Julius Caesar
Il Trovatore	Tam o'Shanter	Karelia Suite
Jack and Jill	Trial by Jury	Khovanschina
Journey's End	What Katy Did	Kinderscenen
Judith Paris	Wild Duck, The	Kreisleriana
Little Eyolf	William Tell	La Sonnambula
Little Women	Women in Love	Le Pere Goriot
Loved One, The	Wrong Box, The	Les Huguenots

WORKS OF LITERATURE AND MUSIC

Les Sylphides
Linz Symphony
Little Dorrit
Locksley Hall
Lost Chord, The
Madame Bovary
Major Barbara
Manon Lescaut
Moll Flanders
Moonstone, The
Old Mortality
Owen Wingrave
Paradise Lost
Piers Plowman
Porgy and Bess
Precious Bane
Private Lives
Prothalamion
Rheingold, Das
Rip Van Winkle
Rogue Herries
Romany Rye, The
Sardanapalus
Spring Sonata
Trout Quintet
Twelfth Night
Valkyries, The
Whisky Galore
Albert Herring
Almayer's Folly
Andrea Chenier
Angel Pavement
Arms and the Man
Art of Fugue, The
Bab Ballads, The
Black Arrow, The

Black Mischief
Blue Danube, The
Boris Godounov
Brave New World
Cancer Ward, The
Carmina Burana
Chanson de Nuit
Clock Symphony
Crown Imperial
Death in Venice
Der Freischutz
Dido and Aeneas
Doctor Faustus
Doctor Zhivago
Fame is the Spur
Finnegans Wake
Ghost Train, The
Gondoliers, The
Harold in Italy
Hatter's Castle
Jungle Book, The
Just So Stories
La Cenerentola
L'Elisir d'Amore
Mabinogion, The
Magic Flute, The
Magistrate, The
Mansfield Park
Metamorphosen
Nutcracker, The
Odessa File, The
Orb and Sceptre
Path to Rome, The
Peg Woffington
Private Angelo
Religio Medici

Schindler's Ark
Sketches by Boz
Songs of Travel
Sons and Lovers
Stamboul Train
Tarka the Otter
Timon of Athens
Under Milk Wood
Utopia Limited
Virginians, The
White Devil, The
Winnie the Pooh
Winslow Boy, The
Zuleika Dobson
Ambassadors, The
Andrea del Sarto
Battle Symphony
Bees Wedding, The
Book of Snobs, The
Brief Encounter
Chanson de Matin
Choral Symphony
Cider with Rosie
Claudius the God
Coral Island, The
Country Wife, The
Crotchet Castle
Darkness at Noon
Decline and Fall
Deep Blue Sea, The
Die Zauberflote
Ein Heldenleben
Emperor Quartet
Entertainer, The
Eroica Symphony
Forsyte Saga, The

Four Just Men, The
Gay Lord Quex, The
Golden Bough, The
Goodbye Mr Chips
Great Gatsby, The
Handful of Dust, A
Horse's Mouth, The
Jude the Obscure
Kreutzer Sonata
Le Morte d'Arthur
London Symphony
Loom of Youth, The
Lord of the Flies
Lord of the Rings
Lost Horizon, The
Lyrical Ballads
Madam Butterfly
Man and Superman
Masterman Ready
National Velvet
Nightmare Abbey
Nine Tailors, The
Of Human Bondage
Our Man in Havana
Pickwick Papers
Plain Dealer, The
Prague Symphony
Quentin Durward
Rhapsody in Blue
Rights of Man, The
Robinson Crusoe
Roderick Random
Romeo and Juliet
Separate Tables
Shropshire Lad, A
Siegfried Idyll

Sinister Street
Sins of my Old Age
Slavonic Dances
Spring Symphony
Stones of Venice
Time Machine, The
Town Like Alice, A
Tragic Symphony
Treasure Island
Tristram Shandy
Uncle Tom's Cabin
Venus and Adonis
Vicar of Bray, The
Voices of Spring
Water Babies, The
Widowers Houses
Winter's Tale, The
Woodlanders, The
African Queen, The
Allan Quatermain
Ariadne auf Naxos
Bartholomew Fair
Beggar's Opera, The
Child of our Time, A
Christmas Carol, A
Clarissa Harlowe
Dangerous Corner
Daphnis and Chloe
Divine Comedy, The
Emperor Concerto
Emperor Waltz, The
Essays of Elia, The
Faerie Queene, The
Fanny by Gaslight
Farewell to Arms, A
Frenchman's Creek

From the New World
Golden Legend, The
Gone with the Wind
Goodbye to Berlin
Gotterdammerung
Haffner Symphony
Hansel and Gretel
Heartbreak House
Huckleberry Finn
Iceman Cometh, The
Invisible Man, The
Italian Symphony
Jupiter Symphony
Le Nozze di Figaro
Letters of Junius
Life for the Tsar, A
Look Back in Anger
Moonlight Sonata
Northanger Abbey
Old Wives Tale, The
Our Mutual Friend
Passage to India, A
Pearl Fishers, The
Peregrine Pickle
Peter and the Wolf
Puck of Pook's Hill
Put out More Flags
Raindrop Prelude
Rite of Spring, The
Rupert of Hentzau
Samson Agonistes
Samson and Dalila
Scholar Gipsy, The
Serenade to Music
Simon Boccanegra
Soldier's Tale, The

Tanglewood|Tales   Waldstein|Sonata
Three|Men|in|a|Boat   Weir|of|Hermiston
Titus|Andronicus   Woman|in|White,|The
To|the|Lighthouse   Yarrow|Revisited
Waiting|for|Godot   You|Never|Can|Tell

Writers

Fry	Hume	West	Freud	Moore
Hay	Hunt	Wren	Gogol	Noyes
Kyd	Kant	Zola	Gorki	Orczy
Lee	Knox	Aesop	Grimm	Ouida
Poe	Lamb	Auden	Hardy	Paine
Amis	Lang	Bacon	Heine	Pater
Baum	Lear	Bates	Henry	Pepys
Bell	Livy	Behan	Henty	Plato
Bolt	Loos	Blake	Homer	Pliny
Buck	Lyly	Burke	Ibsen	Pound
Cary	Mann	Burns	Innes	Reade
Dane	Marx	Byron	James	Rilke
Dell	Mill	Camus	Jeans	Scott
Elia	More	Capek	Jones	Shute
Eyre	Muir	Clare	Joyce	Smart
Ford	Nash	Dante	Kafka	Smith
Gide	Ovid	Defoe	Keats	Spark
Glyn	Owen	Donne	Lewis	Stein
Gray	Pope	Doyle	Locke	Stern
Hall	Saki	Dumas	Lodge	Stowe
Home	Sand	Eliot	Lorca	Swift
Hood	Shaw	Ellis	Lucan	Synge
Hope	Snow	Evans	Mason	Tasso
Hugo	Webb	Frayn	Milne	Twain

WRITERS

Verne	Cooper	Mailer	Anouilh
Waugh	Coward	Malory	Aquinas
Wells	Crabbe	Miller	Beckett
Wilde	Cronin	Milton	Bennett
Woolf	Daudet	Morgan	Blunden
Yeats	Davies	Morris	Boswell
Young	Dekker	Musset	Bridges
Zweig	Dryden	Newman	Campion
Anstey	Empson	ONeill	Carlyle
Archer	Evelyn	Orwell	Carroll
Arnold	Farnol	Parker	Chaucer
Asimov	France	Pascal	Chekhov
Austen	Frazer	Pindar	Cobbett
Bailey	Gibbon	Pinero	Cocteau
Balzac	Goethe	Pinter	Colette
Barham	Gordon	Proust	Collins
Barrie	Graham	Racine	Corelli
Belloc	Graves	Ruskin	Dickens
Benson	Greene	Sappho	Dodgson
Binyon	Hawkes	Sartre	Douglas
Borrow	Hemans	Sayers	Drayton
Brecht	Henley	Seneca	Dunsany
Bridie	Hesiod	Sidney	Durrell
Bronte	Hobbes	Squire	Emerson
Brooke	Holmes	Steele	Erasmus
Browne	Holtby	Sterne	Flecker
Bryant	Horace	Tagore	Forster
Buchan	Howard	Thomas	Gallico
Bunyan	Hughes	Villon	Gaskell
Burney	Huxley	Virgil	Gilbert
Butler	Jerome	Waller	Golding
Caesar	Jonson	Walton	Haggard
Chekov	Landor	Wesker	Harnett
Cicero	Larkin	Wilcox	Hartley
Clough	London	Wilson	Hazlitt
Conrad	Lytton	Addison	Herbert

Herrick	Spencer	Koestler
Hopkins	Spender	Lawrence
Housman	Spenser	Lovelace
Ionesco	Spinoza	Macaulay
Johnson	Surtees	MacNeice
Juvenal	Tacitus	Mallarme
Kipling	Terence	Melville
Leacock	Thomson	Meredith
Lehmann	Thoreau	Merriman
Lessing	Thurber	Mirabeau
Malraux	Tolkien	Mortimer
Marlowe	Tolstoy	Petrarch
Marryat	Ustinov	Plutarch
Martial	Wallace	Rabelais
Marvell	Walpole	Rattigan
Maugham	Webster	Rossetti
Mauriac	Whitman	Rousseau
Maurois	Andersen	Schiller
Merimee	Apuleius	Sheridan
Moliere	Beaumont	Sinclair
Murdoch	Beerbohm	Smollett
Nabokov	Berkeley	Stendhal
Newbolt	Betjeman	Stoppard
Nichols	Browning	Strachey
Osborne	Campbell	Suckling
Patmore	Catullus	Tennyson
Peacock	Christie	Thompson
Pushkin	Congreve	Tibullus
Rimbaud	DayLewis	Trollope
Russell	DelaMare	Turgenev
Saroyan	Disraeli	Vanburgh
Sassoon	Faulkner	Verlaine
Shelley	Fielding	Voltaire
Simenon	Fletcher	Whittier
Sitwell	Forester	Xenephon
Southey	Kingsley	Aeschylus

WRITERS

Aristotle	Wycherley
Blackmore	Ayckbourne
Boccaccio	Ballantyne
Cervantes	Baudelaire
Churchill	Chatterton
Coleridge	Chesterton
Corneille	Conan Doyle
De la Roche	Drinkwater
De Quincey	Fitzgerald
Descartes	Galsworthy
Du Maurier	La Fontaine
Euripides	Longfellow
Goldsmith	Maupassant
Hemingway	Pirandello
Herodotus	Propertius
Isherwood	Quintilian
Linklater	Richardson
Lucretius	Strindberg
Mackenzie	Thucydides
Masefield	Wordsworth
Middleton	Dostoievsky
Mitchison	Maeterlinck
Montaigne	Omar Khayyam
Nietzsche	Shakespeare
Pasternak	Yevtushenko
Priestley	Aristophanes
Sophocles	Beaumarchais
Steinbeck	Macchiavelli
Stevenson	Quiller Couch
Suetonius	Rider Haggard
Swinburne	Solzhenitsin
Thackeray	Wittgenstein
Trevelyan	Sackville West
Wodehouse	Marcus Aurelius

Signs of the Zodiac

Leo	Cancer	Scorpio
Aries	Gemini	Aquarius
Libra	Pisces	Capricorn
Virgo	Taurus	Sagittarius

NOTES

NOTES

NOTES

NOTES

NOTES

NOTES

NOTES

NOTES

NOTES

INDEX

LITERATURE
Drugs: MEDICINE

Ecclesiastical: RELIGIONS
Employment: TRADE
Engineering:
    MACHINERY or
    PHYSICAL SCIENCES
Entertainment: CINEMA
    or THEATRE
Examinations:
    EDUCATION

Fabrics: CLOTHES
Fashion: CLOTHES
Festivals: RELIGIONS
Figures of Speech:
    LITERATURE
Finance: MONEY or
    TRADE
Flags: HERALDRY
Footwear: CLOTHES

Games: SPORTS
Geology: GEOGRAPHY
Geometry:
    MATHEMATICS
Grammar: LITERATURE

Headgear: CLOTHES
Herbs: VEGETABLES

History: LITERATURE
Hobbies: PASTIMES
Hospitals: MEDICINE

Illnesses: MEDICINE
Instruments: MUSIC

Journalism:
    LITERATURE

Kitchen: HOUSEHOLD
    ITEMS

Land Formations:
    GEOGRAPHY
Language: LITERATURE
Legal Terms: LAW

Maps: GEOGRAPHY
Market Terms: TRADE
Metals: MINERALS
Monuments:
    ARCHITECTURE
Motoring: TRANSPORT

Nautical: MARINE or
    TRANSPORT
Numbers:
    MATHEMATICS

Operas: WORKS OF
    MUSIC

Operatic Characters:
LITERARY
CHARACTERS

Pastimes: SPORTS
People: OCCUPATIONS
Philosophy: EDUCATION
Photography: VISUAL
ARTS
Poets: WRITERS
Pottery: VISUAL ARTS
Printing: LITERATURE
Professions:
OCCUPATIONS
Psychiatric Terms:
MEDICINE
Punctuation:
LITERATURE

Radio: CINEMA AND TV
Railways: TRANSPORT
Reptiles: INSECTS
Roads: TRANSPORT
Rocks: MINERALS
Rooms: FURNITURE

Sculptors: ARTISTS
Seas: OCEANS

Seasons: TIME
Ships: MARINE or
TRANSPORT
Shrubs: TREES
Signals: TRANSPORT
Speed: LENGTH
Stars: ASTRONOMY

Teaching materials:
EDUCATION
Television: CINEMA
Towns: CITIES
Travel: TRANSPORT
Trigonometry:
MATHEMATICS

Vehicles: TRANSPORT
Volume: LENGTH

Weapons: WARFARE
Weather:
METEOROLOGY
Writing Materials:
EDUCATION

Zoology: ANIMALS or
BIOLOGICAL
SCIENCES